The People Hitler Left Behind

The
People Hitler
Left Behind

LARRY B STELL

Library of Congress Control Number: 2021904341

HARDBACK: 978-1-954673-96-0
PAPERBACK: 978-1-954673-95-3
EBOOK: 978-1-954673-97-7

Ordering Information:

For orders and inquiries, please contact:
1-888-404-1388
www.goldtouchpress.com
book.orders@goldtouchpress.com

Printed in the United States of America

Contents

Chapter 1

Germany Recovers After World War II

In 1955 I was in my sophomore year of the University of Arkansas, Monticello. My mother and father owned a soft ice cream parlor in Warren, only 15 miles from the university. I often worked there, relieving them both of the inactive winter months. Hot dogs, hamburgers, and barbecue sandwiches were served to enhance low sales of ice cream over the winter months.

One day a young veteran came into the establishment and I learned he had spent two years in the occupation army of post II World War in Germany. I, knowing little about the German culture, except for anti-Nazi films, and what I had read, began to quiz this young man. I asked about climate, the people, drink, and food found in Germany. I also learned that he had married a German Fraulein, and brought her back to the United States.

The fascination I had for Germany was almost beyond description. I picked the veteran's brain every day he frequented my parent's business. The descriptions of the occupation army and American military visiting the various villages and war torn cities of Germany gave me a thrill of the highest degree.

This particular farm lad had nothing but good things to say about his newly acquired German wife. His wife's blending in with his family and even the locals of Warren, Arkansas was optimal. She seemed to love the experience of living in a country, which had not been blemished by the atrocities of war.

His house, according to him, was the cleanest, best kept house any one could find in the United States. In an overtone of subservient implication, he also told me his wife polished and shined his shoes. But when I married my German wife, Brigitte there was no such thing as shoe care for me. That was my own responsibility!

The conversations, between him and me continued, and he made several visits to our business, ordering milk shakes and hot dogs, which I eagerly made because I wanted to hear more. His tales of the German villages, the snow covered mountaintops, wine, beer, and outstanding Wienerschnitzel, Sauerkraut, potatoes, dumplings, and fantastic apple dessert dishes, made my mouth water. Also the continual ravings about the tremendous meals at the guesthouses, and at such a post war price, made my head spin.

On top of these frequent conversations about Germany, and lectures by dear Dr. Claude Babin and Dr. Annie McCarrol, professors of European History and World History at the University of Arkansas, Monticello really cinched my goals to visit Europe, and especially Germany.

After two years teaching, one year in Arkansas and one year in New Orleans, my mind was set. Rumors and tales of teacher scarcity for the Overseas Dependent Schools program, under the Department of Defense (Army, Navy, and Air Force), really lighted my fuse.

After completing my Master's degree at Vanderbilt Peabody University, Nashville, Tennessee in 1959, I journeyed to California, substituted for a semester, and by August 1960, I was signed up with the Air Force to spend a year in Libya.

The duty station was in North Africa, along the Mediterranean Sea. The school was at Wheelus Air Base right outside of Tripoli, Libya. After a ride on a Constellation, 4-engine plane of the U. S. Air Force for about 10 or 12 hours with about 65 teachers, I landed in Tripoli. We made two stops. One stop was at Bermuda and the other was the Azores.

Remaining for only one semester in Tripoli, trying to learn some Arabic, and flirting with Italian and British secretaries, and driving along the Roman ruins of the Mediterranean coast, I was again on an airplane to another country. The assignment was Ramstein Air Base, Germany. What a thrill, and I was the envy of every teacher at Wheelus Air Base, Tripoli! All this happened because I was deficient of about 4 semester hours of Biology, which I was teaching at the high school level, and the North Central Association is very strict about schools they evaluate in the Overseas Dependent Schools.

The airplane we flew on was "plush", as they were called because it was a DC-4, used by King Idris to fly to different parts of North Africa and Europe. Along with me on the plane was the Director of the Air Force branch of the Overseas Dependent Schools. He was along with his lovely wife, Sue Mason. Meeting him, because of his dedication and confidence in teachers, as a main component of the education process, was a pleasure. The meeting turned out to be a political advantage later in my school career.

We had to land in Marseilles, France because of a compass problem so we had a delightful night in a quaint hotel and ate in a great restaurant before journeying on to Wiesbaden,

Germany the next morning. Wiesbaden was our final destination.

After a 2-hour train ride, I reached Ramstein Air Base, and it was now late January, and there was about a 25 centimeters of snow on the base and I had no means of transportation. I walked in the snow to the Officer's Club for dinner since it was then about 5:30 p.m. in the evening. It only took a few minutes in the Officer's Club, and I met several teachers from the junior high school where I was now assigned.

It was January of 1961 and near enough to the ending of the 1950's decade where allied occupation troops had provided a more pleasant setting than their counterparts, the Russians of East Germany. For most of western Germany, things were beginning to stabilize and economic surges had begun.

Within one week of my arrival, I managed to procure a 1952 Volkswagen with a non-synchronized transmission. The manual transmission sounded like a coffee grinder when shifting down from first gear to second. But the car was dependable.

I bought the car from a colonel who had used the vehicle as a second car but he was buying a Mercedes, and he was pleased when I paid him $500 cash for the auto. It was the first vehicle I owned in Europe and I hit the road the first weekend, with Jerry cans (10-gallon spare cans used by the military) filled with Quartermaster gasoline at only nine cents per gallon. We all bought gasoline from the Air Force Exchange because fuel from the economy was far too expensive. We had choices of Esso coupons or the cheaper Quartermaster (PX) gasoline. The Esso gasoline was about 5 cents more expensive than the Quartermaster.

Our salaries were not so great, but the tremendous advantage of living in the Bachelor Officer Quarters was absolutely magnificent! Warm sleeping quarters, a bedroom, bath, and living room made the adventure of living in Germany a very splendid experience, especially in the early 1960s.

Venturing out to cities like Heidelberg, Mannheim, Ramstein (a small village outside the air base), Landstuhl, Bann, Sauerbrücken, Metz, France, and many other charming German or French sites was a delight which I, as a young man, had dreamed about.

To enhance my stay, I immediately enrolled in a Berlitz German class, asking for a female private teacher because of my harrowing experience with a male Arabic instructor in Libya. Berlitz assigned me a lady named Frau Scmidt and she was one of the most delightful teachers of language I had yet experienced. Unfortunately she remained with me only 4 weeks and I got a male replacement, but he, though the wrong sex, was a superb scholar, especially in grammatical skills. I quickly learned the difference in the indirect objective (dative) and the objective case.

After having about 3 months of conversational German battered into my reluctant skull, I began to wander out to the cities and villages, even as far as Munich, Stuttgart, the Black Forest, and Worms. They were all cities of beauty, and prices, were very suitable for my income, especially compared to my counterparts, the German national teachers at that time.

Getting into the German mind, with some German teachers on our staff, who were teaching German language and culture was very exciting. They were simply enthralled in the discourse about language and discussions of comparative education! Getting to know these teachers who were excellent in constructing grammar, and who taught German in a way which enhanced English also, was great. The grammatical approach to the German language, which is often omitted from English in secondary schools today was refreshing and reminded me of the approach my ninth grade English teacher used back in Little Rock, Arkansas.

The conjugation of verbs was a task of memorization, and after enrolling in the University of Maryland, then logging up about 12 semester hours of German, the haziness of the complex German language began to clear up somewhat.

Later on, in the late 1980s, I was to take more courses of German at San Diego State University and University of California, San Diego. Some of the advanced writing in science research, and a stiff course in Kafka (German Literature) really convinced me of how difficult grammatically correct German is. Franz Kafka was a difficult writer of German literature, so the course was not easy because of his intense and complex style.

I was to later meet my delightful wife, Brigitte von Jagow, then really get a saturation of a clear, high spoken German language from her. My University of Maryland instructors praised Brigitte because of her clear, articulate, and proper use of the German language.

Brigitte, though her writing, as I suspect of many working Germans, could always stand improvement. My written German still demands constant practice if I am to utilize the finer elements of the intriguing and difficult language. Nevertheless, Brigitte the German language, almost at a very rapid rate, and verbalizes today in such a fast manner that many Germans must really focus to keep up with her.

The spring of 1961 brought smaller villages and me together quite often. It also brought me to the German Gasthäuser (guesthouses) where German beer cost about 25 U. S. cents. A glass of wine cost no more than 50 U. S. cents, and a delightful dinner in the loveliest restaurants cost a little more than $2.80 to $3.50. Add a bottle of wine and a great meal was no more than $5.00.

As a young teacher, and with the respect that Germans have for teachers and all educators, I was meeting some very lovely German ladies in Heidelberg, Mannheim, and even around Cologne. My weekends, with a never ending thirst for viewing beautiful architecture, cathedrals, and even Roman aqueducts, and Roman walls never seemed to cease. The weather in the spring, after April, was inviting and frequent drives out of Ramstein to nearby Mainz, Wiesbaden, Frankfurt, and even Nuremberg, only enticed me to explore more and more of the German countryside.

Several trips down to Bavaria, with an inquisitive dissection of Munich and its cosmopolitan atmosphere extracted even more wanderlust from my psychic. The wanderlust was surpassed only by desire for more social encounter with all types of Germans. The city of Munich is beautiful, and the outlying, snow covered mountains are magnificent to behold, so it satisfied my longings for magnificence in this great and beautiful country.

During spring of 1961, I ventured into the elitist hobby of hunting, which was propagated by the Status of Forces agreement between the U. S. military and the German government. The course was stringent, but not nearly as extensive and detailed, as the one native German hunters must endure. I failed the first try at the test, along with 15 other flunkies but after the retest we passed, and the 45 new Jägers (hunters) were ready to join the Germans in the forests of Deutschland.

Hunting is a passion I have had since I was fourteen years of age. My father who hunted duck, quail, and geese in the state of Arkansas passed it along to me. My father and I hunted ducks and geese around the White River area of Arkansas during World War II and through the 1960s, so I had already acquired a strong desire for hunting, along with extensive experience.

Venturing out into the forests and fields of Germany, obeying the strict hunting customs and laws was an experience I shall never forget. American hunters, especially the new ones, would wait patiently, around the Rod and Gun Clubs of Ramstein and Kaiserslautern, Germany, until an invitation was extended to them. The invitations would come from private land owners, but some of the hunts would take place in the German national forests, and were conducted by the Foresters, who were civil servants and all of them possessed the Jäger Brief (hunter's diploma) as a part of their profession.

Americans learned soon that the strict customs, rules of etiquette, proper forest-green clothing, and lady or gentleman like conduct was the proper mode of behavior. The Germans, as hunters, were only in the top 6 to 10% of the population, so it was not a hobby where anyone can get a gun and go to the great outdoors and hunt. The strictest of safety rules were applied, and especially in shooting game. Shooting at game in a drive hunt or standing and remaining at the proper location was done in the most regimented fashion. There was always ample game, especially in the 1960s and 1970s, in many parts of West Germany, and especially the Rheinland-Pfalz area where I hunted most frequently.

Through this schooling, I met doctors, Gymnasium teachers, lawyers, dentists, and many business owners. The hunts were highly social because whether they were sponsored by private landowners or by the government, there would always be food or drinks served afterwards. Some of the hunts would have hot soups, sausage, beer, wine, and schnapps furnished after the great event.

The game would be laid out in a methodical, prescribed manner, with certain high game (Hochwild) laid out in priority.

The smaller game such as European Hare or partridge placed below the Roe Deer (Rehwild) or Red Deer (Rotwild). These ceremonies were serious, with a proper respect for the game.

In German hunting, the training and control of guns is so much more advanced over the "Wild West" type of hunting in the United States. The experience is fascination and rewarding. If a shot is fired, the landowner or government forester (Förster) is aware of each and every one that rings out. If someone makes a mistake and shoots at the wrong time during a drive hunt (human beaters and dogs drive the game forward in a designated area), the hunter must buy rounds of beer or wine at the Gasthaus as a penalty.

Americans, however, do not respect the concept of drinking while shooting, but German hunters often mix the two. The control is so thorough and extreme that the landowners and foresters know almost everything that happens on a hunt.

The connections through my hobby of hunting brought me into contact with a social realm I would never have met had I not have used hunting to become acquainted with some of the social elite in German society.

Along with my quick grasp of the German language, and a strong desire to soak up any and all of the customs, I laid the groundwork for valuable connections. The connections are still viable for my frequent visits to Germany because they are lasting friendships. On future trips I can again hunt if I so desire, but must obtain a temporary license. One of my contacts writes articles for hunting magazines in Germany, and he flies to Alaska every couple of years, just to fish and make big game hunting expeditions.

My friend is Herbert Dietrich, and he lives right in the middle of Karlsruhe, Germany, near Karlsruhe American High School, where I taught for about six years. The entrance to his quaint home is covered with hunting trophies, and his wife has a hobby of making Black Forest souvenirs. Herbert is an engineer for the city of Karlsruhe, and is one of the most fascinating persons I have encountered in my life. He is friendly and has an unusual sense of humor, but passionate when it comes to hunting and fishing.

In 1975, Herbert and I had the pleasure of hunting together, in a high seat in the Ardennes Forest, close to where the Battle of the Bulge, II World War took place. We were invited by a hunter, and friend of mine, Dr. von den Driesch, who lives near the Dutch and German border, for an overnight hunt. At about 3:00 a.m. I had the somewhat rare experience of shooting a wild boar, about 65 kilograms in mass, but we did not find the animal until we took a dog the next morning and found the animal just a few meters into the brush under the high seat.

The whole aura of hunting wild boar in Germany is a high light in my life and if I never get to hunt again, it is something I can always boast about. Such episodes certainly contributed to making my stay in Germany unusual.

Not only did my friend Herbert and I experience such exciting trips together, but we attended many magnificent events (social and hunting) in the fall hunting seasons near and around Karlsruhe and the Black Forest from 1971 until I transferred out of Karlsruhe American High School in 1977.

One of the Reviers where we received invitations to was one owned by a businessman who owned one of the largest bakeries in Germany. The owner's name was Max Griesinger, and his bread and cakes were sold all over West Germany. When one was so fortunate as to have an invitation to a hunt hosted by Max, the food, wine, beer, and schnapps flowed incessantly at these great galas. The beautiful fall mornings highlighted the beauty of forty or more hunters parading around in their forest green uniforms.

Most of Max Griesinger's hunts were generally for pheasant, one of my favorite types of hunting. Pheasant are exciting to hunt and are one of my favorite game birds for eating. They go great with the Rhine wines. On some of the hunts we would shoot over a hundred birds.

The beautiful fall weather, with an early morning hunt, some beginning at 7:00 a.m. were almost storybook events. The hunters, mostly men, but some women, were dressed in their exclusive green uniforms and most of them shooting with expensive side-by-side .12 gauge guns, or over-and-under weapons. Some of these weapons cost well over $2,000 and some even more. Watching well trained all-purpose dogs in the field, on a beautiful fall or winter day is beyond description. The German hunting dogs are usually well disciplined, and happy to do their jobs for their masters.

In some of the German hunting areas, one specific area around Speyer, Germany would have cornfields that had literally hundreds of pheasant. In the 1960s there were ample populations of pheasant. Today, from what the hunters have told me, the populations, because of increased housing developments, are ever decreasing.

Usually on these hunts, the cocks, or males, were the only ones we were allowed to shoot, unless we were given the permission by the landowner, and sometimes we could shoot the hens. This was just another element in the tight control the Germans used in what is known as the "Abschuss Plan," a system that maintained balance between the wildlife on the land, and the food supply. Diminishing the roosters or cocks did not reduce the population, but too many hens being shot would be detrimental to the next season's population.

The German hunting system is systematic, conservation oriented and one of the most highly controlled of any hunting system in the world. Many of the laws, from what I have heard from the older hunters, were enacted by Herman Göring, the Air Reichs Minister, Minister of the German Air Force, since the 1930s. He was an avid hunter and was instrumental in dictating some of the conservation laws that helped maintained high game population.

On one of my hunts, in 1963, near Ramstein Air Base, where I got to know the landowner quite well, I was allowed to bring along my dog, Suzy. Suzy was a beautiful longhaired, Dachshund, and they are supposed to have the in-bred characteristic, which makes them great wild boar hunters. My dog Suzy enjoyed the adventure so much, she started the hunt, then disappeared into the woods and I thought she would never be found again. She proved me wrong! After about an hour in the woods, with only about 8 hunters and 5 other dogs, we returned to the local hunting lodge for food and drink. What did we find at the lodge, waiting with wagging tail, my dog Suzy?

Insights gained by meeting some of the elite hunters of Germany give one the time to have conversation, talk about economics, politics, and even the past wars, especially World War II. Many of the hunters, some who were in their forties in 1960s and 1970s, had served in the military, and made their confessions that they knew Hitler was going down the wrong path, even in the mid-1940s. They lamented the fact and knew, toward the end of the war, that the blind following of Hitler would only bring devastation to their homeland. Their demeanor was almost like acts of contrition when engaging in conversation with my military friends or with me. But one thing about the German nature, or upbringing, they respect authority, and the U. S. military was, at that time (post WW II occupation) still wielding quite a bit of power around Germany. Many U. S. military personnel were still providing a boost to the Germany economy, whether it was in house/

apartment rentals, automobile sales, or merchandise sales in general. Business with the military and American civilians was a boost to their economy.

Many of the German civilians, no longer a part of Hitler's military might, were working for the military bases, whether it was working as electricians, vehicle drivers, mechanics, construction workers, lawyers, doctors, or teachers in an upward moving economy. The dollar went a long way, with a 4 German Mark to the U. S. Dollar exchange rate in the early 1960s through 1969 or 1970. Americans were well liked by the Germans with seldom incidences of conflicts that I ever read about or witnessed.

The German government tightly controlled the deflated German Mark, and wages were still quite low for the German citizens, compared to those of the Americans during the 1960s. Our dollar went a long way, and Americans, both military and civilians like me, had a tremendous opportunity to travel, purchase nice automobiles, go to operas, and shop in the up and coming department stores. Even credit cards, especially in the 1960s, were a rare item among Germans. I did not start using the American Express card until the early 1970s, and the use of credit cards was definitely a rarity for the Germans.

I always had a new automobile, even though it was a Volkswagen, and by 1966, I owned two automobiles. I purchased one of the cars with tax-free price tag through the American Post Exchange. After early 1970, the American government would ship cars to Germany, from the United States, and also ship American cars back to CONUS (Continental United States). Civilians and military personnel were entitled to one shipment per year, but only after the balance of payments status with the United States became a problem. At this time the American base exchanges went on the "Buy American" campaigns in order to stem the flow of American capital, thereby keeping our dollar stronger.

The post exchanges, Navy, Army, and Air Force began to push American products in order to help reverse the balance of payments problem in the 1970s. It was fine driving American cars in Europe because the cost of gasoline, with about a hundred gallons (400 liters) per month for each family car was sufficient. If one needed extra allowances, it was relatively easy to get if one merely obtained leave orders from the local base commander, and sometimes merely from the principal of our school on base.

Many Americans, civilians, and military, made friends with the German civilians, brought them to Officer Clubs and NCO Clubs as a way of interacting. Germans enjoyed the opportunity to meet Americans and readily accepted invitations to attend on-base functions.

The Germans, historically strong in military past, really respected the American military stance, with bases interspersed throughout West Germany during post World War II because they expressed gratitude for the buffer established against any possible Russian threat. The German citizens always gladly participated well in American military exhibitions, parades, or air shows, showing their support of the strong military defense in West Germany.

Even references and tales of past experience during the Third Reich by many of my German friends were described in almost guiltless overtones, because their military status during the war was a state and patriotic duty. If one discussed the events involving the persecutions of six million deceased Jews of World War II, many veterans, who spent years on the Russian front, obeying orders of the state, would guiltlessly immerse into dialogues regarding experiences related to the war. Most were tales of the encounters on the Russian front, where great numbers of German soldiers served. Many claimed to have little knowledge of the extreme persecutions going on in the interior of Germany and of countries under German occupation.

Many conversations I held with my Uncle Walter Kiesel, who was a prisoner of war around Bremerhaven, had tremendously comic overtones as he described encounters with some of the American sergeants with whom he dealt. Walter Kiesel was my uncle because I married his niece and I happily called him Uncle Walter.

Walter's command of the English language was quite good and though I spoke German with him about 90 per cent of the time, he would often describe his experiences in English. He would often imitate some of his old U. S. Army sergeants who commanded German veterans who served on work forces during the transition back into the economy during U. S. occupation.

Uncle Walter later transferred his military tenure, as an administrator, to a job with one of the national health insurance companies in Mannheim, Germany. I met my wife with his daughter in the city of Mannheim and later, after marrying Brigitte, his niece, became a frequent guest in his and Tante Else's modest one bedroom apartment overlooking a park in a great location of the city of Mannheim.

Uncle Walter and I became great friends from 1961 until I left Germany in 1983, and over twenty years of friendship bonded us. He and, sometimes his wife, Tante Else, visited me in locations of Ramstein, Karlsruhe, and Brunssum, the Netherlands. Our time was most memorable because of the familial relationship and respect I had for this person.

His benevolence was almost religious. He had a deep understanding of people, family, and friends. His social contacts were tight, almost solely with family but the interactions were intensive, introspective, deep rooted, by his keen family perception. It was always a pleasure to get out into various parts of Germany, enjoy wine, excellent food, and enjoy the fast pace of the German Autobahn. We would drive to many villages in the Rheinland-Pfalz region of Germany with anticipation of exciting scenery and quaint cities or Dorfs (villages).

The intensity of appreciation I had for Germany and its almost visible reincarnation to democratic value mixed with a regimented pace was uncanny. Business owners and restaurant or Beer Stubes (beer halls) rallied in their reassertion of economic achievement. Germany was definitely getting back on its feet economically in the early 1960s.

The most enjoyable meals, even in small villages were attainable because of the recuperative pride the Germans had in reestablishing themselves in the early 1960s. Beer and wine were at such minimal prices that it was unbelievable. I putted around in my old Volkswagen with a satisfaction attainable only through my basic "wanderlust" and curiosity about this magnificent country and its magnetic progression toward economic recovery.

Political assertion into the remolding of Europe had begun with the first chancellor of the Federal Republic of Germany, Konrad Adenauer. He resided over the reconstruction after World War II (West Germany; 1949-1963). Since I arrived in Germany in January of 1961, it was easy to get a sense of the conservative, solid currency approach to recovery. Citizens of West Germany were working diligently, taking jobs around the military bases, rebuilding bombed out buildings, although most of this was completed by the time I arrived.

One could, from 1961 through the late 1960s, ride in a taxi in Wiesbaden, and most other cities, then pay with the American dollar which commanded an immediate rate of 4

D-Mark. Our currency was strong up until the 1970s, when the dollar began to lose value against European currency. Many restaurant owners loved to take American dollars if we did not bring enough German currency, especially in the late 1960s. The ready exchange of U. S. Dollars to German Marks later changed as the U. S. dollar lost its value because the diminishing exports of American goods abroad.

How I loved to take a train, or drive my old Volkswagen to nice resorts, order a nice meal and wine, enjoying the excellent service. After battling with waiters in the United States in the 1950s, this was paradise, just enjoying the immaculate continental flare in countries of Western Europe.

I visited West Berlin in 1963, and stayed in a nice German hotel, dined on the Kurfürstendamm, the main street of West Berlin. This proved to be one of the most delightful meals I ever had in Germany. We had pheasant under glass with sauerkraut, and with a great white wine from the Rhine, and this fantastic meal cost less than 60 German Marks or an equivalent of $15 in the early 1960s.

During the Berlin visit my wife and I knew we had to see East Berlin so we planned a day tour of the other half of the city. The tour proved to be a highlight of the trip because we witnessed what we had so often heard about the sad status of the citizens of Eastern Berlin.

I had to take a tour on a separate bus from that of my wife, Brigitte, in order to see East Berlin. The difference between the west part of the country from the east was so quite dramatic. Why the United States obliged the USSR, and endured the economic deprivation, and turmoil rendered upon the satellite countries during the Cold War is difficult to grasp.

The sadness, degeneration, despicable, unimaginable, and complete waste laid upon the East German people by the daunting, failing experiment of communism could be read in the faces of people on the streets of East Berlin in the 1960s. Civilization can only be thankful that this experiment failed, and failed miserably.

My wife and I waved at each other as my tour passed hers on that day in East Berlin. My wife, a West German citizen, could not ride on the same bus I rode, because of the tight control the East Germans had on West German citizens coming into the deteriorated eastern half of Berlin.

My wife's German citizenship also affected a possible career change I pursued in the 1970s. Ten years down the road I was to apply for a position in another field of work.

At that later date I was to learn that an application with the CIA (1971, Brunssum, the Netherlands) disallowed me to become part of that agency because of my wife was a citizen of West Germany. There was, obviously, a policy preventing an American citizen from joining this agency because of the great risk of either revealing information to the East or the danger of East German relatives attaining military information. Nevertheless, it was an obstacle to my transferring from my teaching position to this particular branch of government service.

While in East Berlin, I did do a stupid thing, and that was exchange, in a restaurant, forty German West German Marks for East German Marks, and this could have been tragic, had I have been caught. I was young, and much more adventurous than I am today. The waiter accepted the money, and the exchange went on under a napkin on his tray. Fortunately I was not caught in the act so I was not apprehended by the secret police of East Germany. That could have caused a political catastrophe.

I remember, when leaving the Eastern sector, talking with an old gentleman, after I asked him what he thought about the political situation and his being a prisoner of that city. He said, in German, "The Germans of the east would ride out the storm, and someday there would be a change." I thought he was wrong and trapped in the setting forever, but he proved to be right because the fall of the Berlin Wall in 1989.

I have since the 1960s, visited various parts of Eastern Europe. I visited Eisenach, Erfurt, and Weimar in 1993, and the contrast to West Germany is absolutely unbelievable. Except for the remaining psychological stress ingrained into the citizenry, things are beginning to improve. The economy is turning around, especially contrasted to the tragic cloak of communism imbedded into the Germans and others in Eastern Europe during the time of the Eastern Bloc.

In 1994 I visited Budapest, a city I often dreamed of because of its acclaimed charm. The charm is almost unbelievable, and the food in restaurants superb. I enjoy spicy food, and it can be found along with the enjoyable Gypsy music, in any restaurant. I visited a most exclusive restaurant known as The Gundel, and it was enchanting. The owner, a Hungarian, and owner of one of the large cosmetic firms, I was told by one of the managers, is from New York City. He happened to be in the restaurant on the evening, August of the year I visited, but I did not get to talk with him.

When the manager found out I came all the way from San Diego to enjoy a Hungarian meal, I was given the royal tour of the fantastic establishment. The food was terrific, as well as the wine. My meal cost about $60, with the bar bill, and I shall never forget it because of the exclusiveness and the charm of the building.

My lovely Hungarian hostess escorted me to the banquet room upstairs and she clarified every nook and cranny, describing the groups of city dignitaries who often frequent the location.

After full exploration of Buda and Pest, then my impressive ride along the Danube, I concluded my three exciting days of visiting a city filled with history and architectural splendor. The mark in my visitation book in the next year or two was definitely going to be Prague, and I carried out my promise to myself a couple of years later.

In 1998 I visited Czechoslovakia, and found the city of Prague to be also exciting as well as charming. Some Americans like the city better than Budapest because it is more concentrated as opposed to the Buda and Pest entities of Budapest. I was captivated by the food of Budapest, though the charm of both cities is overwhelming.

When visiting the eastern part of Europe since 1989 and the fall of the Berlin Wall one acknowledges the fact the communists have lost their hold on these countries. This is a breath of fresh air because there was such a restriction, especially on people from the West. The interaction between any foreign visitor, especially Americans, while in those areas was limited because of the secret police. We Americans do not like to be restricted, especially by an inferior sociopolitical system created by unsuccessful Marxist fanatics.

My move into West Germany, in 1961, was the most broadening experience of my life, and I would not trade it for any cultural exposure of a young man in his 30s. The continual acquisition of the German language, travel, dining, social interaction, and exploration of hunting along the Rhine river gave me an almost "Hemingway" thirst for more adventure in my young life. I wanted to see more, travel more, and learn more about Europe.

My income in the 1960s, though only about $6,000 a year, elevated in take home pay by government subsidized housing, eventually reaching, in the 80s, about $10,000 extra dollars, tax free, so this made my pay extremely good. In relation to the existing, but upcoming economic status of the Germans, I did quite well. I had a millionaire German brother-in-law, Otto Stöben, realtor in Kiel, Germany, who praised my income at that time, because relative to that of German professionals, he thought I did quite well, especially since I was supporting his sister-in-law. He is one of the most successful independent realtors in northern Germany, and I spent many great evenings with his now deceased wife, Christiana. She is the sister of my ex wife, Brigitte von Jagow Stell, and had a charm and confidence most becoming. After enjoying many great meals and wonderful wine at their lovely home outside of Kiel, I have only positive and fond memories of our frequent celebrations.

Otto is about my age, but his economic success, with several acres of beautiful German farmland and great stables with beautiful jumping horses, is enviable. I respect him to this day, and it is my understanding that Otto, though approaching seventy is still working. I am sure his fine three sons, who are taking over the real estate business will continue his acute and successful accomplishments.

Otto Stöben's business success was highly attributed to his also successful father and there are many Germans who continued such successes and with the profitable injection of the Marshall Plan, continued the positive achievements of the very productive West Germany. This is especially true in West Germany because of the free enterprise system. The Marshall Plan boosted that half of a great and progressive nation after World War II.

The West German recovery from World War II was remarkable and I feel certain, that after a few more years, the Eastern Germany will also be great. The tendency for Germany to lead the way in Europe is definitely occurring today, even into 2014!

The building of a new infrastructure of East Germany will certainly, someday in the future, lead to a great renaissance in that half of Germany. Except for the scar left on the East Germans, by the degrading Communistic regime, there is great hope for that half of a great country.

I see Germany, as a whole, the up-and-coming leaders of Europe. This accomplishment is mainly because of the innate tendency of Germany to be progressive. Their technological capacity, and historically great workmanship, with specialized schools meeting needs of all their citizens, will lead them to great things.

One needs only drive a Mercedes vehicle or a BMW, and you will witness the solid quality of great machinery. Germans take pride in their products, and I feel that, with the right balance in politics, and economic assertion, the great German mind and people will achieve at their highest potential.

The recovery of West Germany, after World War II was, with the aid of the Marshall Plan, one of the greatest achievements in Western Europe. Germany utilized the aid of the United States in the essence of capability. The only unfortunate event was that the USSR tied down East Germany and detained its development and achievement for forty years. The western part of Germany, in the 1960s was remarkable in its growth, focus, and socioeconomic development, along with its political stability.

Its people were progressive, apologetic, democratic, and gracious after the sad events of the Third Reich. Today, the apologetic overtones still exist in many world political events. This is most obvious when events related to any minority infractions occurring in Germany. The German government is very sensitive and responsive to any negative political events. Maybe this is why I found their courts to be so humane and democratic during my one experience in a German court.

There are, however, some underlying conservative elements of Germany, which, if not controlled and kept in balance, that could again surface if ultra-conservative tendencies were to ever get the upper hand of the political dynamics existing.

The overall achievements are remarkable and the modern and democratic Germany in the twenty-first century should succeed with the greatest possible surge. Its people will continue to achieve, because the opportunity for West Germany after 1945, to attain economic stability, was successful.

The modern technological progress attained after the war made the country one of the most enjoyable to visit in all of Europe, and I can only praise their success and achievement, which should continue. Germany, as one nation will take advantage of its post war success. The postwar success and the movement into the twenty-first century should elevate to one, along with the United States, one of world leadership!

The people Hitler left behind are certainly utilizing the democratic principles adopted after the end of World War II, and are magnifying the country in a positive light that can be envied by any country in Europe today!

Chapter 2

~ ✡ ~

Americans And Germans Blend

In the overseas setting, Americans are often awe-stricken when entering into a different country. Actually the Americans and Germans, during the days after the occupation, got along quite well. Sometimes I, as an American in a strange country, had more trouble dealing with rank conscious military than with the general German population.

On the first day I entered Ramstein Air Base in January of 1961, I felt much at home, and very secure, especially because of the military community surrounding me. When I lived in the BOQ (Bachelor Officer Quarters), I knew I had the support of the American military behind me for security, and when one is just moving into the overseas environment, security is important.

After living in the BOQ from January, 1961 until spring of 1962, when I married my wife, Brigitte, I left the bosom of the U. S. Air Force, and sought housing on the German economy. I found a nice 2-bedroom apartment, which was actually the lower half of a German house, in Bann, Germany. Bann is a small village near the airbase and had only about 800 or so inhabitants, at that time. My landlord and landlady were

Frau and Herr Kusel the name I remember to this day, as being Frau and Herr Kusel. They were my first landlady and landlord and were most accommodating.

The apartment, or lower part the house, had a heater, which was sustained by fuel oil (kerosene), and I had to bring in the oil from a neighboring village. Bann, at that time had no source of fuel oil. About every two weeks or so I would have to purchase a new oil supply in order to keep my 2 bedroom apartment warm. The kitchen source of fuel for the stove was propane gas, and I also had to buy the filled containers every 4 weeks or so.

My wife-to-be, lived with me from February1962, until May, the month of our marriage. The living was somewhat difficult because we did not have natural gas or electrical heat. But we survived until the fall of 1962, when we moved to on-base housing and had all the amenities we needed. What a difference, living in warm quarters with abundant heat and hot water provided by the U. S. military. These quarters were set up to support our military and civilians who sacrificed their time to protect Europe during the post occupation years of the 1960s.

Living on base proved to be quite an experience for a 30 year old teacher who was full of idealistic ideas, eager to mix with the German culture, learn the language, and travel to all the villages and interesting cities of West Germany.

During the week I was preoccupied with the processes that normally take place in an American Dependent School setting. I was teaching in a junior high, which was regarded as one of the best in West Germany. The junior high school had an enrollment of over 900 students, and had the best equipment, and a wonderful teaching staff.

Many of my afternoons were spend drinking beer at the local beer taverns Gasthäuser) in neighboring villages or Ramstein, Landstuhl, and Kaiserslautern. Many of the American teachers, also eager to learn the language, and the culture of Germany, frequented various places that were identified as popular meeting places after school. The newcomers, teachers new to Germany, were curious about what was taking place in the local communities so they frequented them often.

To be frank, the most significant thing taking place in the early 1960s, with the Germans, was the business of getting Germany back into a normal, Western European economic status. The local merchants were happy to do business with military and civilians. Credit cards were seldom seen at that time, and cash was the mode of doing business with the Germans and most Americans paid cash also. The department stores of Germany had not yet started using credit cards, though they were popular in the United States.

I remember one Friday evening, after work, I wanted to purchase a new top coat, since most of my clothes were those brought over from California, and heavy winter clothing was a minimal part of my wardrobe. I was persistent in my search and wanted to purchase a new topcoat to protect me from the forthcoming cold winter of 1962. I bought the coat, somewhat tweed in design, and when I saw it in the light, I was shocked because the illuminated green, mixed with the white was obvious and I had wanted black and white. I am color blind in shades of grays and greens so I definitely erred in my choice of a coat.

I kept the nice topcoat, costing not much over $25 at that time, and took it home with me to receive my German wife's approval. When she told me it was dominantly green, I was shocked. At any rate, I kept the coat, only to wear it for about a year before giving it to a Diakonie, which is similar to our Salvation Army or Good Will outlets.

I experienced many adventures and encounters, in my gregarious manner, with various German citizens. One particular event I remember is contact with a German police officer whom I met through my landlord. Someway we made a deal and he accepted a 5-gallon Jerry can full of Post Exchange gasoline, for helping me repair one of my cars. That auto the gentleman worked on was a 1962 Volkswagen, light green in color and absolutely perfect for driving in Germany at that time, especially in the snow. They, with the weight of the engine in the rear and being a rear wheel drive, really maneuver in the snow.

I could not believe that a German police officer would accept such an offer since it was somewhat in the realm of black market, or to say the least, gray market. But I assumed he was ready to take the risk so I made the deal because the gasoline was cheap for me and expensive for him. Later I began to barter often in this way, but not on a grand scale.

Later, however, I was to learn that my wife, Brigitte, would be making such gray market deals quite often in the near future. Gratuities or barter items such as cigarettes, alcohol, and coffee were items, which could make things happen in Germany in the 1960s through the 1980s. Such practices, no doubt, still go on around the U. S. military bases throughout the world.

My wife, Brigitte, when I met her in the spring of 1961, was working as a dental assistant in Mannheim, Germany. She also had a job as a waitress in a Konditorei (high-class coffeehouse) in downtown Mannheim. She served coffee and Kuchen (cake) in the Konditorei, and supplemented her dental assistant salary. Before we married, I visited her each weekend in Mannheim, Germany. Later I coaxed her into living with me before I made the vows, and assured "Mutti Jagow", her mother, that I would marry her daughter.

While visiting Brigitte in Mannheim, I would bring her, and her aunt and uncle, cigarettes, coffee, and alcohol. When they learned I was happy to present such gifts I was the greatest creature on earth because of my generosity. Later, such items proved to be the bartering ticket for all sorts of services in Germany, as previously mentioned. They were convenient in small business deals, hunting, and it was always nice to present a bottle of liquor to hostesses and hosts who invited us to dinner.

Also, post-exchange items were great to use in purchasing wild game especially, which had to be paid for after the German hunt. The German hunters, whether private land owners or State land managers, had to be reimbursed for the game taken off the Revier (hunting area), and the money used for purchasing food or for normal costs in the operation of the hunting area.

As I reflect back on particular hunting associates in my past twenty years of hunting in Germany, one gentleman whom I respected and really loved was a previous Bürgermeister (mayor) of the village of Gangelt, Germany. Gangelt was a town of a few hundred residents, and was located just East of Schinveld, the village where I lived in the Netherlands, while teaching for NATO. The gentleman's name is Dr. von Den Driesch. He had served a Bürgermeister of Gangelt for several years, and was the most gracious hunting friend I have ever known.

In 1969 I was invited to his home and was introduced to his wife, and son, both being delightful people. He took me to his hunting Revier in the Eifel Mountains many times, after I met him, because he had a great hunting area with over 2,000 acres. This location was not far from the Belgium border, and near where the Battle of the Bulge took place during the heavy fighting of WW II.

We also hunted pheasant near the border of the Netherlands, and in the vicinity of Gangelt, but the great hunting was for wild boar and Roe Deer (Rehwild) near the Ardenne Mountains near the border of Belgium.

Our hunts would usually have the longevity of about two nights, where we spent the spent the evening in his cabin on his hunting Revier. There was a caretaker for the game and the cabin so everything was always in good shape. There would be drinks, meals, and just good old times with plenty of pleasant conversation, in German, with him and the other guests who were also invited.

The doctor, a great provider for us, the eager hunters, was well off enough to furnish all the food, drink, hunting dogs, and lodging. Usually when invited by such a host, it was a full invitation, with no cost to the guest. The hunter had to pay for the game only, and sometimes he did not charge, even for the game. Dr. von den Driesch had a game manager who lived in the local area to keep track of the game population and habits. One would always shoot a deer, and sometimes luck up on a wild boar.

My first time to shoot a wild boar happened on a cold December snowy night in 1976, several years after I left the Gangelt, Netherlands region I lived in from 1968 to 1971. I was invited to the Revier, along with my friend, Herbert Dietrich, the avid hunter and friend from Karlsruhe, Germany.

We called the doctor, drove up to the revier, and spent two nights in the hunting lodge. We also bought a 20-pound turkey at the U. S. Army commissary, and took it along as a gift and as a return gratuity for the invitation, though with this gentleman, gratuities were never necessary. He, of course appreciated it, exclaiming that it was in no way necessary.

This doctor, who was my very good friend and hunting friend had done me a great favor while I taught in the NATO secondary school, known a AFCENT (Allied Forces Central Europe, a part of the NATO organization). I had gotten involved with a lovely teacher in the AFCENT secondary school, had an ongoing love affair, made the lady pregnant while teaching in the school there. We spent many cold snowy nights under her silk sheets making love; obviously I was not faithful to my German wife, so she, my teacher friend, ended up pregnant! Dr. von den Driesch, not only being a respected doctor but the Mayor (Burgermeister) of Gangelt for several years, came to my rescue and had the lady go to a location, via his connections, in one of the Dutch hospitals near Brunssum and abort the child. That was my best solution, rather than break up my marriage, leaving our young gorgeous daughter without a father.

This lovely lady teacher had her second abortion, due to my playing around, sleeping around with her, done in the United States the next summer while she was home on leave, somewhere in Indiana or near Indiana. Abortions were not legal everywhere in the U. S. in 1968-70. I was a slow learner and our affair went on for almost two years.

The time frame for Herbert's and my hunting trip was during winter holidays of the Overseas Dependent Schools, so I had about 15 days free so must have been about 1972 or 1973. Hunting still being my favorite hobby at that time, I utilized many of those holidays for such enjoyment.

Herbert Dietriech was an excellent hunter, knew all the characteristics and habits of the various wild game, including wild boar, red deer, roe deer, pheasant, and others existing in Germany. We were sitting in the high seat on the Saturday evening of our hunt, and a huge stag (male red deer) walked right under the high seat so Herbert, being a gentleman and fried, gave me the opportunity to take aim and shoot the beautiful animal. I had the typical "buck fever," so I shaking like a leaf hit the sling of my rifle against the wall of the enclosed house like high seat. From the sound of the sling hittine the inside wall of the high seat, the huge animal turned and slipped, immediately, and quietly, back into the forest.

Disappointed with my first opportunity to take a trophy, one of which I was to never have again, I extended my heartfelt apologies to Herbert. Herbert, of course, had many trophies, though the one we saw must have been in the class of about 1-A, or highest rated in the German system. (The trophies are classed in the German hunting program). He wanted to give me, his American friend, the opportunity to make the kill. I lost the chance forever!

But all was not lost because the next evening, the last day of our visit, provided me with an opportunity to shoot an animal I had never shot before. It was the wild boar! Again, during a freezing rain and snowy night, I got my opportunity. A young wild boar, about 60 kilograms mass (approximately 132 U. S. lbs. weight), came ambling up to a feeder under the high seat. I took aim, with a .308 lever Winchester rifle, put the cross hairs onto the designated heart ("Blat") or heart area, squeezed the trigger and heard the loud report of the .308 Winchester. The animal appeared to turn and run away, so I was not sure I had made a complete kill, as hunters in Germany are supposed to do. The hunters, under the German hunting program (Abschussplan), must shoot all game, if possible, with one shot so it will not be wounded, run away and be consumed by predators. Also, the Revier owners do not like to lose the meat that is sold to the hunter, or that is sold to various restaurants. Conservation, with balance of food supply and game population, is the main concept of the whole hunting plan in Germany.

We could see very little at night, so we walked back to the lodge at about 3:30 a.m., fell into our cots and slept until about 8:00 a.m. the next morning. The Revier caretaker took us back to the spot, with a proper dog, and we searched the area for the wild pig.

After walking under the high seat where Herbert and I had been sitting, wrapped in our sleeping bags for warmth, the night before, the dog picked up the scent. The animal had jumped and run, as many animals do before they die, after a large caliber hit. He ran into the thick underlying bush, only about 10 meters from the feeding trough, cold, stiff, and quite dead. He was killed with the one shot, almost instantly, but had a few moments of life to run for protection.

There were many experiences, such as high seat hunting, still-hunting (walking silently through the woods), and the colorful drive hunts I remember in Germany. The fascination of the German hunting culture is almost beyond description. The dress, colorful-fall and winter days, working dogs, stand locations (for drive hunts), and social interaction during and after the hunts are magnificent. The horn blowing, laying out of the game, with high game and lower game having specific patterns or order, is so different from the almost frontier mode of American hunting. One must participate in the German hunt to attain the gala of the day because of the tremendous network of customs interwoven into the beautiful "conservation mode" of their particular type of hunting.

The intimate association with many German aristocrats, and some Burgers (middle-class citizens), or business owners, exposed me to a cross section in Germany, which most Americans living abroad seldom have a chance to experience. The invitation into many German homes activated an interaction with the citizenry of the host country that was profitable in its richness for future contacts.

Many of the American military also participated in such interaction, forging lasting friendships which are excellent for German-American relations. Herbert Dietrich, whom I still continue contact with when visiting Karlsruhe, Germany was and still is a friend of mine. He made another acquaintance with a dentist from the U. S. military dental clinic in that city and the two still communicate. The dentist, after the 70s (practice in Oregon) returns to Germany often and always visits Herbert and his wife. My ex wife and I also visit Herbert each time I return to Germany. It is always pleasant to visit the Karlsruhe area because of its beautiful memories.

These two particular hunting friends, the American dentist, Rich, and Herbert send Christmas cards, speak by telephone, and if both have access to the Internet and E-mail, I am sure they utilize that mode of communication also. There were many such bonding processes, especially if the Americans learned the German language. The acquisition of the German language opened a door of more extensive depth than those relationships where the language key was missing.

The blending of the two cultures was quite easy for the general U. S. military population and U. S. civilian population because of the German festivals and German-American organizations. These festivities were in the form of wine festivals, beer festivals, and the famous "Karnival." This is what we call Fasching, and is similar to our Mardi Gras in New Orleans or Mobile, Alabama each year.

The Germans love celebrations, and have festivals or Karnival celebrations throughout the country continually, whether in villages or cities. It is an opportunity for people to relax, enjoy beer and wine, parades, costumes, dancing, and great times together.

My participation in such events were frequent, and it was seldom that I saw an uncontrolled brawl or friction, even though the crowds were sometimes shoulder to shoulder, and in the thousands. The Germans knew how to enjoy life in their free time of celebration and leisure. Once, however, in the 1970s, I was told that a drunken citizen was hit and killed by a streetcar in the city of Karlsruhe, but this tragedy was somewhat rare, or unusual. The local Karlsruhe Zeitung (newspaper) verified the incident the next day. It is amazing that there are not more accidents with the numbers that gather for the German celebrations, especially in the larger cities. Brut this is also a reflection of the order and control maintained in German society.

When writing about German structure, organization, and order, is not difficult to understand some of the past regimented behaviors of the German citizens, such as the events leading to World War II, because the Germans tend to believe in strict authority and strong leadership. It is obvious that other European countries watch closely at political developments in Germany, and any gestures or overtones toward strong military or political assertions. In the twenty-first century these neighboring countries will cautiously, no doubt, observe German political activities and their influence on Europe.

Another observation I made during the Vietnam War, was the reaction of my landlord, where my family and I lived, in a small village called Hagenbach, and near the Rhine River. He made a comment to me that I felt was typical about the German attitude toward use of military strength. Good old Herr Weschler commented, "The Americans should take the atomic bomb, drop it on Hanoi, and be done with the war!"

At that time I was working for the Department of Defense, and certainly supported the military because but knew they were ham strung by the political forces during that period of history. I often had doubts about increasing the number of troops in Vietnam, and seeing young men sent home in body bags.

University students, especially in the immediate vicinity of Karlsruhe, which has a university, were often protesting our actions in Vietnam in the early and mid 1970s.

It was comforting to me when Nixon got us out of that fiasco in 1975. The Europeans, in general, did not sympathize too much with our involvement in Vietnam. The Germans, as a nation, tried to find empathy, and often used the Vietnam argument when confronted, in social conversations, as a justification for their past alignment with Nazi Germany.

The farther one moved toward Scandinavia, the more intense the Vietnam social stigma became for traveling Americans. The Swedes, whose country was one that our draft evaders often ran to, tended to be quite vociferous in denouncing our actions in Vietnam. Many of our politicians had to find justification for our actions when touring about Europe, especially when on official business. Visiting military bases abroad is a favorite junket for American Congresspersons.

I had numerous conversational encounters with Swedish citizens, especially on one occasion when traveling aboard a Swedish ship, headed to Norway. These people expressed their disdain for our involvement in Vietnam, and rather explicitly. I sometimes found it rather difficult to justify such a policy, but because I worked for the American Department of Defense, I felt obligated to at least defend our military women and men.

I found it to be rather cumbersome, eternally having to try to explain why our country got into a land war in a land so many miles from home, and one that was not attacking our shores at home. Had the Vietnamese have been doing so, I feel there would have been more justification for such a venture.

There were many instances I witnessed, working with the military in Dependent Schools, which placed the status of our military in an awkward setting. One particular instance I remember was when my friend, a major, married to one of our schoolteachers in the Netherlands. He was sent to Vietnam, put in harm's way, because he had made problems in the Pentagon regarding his rank. It seems the major thought his rising to the level of light colonel was being obstructed, or taking much too long, and wanted to make inquiries regarding his status, with the help of his congressperson.

About one month after he started inquiring, he was sent to Cam Ranh Bay, Vietnam. Within a month of his being stationed there, he was killed in a rocket attack. It appeared, from the explanations of several of his friends, that one does not question one's status in the U. S. Army. The friends of the major, with whom I spoke with while assigned to AFCENT, Military Dependent School, the Netherlands, were convinced that the reason of his assignment to a dangerous area was because of his persistence and questioning of military authority.

Other stories I heard from pilots, usually captains and above, involved the concept that the politicians in Washington D. C. tied the hands of the military and our troops or pilots could not really finish the war in Vietnam. It was a political war where pilots could only hit certain targets, and not go for targets to expedite their needs to cripple the enemy. If Vietnam was really our enemy? I often heard such comments from officers who were questioning the political control of the war by politicians. The military felt they had the expertise to either finish it or get out.

The "Butter and Guns" economy under President Lyndon B. Johnson set up a polarized effect in our society whereby part of the nation felt the patriotic need to support troops, and the students, along with the most of the rebelling youth wanted to get out of the war altogether.

When Nixon got so much pressure from the intelligentsia, and the rebelling youth of America, the war was finally ended in 1975. When the draft started selecting college students whose parents were well enough informed about our mission in Vietnam, the protest factor became overwhelming. Also, the disgust with body bags coming home, Americans began putting pressure on the politicians and it began having a notable effect in Washington D. C. People with reasoning ability and those who were educated enough to begin to question our mission had seen enough the Vietnam fiasco.

I, being a veteran of the United States Navy, Korean War, vacillated in my opinion about this sociological phenomenon of the Vietnam War when our country was not threatened as we were in World War II. The mission and cause was entirely different!

Why would a great nation like the United States prolong an unpopular war when our nation was not threatened? Even with the so called "Domino Theory," reflecting the possible loss of the other Southeast Asian nations to communism, there did not seem to be a logical reason to continue spending billions of dollars, and losing young lives in a distant country.

This is exactly what most Europeans questioned about the United States and its involvement in the Vietnam War. It was a continual thorn in my side when dealing with German professionals, and even everyday laborers working in German society, or other Europeans whom I met in my travels.

With intellectual dialogue among my German friends, I was sometimes like an ostrich with its head in the sand, hoping the conflicting dialogue would go away. "Have another beer, and let us talk about beer, bratwurst, and fun German living. I was thinking, I hope they do not bring up that damned war!"

Finally, after the end of the Vietnam war (1975) in the mid-1970s, we, who were employed with the Department of Defense, in Europe, got about our business justifying why the Americans remained in Europe, especially in conversation with the people back home, when we returned there on leave. Many times the inevitable question, "Why are dependents overseas?" came up, especially back in the United States.

Many of the military with whom I worked, asserted that NATO had its foot in the door in Europe, and especially in Germany, utilizing their military acuteness in a manner to create a strong buffer against the reigning bad guys, the USSR. I felt this was a much more useful cause, and feel, even now, it was a worthwhile adventure, vying with the degrading virus of communism in Eastern Europe. Maintaining dependents might still be questionable because the recent trend of the United States has been to reduce military dependents abroad, at least from what I have seen with the closing of many of the schools about Germany since the 1990s.

Unfortunately, I was in San Diego teaching when the Berlin Wall fell in 1989, and the East Germans, Czechs, Hungarians, and other chained countries starting letting their citizens come and go, as they pleased throughout Europe. The scathing existence and plague of Communism only held those poor citizens of Eastern Europe back from progress for many years. The sight would have been enjoyable and I missed feeling the joy the East Europeans must have expressed.

I feel that the great fusion years between Americans and West Germans, from late 1940s through today have tended to increase the bonding effect between Germans and Americans. The blend that occurred in the postwar years, with the various military bases being immersed in the heart of Western Germany was a fantastic opportunity to temper the positive new alloy that was created between our two nations.

One of the most pleasing experiences I believe I have ever enjoyed as a dependent school teacher was an encounter with the NATO advisor, retired General von Steinhof, an ex jet pilot who was injured in a crash of his plane, and suffered numerous scars on his face and head. I often saw him on German television because he was used as a sounding board on NATO policy and administration in the 1960s through the 1970s.

I had the good fortune of meeting him and his lovely wife while looking at investment condos in Southern Spain, near Malaga one summer. He was on the beach writing, and I recognized him, then wandered over to him and started a conversation in German. When he discovered I was an American school teacher with AFCENT (Allied Forces Central Europe), and had taught in Brunssum, the Netherlands, he conveyed to me that he was a member of that local school advisory board there in 1970, the time I was teaching at that fantastic school.

We had a long conversation, and the fact that he had been scarred but plastic surgery did a great job to mend his burned, and scarred face, did not distract one from such an intelligent person. One never even noticed the affliction because of the powerful manner and dedication he exuded as he talked. Later that evening he was eating dinner with his wife and invited me to sit with them and enjoy a drink together, since they had just completed their meal.

We talked about NATO, the Cold War with the USSR, and various social aspects of German American relations. I was alone on the trip, but explained my wife was from Kiel, and originally from East Prussia, so this brought on other tidbits of conversation. Nevertheless, the conversation was invigorating, and I got to pick the mind of a once Nazi Luftwaffe pilot who was a consultant with the existing NATO contingencies of post World War II Germany and Europe.

Actually, General Steinhoff crashed a German Messerschmidt 262, one of the World War II jets produced for the German Luftwaffe. From my Internet research, I discovered he was taking off in the plane and hit a bomb crater on an airfield near Munich, Germany. The airport was Reim field. He was burned severely and hardly recognizable when taken to the hospital. But after, what must have been a series of skin grafts, and much medical care, he still functioned well after the war, becoming a great sounding board for German/American NATO ventures up through the 1970s, in and about Germany.

This gentleman was a gracious person, who contributed well to the German/American NATO setting of the 1960s and 1970s. He and his wife were quite gracious, and were most cordial to me when we conversed on the Mediterranean known as the Costa del Sol, in the early 1970s.

I find, even today, the German people to be the most cordial in social interaction, and continue my close friendly contacts as often as I can, each time I visit Germany. I also have a standing invitation from the German Volkshochschule administration in Bad Kreuznach, to teach English as I did for almost six years (1978-1984), in evening classes. There are many German business people who love taking classes from Americans who can deliver the "idiomatic" approach to the lessons. I look forward to future teaching encounters just so I can continue and expand my German contacts.

When I taught these classes in the 1970s, I formed a bond with many of my students. They were usually in the age brackets of 30s and 40s, trying to enhance their knowledge of the English language, and in turn, the teaching gave me a deeper insight into the workings of linguistic and social interaction in German society.

The experience I had in my twenty years of living in Germany provided me with an insight that proves that international maps and barriers are broken through communication, understanding, and social contact. One soon learns after living abroad that the, sometimes, abhorrent conflicts and wars that often occur between people and nations come from lack of cultural understanding. The Second World War certainly emanated from lack of cultural understanding, with the attempt Hitler trying to decimate the Jewish people.

It is almost inconceivable today, to think of myself, in uniform, and seeing a German, perceived as my enemy, in the sights of a military rifle. During the time of World War II, because of the dastardly atrocities levied by the Third Reich, it was understandable that we shot at each other. But with the years of democratization of Germany, and the current positive trends of this Germany, it would be difficult to perceive them as enemies. With my ex family connections, I would abhor conflicts, or another war, and especially with Germans. I see war as an agonizing solution for world conflicts, especially as I grow older.

The blending, German/American processes created by the fifty-year interactions, military, politically, socially, and economically, has come to be one of improved understanding. The only possibility I ever see for Germany to experience what happened during the Second World War would be for a drastic economic change in the direction German society is now headed. The Germans have the potential to be cooperative leaders in Europe. With their current progress socially, politically, and economically, I expect to see great achievements by them in the future of European cooperation.

As far as the blending of Germans and Americans, since the Second World War, I feel that much has been accomplished.

Much of this has been provided through the structure of NATO, the tremendous thrust of military German/American programs promoted and supported, via the U. S. military bases created after World War II. Such military investments have enhanced our status with the German people.

It is too bad that the programs created by the military, and the civilian appendage, did not reach into East Germany. But now they, East Germans, are safe from the dastardly scars inflicted by the communist processes ruling their society since the end of World War II. The sad thing is that their citizens did not have the opportunity, as West Germany did, to enjoy the fruits of both countries' labors between 1945 and 1989.

With the economic processes evolving from a centralized Germany, the eighty plus million citizens will now have the opportunity to utilize the blend of German-American relations created in the last fifty years. It does not take long for half a nation to pick up on the tremendous opportunities created by the two positive elements of capitalism and democracy. Though the citizens, of many of the areas I visited in the eastern half of Germany, were set back, by the plague of communism, things are changing rapidly. The smiles come to the faces of East Germans as the U. S. and other tourists, U. S. military personnel, U. S. civilians continue to travel throughout the eastern half of this great country.

All in all, the Germans and Americans are coming together, finding more similarities than we ever knew. The strong "work ethic" injected by the German people, through historical immigration has also contributed to American society here at home. The healed scars existing since the end of World War II, are becoming more apparent as tourists begin to explore and travel the autobahn, fantastic "on time" trains, and other modes of traveling in Germany.

The internet, with its chat programs, jet travel with quick contact, cultural exchange programs, and modern communication devices should continue to break down any barriers recreated by the grim "Saving Private Ryan" realism so well depicted in the recent Spielberg film. We hope the memories of World War II will soon be overcome through mutual understanding from exchanges, the past U. S. military involvement, and future exchange programs.

For me, going back to Germany is like going back home. It is my second home, and I feel as safe and secure there as I do any place in the United States. Their fantastic beer and wine enhance the warmth of the German people, in their fun loving and festive manner! The blend between the two countries and their people has now emerged, and great things will continue to happen because of it.

The people Hitler left behind have now, through fifty years of close contact with Americans, should continue to extend the understanding needed to forge future relationships between two great countries. The constant movement, back and forth, of the two populations can only bring broader understanding and continued trust. The two governments, in the twenty-first century have a great start for unlimited exchanges in culture and between their people!

Chapter 3

Golden Ghettoes, American Style

Many Americans, when abroad, tend to miss the things that make them feel secure. Often that is certain foods such as hamburgers, apple pie, and bacon and eggs for breakfast. The United States Military, when setting up their bases in Germany and other countries tried to establish home away from home so, especially the dependents would be content inside the bases.

Actually that is what the American did with their dependent military schools also tried to established in their programs when they were built throughout Germany, France, Spain, Italy, Japan, Korea, Libya, Turkey, and many other countries of the worlds. The schools were built so they could deliver the same programs that schools in the United States have. The U. S. government did provide the security for the military and civilian dependents in their designs and programs, and the school system was financially well by one of our strongest government agencies, the Department of Defense. Congress financed the programs quite well.

The acting school board of the Overseas Dependent Schools is the Congress of the United States, and they like to take care of the military and their dependents. They do it in a quality manner, and provide the $8,000 plus per pupil allowance/year on these children throughout the world! This amount was roughly a late 1980 estimation, and I am sure the figure would be even more today. I would suspect this figure is approaching $9,000 per pupil/year by now. This is a high amount of per pupil dollars, and compares with better school financed states, certainly better than California which is much lower than it should be.

The Americans who lived in the base houses were well taken care of in a secure and quality manner. There were those, however, who because of base housing scarcity, in the 1960s through the 1980s, had to live on the economy. Many did not like it, but some did, and some even preferred the opportunity to mix with their German neighbors. Many teachers who chose the "living abroad" opportunity in their teaching careers wanted to live outside the bases in order to access the culture and language more conveniently.

Those teachers living outside the American military bases in Germany soon learned a significant amount of the host country language, how to purchase goods on the economy, and how to interact with German neighbors. Was this good? Actually it was probably the best thing that could have happened to them.

The concept of the "Golden Ghettoes", is an idea coined by me, and it was one that provided the security of the military and civilians, so they could do their tasks just as though they were in the United States. The Americans were clustered, on most bases, seemingly for their security. But they were not in the United States so they had to endure, good or bad, another culture when they left base.

Unfortunately, from what I observed, many of the lower paid military personnel did not like living in a strange land.

They were forced to be there because the army, air force, or navy, placed them and their dependents there. Trying to shop, drive, procure furniture, and do other necessities was a real burden for some.

But, for lower grade and higher grade personnel, military or civilian, the Department of Defense tried to make it easy on them abroad, by setting up commissaries, providing furniture, post exchanges and gasoline stations right on base. The lower grade military did not seem to mingle with the host nation environs, as extensively as the officers did, unless they were married to a host nation partner. Then the motivation was quite different. I knew many E-4 through officer grade U. S. Army personnel who were married to Germans, and they did quite well with the German language. They therefore got the most out of the assignments. I knew many civilians and army personnel who lived in Germany, including myself, for twenty years or more. Spouses were usually the deciding influence in seeking extended stays abroad.

The opportunity for gleaning ideas and culture from another nation was the ultimate for me because it opened up the multi-faceted world we live in. To order meals, clothes, gasoline, or other merchandise was a pleasure, especially in another language was a valuable and satisfying experience. My year of living in the choice location of Aviano, Italy, from August 1966 until August 1967, was one of the highlights of my overseas experiences.

I was steeped in the German language but wanted to try a second, so I spent time, with my German wife, acquiring the Italian language via German. The secretary at Aviano American High School, where I taught, wanted to learn German, so she taught us Italian while we, in turn, helped her learn German. It was a most pleasurable experience, and we made real progress by setting up lessons for two to three hours a week.

For the benefit of military and civilians, the same amenities, post exchanges, commissaries and base gasoline stations were located in Italy, similar to those in Germany. The same, on base housing was provided, especially for those military of strategic importance, but base housing was not as accessible as in Germany. We had, of course many more bases in Germany, and availability of quarters was more abundant there than in Italy.

The weather was great in the northern part of Italy, so most of the troops who lived in that part of Europe had few complaints, especially when they ventured off the base and made trips to Rome, Pizza, Milan, Naples, and other charming cities of Italy. Travel in friendly weather was absolutely marvelous. It was like being in Florida or California, only with the magnificent Italian culture, interspersed with ancient Roman coliseums, aqueducts, and other remnants of splendid architecture.

Gasoline was almost $3.00 a gallon in Italy when buying on the local economy if my memory is correct, in 1966-67. We definitely needed, and used the post-exchange, gasoline rations of coupons provided through ESSO or other oil corporations. If one traveled as frequently, and as often as my wife and I did in those days (we had two automobiles), then one needed all the gasoline rations available. Fortunately we could get leave orders, even for weekend trips, and having two automobiles we came out quite well. But we were often seeking, because of our frequent trips, the leave orders that could be issued by the school secretary, then signed by the principal who was our acting commander.

If one ran low on rations while down in Naples, one could drive to the Navy Base, show the leave orders, and get extra rations. This was also one advantage of having the leave orders when traveling out of Germany to such places as Zaragoza, Spain or Madrid. The extra gasoline allowance process was one provision which I thoroughly utilized, and quite frequently. High utilization gasoline was definitely a trait of the travel oriented household, and the military and civilian officials actually encouraged the idea of traveling as a broadening experience, and also a morale builder for personnel on leave.

The idea of protection of our troops via the "Golden Ghetto" was to the advantage of the American military personnel. The concept of the Golden Ghetto complexes is that we never really had to go it alone and the "paternalism" of the military was almost over protecting for the Americans. But is this not somewhat natural with most nationalities in the world? But when traveling abroad, if one does not have the military, then he or she has the home embassy located in the host nation. This is a protective device for travelers abroad because they do need embassy protection, especially in some less democratic countries.

All in all, it is probably a good thing for the American military and Department of Defense civilians to have this protection. I often wondered if the challenge was not much greater if one worked for the corporate world, and really had to strive for existence by being thrown right out amongst the host nation citizens when stationed in a foreign country?

The Golden Ghettoes, however, were elements that continued to spoil the American military and Department of Defense civilians living abroad. All the fantastic support mechanisms, as I described before, were protective devices that spoiled us, but made some of the people representing our country void of learning the language, and local customs. Some were haughty enough to explain they did not learn the host nation language because most Europeans know English, even when they were abroad on extended tours. It was therefore not their desire, responsibility, nor necessary to waste their time with a foreign language. I have actually heard such blatant and arrogant statements, from civilians and military living abroad for extended stay. It is excusable if one travels for short visits to various countries, and not learn a language, but those on extended tours should have the courtesy of trying to learn the host country language.

There was, and often, the explanation that they did not have a knack, or propensity for languages. How absurd! Learning a language, from my experience, is based upon desire, exposure, and usage. I do not think I have ever met a corporate person living abroad-Germany, France, or Italy, who did not acquire a quick communicative ability in the host nation language. The reason was, obviously, because they did not have the protection of the, "back to the womb of my mother country" syndrome of many of the military personnel and civilians employed by the Defense Department.

The Golden Ghettoes definitely protected those who did not want to venture out into a strange land, rub elbows with the host nation citizens, and have fun at their frequent festivals. Missing such an opportunity is a fantastic and unique opportunity for thousands of Americans living abroad. Germany is such a friendly and culture rich country and is located in a historically advantageous part of Europe. The frequent festivals, beautiful forests, and sites were there for the taking. I, highly curious about the German society, took every opportunity possible to mingle and interact with the people.

Bacon and eggs, hamburgers, and the traditional T-bone steak, plus the milk shake and hot dog were traditionally missed foods among Americans abroad. For me, it did not take long to become attuned to the traditional German breakfast of fresh Brötchen, 3 minute boiled eggs, butter, and marmalade or jams and jellies of different sorts. This was a traditional German breakfast or Früstück. I must admit, I sometimes had a yearning for southern country sausage, biscuits, and over easy eggs, and we had the pleasure of purchasing all the items from the commissary on base, in order to assuage any homesick moods.

But, had I have had to survive without the American desired foods, I could have adapted, and did so when visiting such countries as Austria, France, Belgium, Spain, or other beautiful countries of Europe. My family and I often visited other countries while living in Germany, Italy, and the Netherlands, and extracted the most in sight seeing, museum visits, and dining or other worthwhile pleasures.

I even bought the well known, camping or house trailer or German Wohnwagen (made by Wilk) and pulled it to Greece, France, and Northern Germany. I purchased it at the Canadian P.X. during the time I taught in Karlsruhe, Germany, at the American High School. I pulled the trailer with a 1976 Monarch Mercury automobile, until I had transmission troubles because of the constant traveling up and down mountain roads and the hinterlands.

I finally sold the trailer for about the same price I paid for it, and after using it for over a year and a half. American civilians and military had the advantage of getting such items, even American automobiles, at tax-free prices. I purchased the trailer at Baden Baden, Germany. I got it for a reasonable price from the Canadians who are great campers. We had reciprocal shopping advantages in other NATO country bases.

Traveling with the trailer gave my family, and especially my daughter Liane, who loved playing in the camp sites, the luxury of living in secure and warm quarters even in cold and rainy weather, as often found in Germany and Northern France, when traveling. We would just pull into a camping area, found frequently in all European countries, hook up to the electricity, and enjoy the comforts of home. The advantage of having such a rig was that one could unhook, then drive to the nearest city, sight see, dine, or even attend an opera, if close enough to a larger city.

But after over a year of the camping, I began to get tire of the outdoor life and enjoyed various unique hotels in various areas of Europe. Once I left teaching, and went into school administration, I lost my interest in the diversity of the camping rig. I made a little more money, though I endured more stress, but did not want to be bothered with pulling the trailer behind me. Hotels were cheap and so were pensions, so I began to utilize them, especially the pensions, more when traveling. I still take advantages of the pension when traveling about Europe, and mostly because of the fantastic prices. They are not quite as luxurious as many hotels, but are quaint and quite unique.

Many U. S. civilians and military personnel did utilize the advantageous opportunity of living in a foreign land because of its strategic travel potential. Some even made trips to Russia. I know one teacher who took his V. W. Camper to Russia one summer, but he complained of the lack of gasoline stations, modern facilities, and restaurants. I never had the "Russia" experience, and still yearn for a trip in the future.

There were various visa hang-ups in traveling to Russia, and the paperwork rarely made the venture worth while. I also did not feel comfortable at the thought of taking my family, German, especially to Russia. I was adventurous, but not that adventurous, especially with a young daughter. My wife had relatives who were in the Second World War, and I was warned about the possibility of running into difficulties in the Eastern Bloc, especially when traveling with a spouse who is German. The Russians were always looking for familiar names related to World War II events.

Some of the American personnel took trips from Germany, to distant lands as far away as Turkey, and some even made road trips to Africa. Actually I had the experience of living in North Africa, as an American teacher in 1960-61, so the yearning for, especially North African culture, did not grind away at my curiosity, and travel laden brain.

The Golden Ghettoes actually fortified the more adventurous Americans, who were curious, about travel and culture acquisition for their tours of duty. It gave them a place to return safely to, with the comforts of home. Many troops stayed only for eighteen-month, or two-year tour, or whatever was required by the military. The teacher contract was normally, unless in a distant country like Turkey, a two-year renewable contract. I signed two-year transportation agreements with the Overseas Dependent Schools from 1960 through 1984. Places like Turkey had only a one year transportation agreement because of the difficulty of getting, especially teachers, to come there.

I returned to CONUS (Continental United States) once a year, because of my schooling. I returned to the United States almost every year because of federal grants, or National Science Foundation Summer Institutes in order to update my schooling. These were provided because of the intensified upgrading science programs emanating from the "Sputnik" surprise of the Russians in the late 1950s.

Staying abroad for protracted spans of five years or more would not have deterred me from living abroad. I knew that I was in the Overseas Dependent School System because of tremendous economic advantages compared to teachers in the United States. It was also very nice that my family and I were fortunate enough to receive the womb security provided by the military, the Golden Ghetto. I and my colleagues had the economic advantage of receiving American wages, living in tax free housing, and purchasing gasoline at about one-fourth the cost of the Europeans. Relative to the Europeans, the postwar NATO opportunities enhanced the overseas teachers' status.

Other allied countries such as the British, Canadians, and the French also provided for these economic advantages. They had their bases, protected housing, post-exchanges, commissaries, and tax-free living. So the Golden Ghetto setting was not only provided to the Americans but to other allied forces. It was seemingly most protective for Americans, however. Americans are just not multi-linguistic, and are not as exposed to multiple languages on the United States continent, so living abroad because of a foreign language is sometimes more difficult for many Americans.

But we Americans, because of a traditional rugged individualism, open spaces, and "apple pie" living, find it hard to assimilate into the womb of foreign lands without the security of our god old USA protection. We are people who can, in our home country, travel from East Coast to the West Coast, and spend three or four nights on the road. We are accustomed to freedom of the road, laundromats, inexpensive motels, and wide open spaces. It is sometimes difficult for the ordinary, down-to-earth red-blooded American to adjust to other cultures.

But because of my education, with a variety of college courses, related to European history, geography, and languages, my thirst for knowledge in other countries will never cease. I now, because of a twenty-year exposure of Europe, am intensely curious about the Orient. My desire to travel to Japan, China, and Malaysia, is very strong. I am only waiting for the days of retirement, and accumulated monetary funds, to hit the friendly skies and head for the lands of oriental culture. More extensive exposure to Mexico is also on my agenda.

While most of the logistic setup for American military and civilians, abroad was advantageous, there were some disadvantages. Being crowded together, and sometimes too tightly, all experiences were not positive.

Sometimes the close living, while on base housing, was somewhat frustrating for me in the early 1960s on Ramstein Air Base. Although Ramstein was one of the most modern, and by far the largest air base on the continent of Germany, I had the yearning to get out and live with the natives. Some of the officers' wives in their arrogance were so particular about utilization of washers and dryers, it made living among them sometimes unpleasant. My wife being German did not seem to help.

Also, the strict parking rules, keeping the dogs on leashes, and other petty rules made "on base" living sickening. Oftentimes I had run-ins with officers who tried to pull rank. They would chastise me for letting dog off the leash for a few minutes, and I got very upset. All I could do was brandish my civilian independence, but I soon learned they were the ones with the power, although officers did not dictate to teachers. We also had advantages because, they, the military personnel certainly wanted to maintain genial contact with us, the teachers, for obvious reasons. We had their children!

Abiding by the military rules of base housing, driving, parking, or even walking about the base made one feel he was a prisoner, especially while living in such a culture rich area as Germany. I soon grew accustomed to the rules of the very large base, but for much of the time, I was off enjoying the Bierstuben of the villages near Ramstein Air Base. If not the taverns, I was enjoying the many sights of the local area.

One place I remember, in particular, was a place in the woods, near Ramstein Village. That is the village or "Dorf" from which Ramstein Air Base received its name. It was only a couple of kilometers from the base, and if you were as adventurous as I, you soon learned how to get in and off the base through the back woods, and without coming by the sentry, or manned gates.

Many a night I drove over to Lilli's little beer tavern, saturated myself, along with the German speaking teachers from my school, with German beer, which had a somewhat higher percentage of alcohol than American beer. I was driving, at that time, an early 50s vintage Volkswagen Beetle, which had a manual, unsynchronized transmission. I became so proficient at driving the car, without grinding the gears that I could sometimes shift from first gear, to second, even without the clutch.

I would go sailing off from Lilli's after ten in the evening, headed for the base, through the thick woods, barely able to see the dirt roads, then finding my way back to the Officer's Quarters. Most of this happened before I was married and living in the officer apartments. I was only living in Germany for a week before I explored the local restaurants or small beer taverns, almost on a nightly basis. My curiosity about the German people, and the German language was insatiable.

Lilli specialized in great Bratwurst, and sold the large, almost 1/2 liter, pop-top, beer bottles of the Rhineland-Pfalz beer, which was cellar cool. It only cost 50 Pfennig at that time, early 1961. This amounted to about 12 and 1/2 U. S. cents. The costs were almost unbelievable, especially when one compares it to today's prices in Germany.

Hank Weeks, an American science teacher, along with several other teachers hungry for German culture, and language, would be waiting for me at Lily's at about 6:30 p.m., and we would stay there, practice our German with the local Germans who were just as eager as we to exchange knowledge. We would talk about local politics, American and German customs, the Cold War, Germany's post war transition, and various and sundry spicy topics.

Lily, always eager to earn money from her American air base friends, would fix us goulash soup, bratwurst, rump steaks, or potato salad. What a treat, and for prices which were beyond belief, and not even denting our pocket books.

My wages, in the early 1960s, for the Department of Defense, were just over $4,600 a year, but with free housing, one could add another $2,000 to $4,000 (depending on the grade or rank) in perks. The American dollar went a long way in those days, and the boundless areas of European travel were there for us, with the Golden Ghetto always awaiting our return to the bowels of innate American security.

Striking out for areas like Heidelberg, Baden Baden, Wiesbaden, or Bavaria was a favorite pastime of mine, especially before I met my German wife. Filling up the Jerry cans, with extra Quartermaster gasoline, so the kilometer range was expanded, was a frequent practice of other Americans, and also mine in those days. Booking in a Gasthaus with rooms was a joy because they were inexpensive, clean, and the food was always good. The guesthouses, especially in the villages, were clean, with soft down covers (or featherbed) and sometimes service personnel polished your shoes if you set them out at nights. Some of the meals consisted of wild game, Wienerschnitzel (veal slices fried in bread crumbs), center cut ribs with sauerkraut, Bratwurst, potato salad, dumplings, rump steak, roast pork, red cabbage, and various other German dishes.

I seldom met a guesthouse owner who did not come by the table to ask if the meal was satisfactory, or if you had a particular wish. Many times the owners would top off your meal with one of the German pear, plum, or cherry schnapps. Some guesthouses with restaurants would even specialize in trout, which were caught in a private stocked pond. These were rainbow trout, and were fresh out of the water.

With the protection of the Golden Ghetto, thousands of Americans in the 1960s through the 1980s, and even today, have the security of knowing a home away from home is there for them. I often wondered if the centralized, base-housing concept was not wrong, especially if the enemy, the USSR, at that time, could simply drop a bomb in the middle of all the bases during those years, and catch the Americans off guard. Would it not have been better to distribute the Americans throughout the areas, where they were all not concentrated in the same spot? Other NATO countries tended not to concentrate the housing as centrally as did the Americans.

But I suppose the logistics of the military insured that all the civilians and the military personnel were at the ready, were the Russians to attack. Actually, I feel the Russians were never militarily strong enough to really defeat the Americans, had a war have broken out. The Russians had a large showcase of military arms, and spent millions on it but would probably have been readily defeated had we come to a showdown, militarily in the 1960s through the 1980s.

From what I saw in East Berlin, and heard from people visiting Russia and satellite countries, the Russians were never militarily as strong as the Americans were. They had a large showcase but the military-industrial complex of the

Americans would have buried the Russians, just as they did the Germans in World War II.

Today, with the Cold War at an end, the Americans who live abroad, especially in Europe, have the luxury of enjoying the beauty of Western and Eastern Europe. They can now travel to countries like Hungary, Poland, The Czech Republic, Slovakia, and East Germany without worrying about the cumbersome and extensive visa paperwork needed in prior to 1989 years. What a beautiful thought, knowing that the Golden Ghetto is there and one can travel as extensively as Poland, Hungary, the Czech Republic, and other satellite countries are at one's disposal.

All the time I was in West Germany, from 1961 through 1983, I always felt that travel to the satellite countries was to set oneself up for a potential encounter with communist officials. They were, from what I read in the newspapers, always ready to detain Americans, especially those affiliated with the military, as I was, and treat them like the enemy. Detaining an Americans affiliated with the military was no problem for the communists. They had the time. Trains were often delayed when going in to Berlin, or coming out of Berlin. Russian troops were eager to hold up the transportation movement, just to flex their military muscles. Communist military regimes such as the Cold War Soviet Bloc and now China were and are oppressive. They also limit freedom and liberty!

The protection of the military and the Golden Ghetto, home security, were always to our advantage when travelling on the Duty Train, out of Frankfurt. If you had leave orders, which were to be sent in a few days before your departure date, you could travel into West Berlin, possibly take tours into the eastern part of the city, with proper paperwork. It was the policy of the American military and the other allied nations to encourage its personnel to travel into Berlin to see the imprisoned and enslaved people, especially in the eastern half of Berlin during the1960s through the 1980s.

I think it really helped in the pro-western propaganda, when one traveled into Berlin, then got into the eastern half of Berlin to see the degraded state of that city. The difference between the two cities was extremely diverse. One wondered how the people of the eastern satellite countries could endure the Spartan existence, cold water flats, and primitive housing. At least that is what I saw when visiting East Berlin. I did not see the lovely homes and modern buildings I saw in West Germany and West Berlin.

After a visit to Berlin, during the post war years, then a short tour into the eastern half of the city made us Americans feel the gratitude of living in a democracy of our own, and appreciate the democratic existence of other countries of Western Europe.

Returning to our base housing, economy housing, and to the protection of the Golden Ghettoes, made us feel even more secure after visits to East Berlin. How did the Cold War last so long, without the eastern half of Europe not getting message of freedom much sooner. One would think the Berlin Wall should have collapsed even sooner!

Many Americans, however, got to witness the drudgery of Eastern Europe through their tours and extensive travel from 1960 through 1989, and this was a good thing for exposing the degradation of Communism. Then Berlin Wall fell in 1989, and all the people of Eastern Europe sampled a taste of freedom thereafter. Even with the temporary set back of collapsed Communistic governments, people were putting around in their cheap 2 cycle automobiles, driving around Austria and Germany, in the early 1990s, just to sample the air of freedom. They were coming out of the East like flies.

Most of all, I would say that the military and civilian personnel of the United States profited extremely with their advantage of frequent and cheap travel in the 1950s through the 1980s. During this time, the interaction with the people of Germany, and other western nations of freedom was enlightening for Americans and Western Europeans and Britain.

From the time of the inception of the Communistic Bloc until the collapse of the dastardly Berlin Wall there was only a downhill road for the Eastern Bloc of nations. The too could be in the mixture of free tourism and travel to the West. The degrading chains of Communism were no longer there to restrain Eastern Europeans from sharing the ideas of the West!

For the American military and civilian, their chances to tour, via military support, were utilized in the essence, after postwar occupation years. The chances to travel, photograph, enjoy, and explore Western Europe and sometimes Eastern Europe were opportunistic. Americans, who never would have had the opportunity, utilized the military as a fulcrum to gain the tastes of Europe with its rich embellished history, in a manner, which probably has never been exploited since the Romans expanded their empire.

The Golden Ghetto was the protector and savior of military and civilian U. S. personnel who took advantage of their opportunities extensively. A large portion, I am afraid, especially the lower paid troops, did not gain the extensive educational and travel opportunities, which the U. S. Government offered them. More could have been gleaned, and by many more, had they grasped the opportunity. In the modern military and since the 1970s, however, and from what I saw in the late 1980s, the military encourages, more extensively, culture and language acquisition by its personnel. This is a positive move and an improvement of the U. S. military mission in the 1960s.

Whether or not the Golden Ghetto (concentration of so many Americans in ghettoes of the military) was the right formula for inspiring troops to gain the fullest potential of being in a foreign country, especially one as unique as Germany, is debatable. Maybe dispersing the military throughout the local economy would have been better, especially from a cultural standpoint. I am sure the concept of putting all our military and some civilian personnel in central base centered housing, was a military concept, utilized to increase morale and provide a feeling of being at home.

We, as educators, saw a wasted potential for the military. Logistics were, no doubt, the prime mission of the military, and the thought of the troops gaining cultural knowledge was, most likely, not practical. A few, and only a few, took advantage of the language, opera, restaurants, sight seeing, and interaction opportunities. The higher the rank, no doubt, the more extensive mingling processes were, especially with the military personnel in post war Germany. With the innovated cultural programs in the late 1970s and 1980s, the military began to push for cultural indoctrination of the host nation and encouraged language and culture of the host nation. I know this was the case because my ex wife, German, taught culture and Germans to the military personnel in the 1970s. These programs were even expanding more when I left Germany in 1983, and it was the right direction for personnel living in a specific host nation!

The future expansion of NATO, into the heart of Europe, and to the south, in the Balkans, is no doubt a scheme set up for the protection of all of Europe. Since the USSR is no longer the primary concern of NATO, perhaps the missions will turn to those of a more cultural nature. Or perhaps the missions might be militaristic with the Balkan hotspot and the potential threat of such idiots as Saddam Hussein in Iraq. But even with strong military definition, the cultural package of language and culture should be an integral part of each military and civilian training program when entering a host nation.

Today, because of the end of the Cold War, the opportunities of so many Americans, military attached, to live in and explore Europe, may diminish. However, the new ventures of NATO, and the military focus on the Balkans may shift the orientation of the military buffer zone in Europe. With the exception of a NATO stance in Hungary, perhaps much of the military focus might be in the area of Italy and Bosnia.

If, however, the NATO concept refocuses on Europe, and especially a mission of keeping in synchronization with Germany, in a military, "watch dog" style operation, a resurgence of American military might evolve in the early part of the twenty-first century. Germany always has the potential for reacting strongly if political and economical issues are not in balance.

The U. S. military bases and schools are diminishing in numbers in Germany, so perhaps a new focus might begin in the direction of the Balkans, and in a strong cooperative interaction with Germany. Our military brains, especially after two world wars that were centered on Germany, might stick around just to acknowledge the military pulse of Germany. Germany is a country with strong economic potential, and with the proper economic and political shifts, it could again pose either economic or military dominance across the heart of Europe, posed by its strong ethnic tendency.

If NATO expansion evolves, and the cooperative involvement of Americans in the military-political-economic arena of Europe expands, then there may someday be a renaissance of American military and civilian posture in various countries of Europe. There may again be a need for the supporting Golden Ghettoes to maintain our sustenance in the heart of Germany and other European countries.

The people Hitler left behind have positively integrated with the American and military population dominating many areas of Western Germany from 1945 through 1989. The Golden Ghettoes provided the security of the American troops and civilian contingency living there so many years. Now with the whole of Germany beginning new economic indulgences, maybe the more modern Golden Ghettoes will provide a more cultural and integrated approach to their sharing of the whole of Germany.

Chapter 4

Wiedersehen Deutschland, Buon Giorno Italia!

In the spring of 1966, I placed a transfer form for a science/mathematics teaching position in Aviano American High School at the Aviano Air Base in Northern Italy. And I readily accepted for the two-year assignment.

In late June 1967, my wife and I packed our clothes, awaited the movers to come in and pack our belongings so we could move to Italy. The last part of August we drove, from Ramstein, down through the Black Forest, through Basel, Switzerland, then headed toward northern Italy, across the Alps in our two cars. One auto was a 1964 Volkswagen Cabriolet (convertible) which I enjoyed driving and my wife drove the 1966 Plymouth Valiant. We were looking forward to our new location in Italy. We had heard that Aviano, Italy, had the most delightful weather, and we were to be just a stone's throw from the Adriatic Sea.

We drove, with me leading the way in my V. W. Cabriolet, full of clothes, overnight bags, and enough money to sustain us for a month or more. We spent the night near Lugano, after crossing the beautiful Alps. We drove through Milan Italy, then headed eastward toward Aviano. Lugano, and with its beautiful sea was romantic, beautiful, and a delightful area to remain overnight. We woke up the next morning, during the very pleasant end of August and enjoyed coming into a completely new and exciting Italian culture. Our previous exposure to Beautiful Italy was only as tourists.

We drove to the Aviano Air Base, only about three hours from Lake Lugano, where we signed in with Civilian Personnel, later that day. We spent the night near the city of Aviano, near the air base, in an inexpensive hotel, and woke up the next morning, ready to explore the exciting and enchanting new area.

It seemed that things did not work as smoothly, for the military and civilians, in that part of the world. The Italian personnel on base were a little slower than in Germany. The communications were slower, and it seemed that though I was a new teacher, no one really was that concerned about newcomers. People were just content and happy in this exciting Air Force Air Base in the beautiful sunshine of Italy.

For the first few days, after registering with base housing, we went into temporary quarters, and selected the city of Pordenone, a town about twenty kilometers, almost directly south of Aviano Air Base, in which to reside. Aviano was a very small town, but Pordenone was a larger city with well over 40,000 in population. The city is probably much larger today, especially the way it was beginning to sprawl in 1966.

We had the option of living off base and collecting cost of living allowance as long as we were in temporary quarters. Looking for an apartment or house was quite difficult because apartments, of good quality were scarce.

We searched through base housing, which assisted us in finding an apartment, and it took us over two weeks to find one, and it was new, and not yet completed. We found a place near downtown Pordenone but were told we would have to wait almost a month, or longer to get into the building after we signed the contract with our helpful apartment complex manager.

We, being young, and eager for a nice place, looked at the unfinished apartment that had a total of four large four large rooms. We had a garage, two baths, two bedrooms, a lovely living room, kitchen, and balcony. We were located in a very nice neighborhood. We signed the contract, and dwelled, with Dachshund, in our nice hotel while awaiting the apartment completion for our move in date.

Our dog, or "Cane", I believe is the Italian word for dog, Heidi, enjoyed living in the lovely hotel, which had a good reputation according our base housing coordinator. He was right, the hotel personnel and management were very accommodating and loved our dog. We enjoyed the morning breakfasts with great Italian coffee and wonderful rolls similar to the French pastries. There were always soft or hard-boiled eggs, rolls, and marmalade or jelly. The August mornings, and later September, were so pleasant we knew we were going to enjoy our two-year stay in this exotic Adriatic area. Our hearts rung with excitement in this sunny and pleasant paradise.

We immediately began to venture out and explore such cities as Venice, only an hour from Pordenone. We then explored Udine, Morifalco, Lido Di Jesolo, Treviso and other magnificent towns and cities in the vicinity. We frequented such beach towns as Lignano, Bibione, and Caorle, less than an hour's drive from our hotel in Pordenone. What fantastic beach cities. The areas were visited and crowded in the summer, from Germans, Austrians, Dutch, Belgians, French, and even people from the USSR satellite countries. Evening walks around the crowded towns such as Lignano were magnificent, with hundreds of tourists from neighboring countries walking the streets, shopping, and eating in the lovely restaurants. The area reminded one of the Venice, California beach areas, but not quite as freakish. People were buying Italian ice cream, eating pizza, and enjoying all sorts of souvenir shops. It was multi-national in flair and one could hear four to five languages being spoken on any one evening.

The fantastic Adriatic weather up through September and early October was a dream! I thought I had found the paradise, of Europe, I wanted to spend a few years in. The little Volkswagen Cabriolet was magnificent to jump into, and drive along the romantic roads, on a summer night, then visit such towns as Lignano and Bibione, for an evening meal of roast chicken, pasta, or other fantastic Italian meals. Fish dishes were delightful, usually grilled, with wine sauce, garlic and other delightful spices.

As September turned into fall, we finally got into our beautiful spacious apartment that we paid only about $350 a month for. At the time were in Italy, the U. S. Dollar would purchase about 950 Lire, so we made out quite well by living on the economy because our housing allowance was ample for the apartment, along with water and electricity.

The Italians were great, even in shops, to accept American money for a fair exchange rate in 1966. They were extremely friendly to Americans and to my German wife. We bought various pieces of furniture from the local merchants. We bought a bedroom suite, a kitchenette, and various needed pieces of furniture for our new fully marbled floor apartment. We had a lovely balcony, ample parking, and were within walking distance from downtown Pordenone.

We needed quite a bit of furniture and a bedroom set was one thing we did not have in our previous apartment in Ramstein. In purchasing our new bedroom set, with the large wardrobe, dresser, and chest-of-drawers, we made arrangements with a furniture store owner to pay monthly, and he accepted our offer with a substantial down payment. I found most of the Italians, with a long history of trading going back to the Medicis of the Italian Renaissance, to be great merchants. They were great money traders and business people. Not only were they great merchants, but they were extremely friendly business people.

My wife's and my curiosity and interest in the Italian language enhanced their friendliness. With her and me speaking two other languages between us (German and English) they were extremely enthused at our rattling on in the other languages, trying to come upon the proper Italian phrases and congenial Italian expressions.

While teaching at the fine Aviano American High School, I met some interesting American teachers. One, in particular, was the local owner of the Volkswagen dealership in Aviano, and was a retired veterinarian. I cannot remember his name but his wife taught at the elementary school, and they were both quite good in the Italian language, he especially, because of his position as owner of the largest Volkswagen dealership in the area. They were very social, gave many parties for the American teachers, and were excellent contacts, especially as a source of information for restaurants and dining.

The teachers there were into the local customs, and language, seemingly more so than some of their American counterparts in Germany. Maybe it was because of the small base, especially compared to the large base at Ramstein, Germany. Also the weather was exceptionally inviting, so people remained at this assignment for long periods of time. The Italian language was also inviting and exciting to learn.

We had many social events, mixing local Italians with our teaching staff. The officer's club, on base, was quite pleasant, with an Adriatic or Mediterranean motif. The many Italian employees, waitresses and waiters, were friendly, enjoyed having U. S. employment, and always were willing to provide us with information about dining and travel around the Aviano area.

The Volkswagen Cabriolet was a fantastic automobile for the part of Italy we lived in because of the open-air aspects of a convertible. To drive along the Adriatic coast with the top down in my white V. W. Beetle was fun, exciting, and the beautiful weather magnified each drive along the Adriatic seashore. Driving east and leaving the Pordenone area, one could smell the Adriatic after about 30 minutes drive, toward Lignano. Enjoying the ride, stopping at a nice fish or chicken restaurant was so quaint that one forgot about work, home, and any worries of everyday life. The restaurants were storybook.

The year I spent in Italy, except for missing some of the Germanic culture was one of the most fantastic experiences of my life, and at the ripe age of 34 years. How I relished that beautiful sunshine along the Adriatic, the beautiful people of Northern Italy, and convenient vehicle access to any other part of Italy I wanted to visit.

Some pleasure trips took me to Rome, Pisa, Florence, and one teachers' convention took me down as far as Naples. I was readily warned that in Naples, the people would readily jack your car up, then take off all the tires and wheels of your vehicle. Fortunately it never happened to me.

After a few months, up through November, my wife grew tired of only a regimen of pasta, so we begin to again long for Germanic culture. That was no problem because within about 2 hours was the lovely city of Villach, Austria. Within only about 2 hours drive we were at the Austrian border.

As one arrived and entered the city of Villach, one drove by the beautiful Villach Sea and that was something to behold. We enjoyed the wonderful semi-Alpine views, wonderful Austrian food, and the area had just enough German culture to eliminate the longing my wife and I had for Germanic food and atmosphere. Though we loved the laid back, casual atmosphere of Italy, we longed for the orderly and regimented Germanic ways, along with the "serve it properly," mentality of the Germanic people. The strict order and immediate service was quite a contrast to the leisurely and nonchalant mode of our Italian friends.

There was, however, some Germanic influence we found about the northern part of Italy, and it was the infusion of lighter complexioned men and women. The local Italians called my wife, being very beautiful and blonde, "Bella Blondina!" They admired her quick German speech and regimented manners when shopping and interacting with them. The Italians also respected her quick attempt to pick up their language, and complimented her for her efforts, as well as mine.

We spent many weekends, during the fall of 1966, around Villach, Austria, a medium sized city, with many restaurants, and being a spa city, it had a lot to offer. I frequented several different small guesthouses, which were very reasonable in price at the time. The food was always superb, with the usual treats of excellent wine and beer, wienerschnitzel, bratwurst and wild game.

The guesthouse owners were always pleasant, and went out of their way to please in our requests for anything special. Fortunately, at that time I enjoyed a rather good salary, relative to Austrians or Italians. The American Dollar went a long way when exchanged for the Austrian Schilling. I do not remember the value but it must have been as good or better than the German mark. I believe the exchange rate was approximately 20 Austrian Schillings to one dollar.

It was rather a difficult transition from Germany down to Aviano Air Base in August 1966. Though I saved enough money for a month's survival at our new duty station, we ran into some trouble. The transfer of pay grade information turned out to be a big problem since CPO (Civilian Personnel Office) did not receive the transfer of our pay status as quickly as anticipated. It took them from the last week in August until about October 15th to properly align the new teachers' pay status. About ten teachers were new to the area, and we were all inconvenienced by the inefficiency of the Civilian Personnel Office on Aviano Air Base. We, as teachers, and employees were fit to be tied. We complained to the base commander, to Wiesbaden, Germany School administrative services, and to anyone else who would listen to us.

Finally, after a month of not receiving pay, an emergency fund on the base was utilized and we drew five or six hundred dollars for emergency use, and some drew even more. When we finally received our pay, which was 2 months in arrears, we paid back the emergency fund, either totally, or by monthly payments. My landlord graciously awaited the payment, because I was not billed for my rent up through December. Three months rent was, a great sum of money for me since the savings we had for the move were about diminished. After the accumulated late pay finally arrived, we paid our debts and things leveled out in sunny Italy.

But, all in all, the Italian living was even better than that in Germany because food, furniture, and clothes were cheaper there in the Italian area. Financially I had no trouble after all the pay hang-ups were overcome. We sailed right on through the year with very little strain, enjoyed a great apartment, and certainly enjoyed traveling from Pordenone to Austria, to Yugoslavia, and down to Southern Italy.

My wife, who lost two children by miscarriage, decided, with me, to go through the process of adopting a child, but we had submitted the paperwork in Germany in the early part of 1966. We were accepted by the proper agency in Germany, and got a contact in Northern Germany for a possible adoption, once the child was born. My wife was making continual contact with adoption agencies in Germany, and by mid-November, we had a lead for an adoption. We learned of the family through a friend of Brigitte's mother, and started making preparation for a private adoption since we had been cleared through the proper social agencies in Germany.

We made preparations to go back to Germany during the winter holidays (Overseas Dependent Schools have similar holidays as public schools back in the United States), and pick up the child which was to be born in early December.

Our little girl was born on December 7, 1966, and we communicated with the father who wanted us to have the baby because I was a teacher, and Germans have a high respect for teachers.

When we arrived, near Bremen, after driving up through Munich, Germany, we went to the adoption agency. We learned, to our disappointment, that the baby had already been given up to a German family, but we were told that Liane's father and mother were not happy with the family, and they had the option of taking the child back. We proceeded, with the help of the social worker, to take Liane from the other family. We drove to the house of the family that had Liane, only a few days old, and actually took her from the family, though the man and wife were very reluctant to give her up.

But with the social worker in our company, and also the father of Liane, there was very little they could do after the father of Liane explained he was not happy with the status quo and wanted his daughter back. Brigitte and I were nervously waiting in the car outside the house. The father of our child to be, explained that they were not providing the proper care for the child from reports of the social worker, so the tactic proved to be successful.

The father handed the baby, wrapped in a blanket, to my wife, and she was ecstatic. In a few minutes we were procuring proper baby formula from the local pharmacy, and then on our way to Kiel. My wife felt as though she had given birth to the 10 day old little girl, and was one of the happiest women I have ever seen. I was also excited, and awarded the father, who went with us and the social worker to pick Liane up, train fair, and some money for him and his wife and their other child. He was a two year old beautiful boy. Since it was right around Christmas holidays, I felt the gesture was appropriate.

Later we learned that the little boy, the family was also willing to give up, came into misfortune. That is a long story into itself, but when we later transferred from Italy to the Netherlands, in the summer of 1967, the whole episode got to be extremely involved. The German criminal police were given our names as possible suspects for the disappearance of the two-year-old blonde boy.

We, after leaving the Netherlands, in 1971, almost four years later, got into a legal battle with one of the biggest German magazine firms, because my wife's and my picture were attached to a sensation story which depicted us, wrongly, as being suspects in the case of Liane's missing brother. We sued for damages and it was directed against the Burda firm, one of the largest magazine companies in Germany at that time.

We later learned that our picture was one we sent to the father and mother of our adopted baby, because we were potential candidates to adopt Liane. The father, when the police investigated the disappearance of the little boy, in about 1971, obviously gave our picture to the criminal police, trying to direct the guilt in another direction. We were then suspicious of the father in the disappearance of the child but the police obviously found no evidence.

We were also highlighted on a television program which participates in such sensationalism, and we saw it in the Netherlands and all our German relatives were calling from all over Germany when the story broke, especially on European television!

The whole process of the lawsuit dragged out for almost a year, and we finally won the fight against the large magazine firm, with a retraction in the magazine that slandered our name. The financial award, nothing like one would receive in the United States, was menial for the trouble we went through to sue, but I learned quite a bit about legal procedure in Germany, with their codified law, and how complex such cases can be.

The whole adoption episode was complex, and we ended up returning to Italy around December 31, 1966, trying to make it over the Alps with no chains in the middle of winter, and having a little baby with no legal papers in hand.

I started my journey up the mountains, headed for one of the passes leading out of Chiemsee, Germany, toward Northern Italy. The rear tires on our Plymouth were not in the best shape, and with three tries to get up the first large grade, I ended up almost sliding off the mountain,

Good fortune was with me, and 3 helpful Yugoslavian men stopped and helped me turn the car around and head back to a hotel. I helped my wife and child out of the car so they could stand on the roadside, out of danger of the car sliding off the mountain. We got the car back into the road, then picked

Liane and Brigitte up then drove about 2 kilometers to the hotel, and spent the night in a warm and safe place.

I left Liane and Brigitte in the warm hotel with food and warmth, then I proceeded back to the military service station near Chiemsee, bought chains, as I should have before the journey began, then proceeded across the steep snowy Alps toward Italy. With the chains, there was little danger of slipping off the road again.

We drove into Italy, crossing the border, with an illegal child in the car, because the paperwork for the adoption was not complete. Later, during early January1967, my wife returned to Germany, with the baby, and procured the appropriate papers, after two intensive weeks of chasing around from one government office to another. On her return to Italy she had all the adoption papers so there was no problem getting our daughter back into Italy on this trip.

With proper papers in hand, and an overnight stay on the border, due to bad weather, I finally had my wife back in Italy in late January 1967. We were given an appropriate baby shower by the Aviano Elementary and High School faculty. My wife was as excited as any mother could be over the generosity and kindness of the fine American teachers from that school.

Spring came early in Pordenone and Aviano, so we enjoyed making weekend visits to Venice once or twice a month. Once we got a young Italian lady to baby-sit for us while we took a day trip to Venice, but when we returned, we found the baby wet from head to foot, and crying. It seems the young lady had little experience in baby sitting, so that is the last time we left our child with a baby-sitter until she was about 2 or three years of age.

In order to feel secure, we took a portable bassinet with us to every restaurant, and Liane slept peacefully, but we dared not leave her with a baby-sitter because of the guilt we suffered for her not being cared for properly during the previous Italian baby-sitter experience. People were so considerate when a baby was around, and the waitresses and waiters were always willing to accommodate us by heating bottles or what needs we had for our baby's care. I thought then that only Italians showed appropriate respect for a baby, and being a new father, I learned that people respected babies regardless of the location. Baby admirers are not only found in Italy but also worldwide!

Regardless of the tremendous beauty of Northern Italy, and the fantastic sights, my wife still had the longing for visiting her family in Germany. Whether we were visiting Tante Else, Uncle Walter, brothers and sisters, or especially her mother, we took the spring vacation in 1967 as a time to revisit our Nordic connections and show off our child.

Often when driving toward Germany and the Alps, or just a visit to Austria, I reflected on the area north of Udine, and the river valleys in that area, realizing it was the setting of Ernest Hemingway's novel, <u>Across The River and Into The Woods</u>.

Hemingway also spent some time around Harry's Bar in Venice, and we went into it several times as we visited the beautiful and romantic city. But I especially remember, as I was driving through the valleys and rivers in that area that the retired military officer, the primary character of that specific book shot ducks out of a barrel in the river near the highway we were driving on. Being a hunter, that specific reflection of Hemingway, was especially interesting to me as a reader. Shooting from an obviously anchored barrel in a river or river bed is unique and contrasted to the traditional blind shooting found world wide.

There is always something fantastic about being near a setting of such a great writer as Ernest Hemingway. And that

I had the privilege of living near the setting, one could only be thankful for the opportunity to live in and enjoy such an area. Hemingway, especially, because of his love for hunting, is one of my favorite authors.

Unfortunately, on one of my trips through that area, and along that specific river, I was given a speeding ticket by one of the Italian highway patrols. I had very little cash with me so I wrote him a check on my hometown bank of Warren, Arkansas, U.S.A., and he took it. I suppose the check cleared since we estimated the rate of the Lira against the dollar and he accepted the payment. I thought to myself, the Italians are certainly trust worthy, and great money exchangers if they would do such a thing right on the open road, and in such an isolated place.

The visits to Germany were as frequent as my wife could coax me into taking, and to be honest, feeling much at home with the German language, I relished my visits to Germany. The only regret I have is that I believe a five year stay, or longer would have fortified my Italian, and made me a solid tri-lingual speaker, and I would have profited from that more than any other experience I could have achieved from living abroad.

My contract required me to remain in the Aviano High School for two years before transferring, but another event arose in my career that I did not anticipate, and I did not have to meet the two-year obligation. A new school was being completed in Brunssum, the Netherlands, and a 4 nation NATO elementary-high school was being completed in the fall of 1967, and it was to be the state of the art, with hand picked teachers to run the U. S. sector. I was watching the development via school bulletins with great interest.

The school was to consist of 4 nations, and they were Great Britain, Canada, Germany plus the United States. The school was to be named AFCENT, standing for Allied Forces Central Europe, and was to be budgeted by NATO, with supplementary funds being contributed from each of the four host nations.

I submitted an application from Aviano High School, and was selected to teach biology and physical science at the high school, American section of course. The enrollment, elementary and high school with 4 nations was well over a thousand students, and everything was new, and at that time, state of the art supplies, rooms and facilities.

My profitable experience in the Italian culture was to come to an end, after my return to the United States, and a summer school of additional National Science Foundation physics courses at St. Cloud College, St. Cloud, Minnesota, in the summer of 1967.

In late June of 1967 we left our automobiles in Italy, along with our beautiful longhaired miniature Dachshund, Heidi, with a family, and flew out of Milan on Pan American Airways. On that day in June, my wife held up the flight of the 4 engine jet because she was out shopping with our daughter, only 6 months old at the time, but finally made it aboard, with my chastising her in German, when she did return to the departing gate.

After a summer of studying and with my wife remaining in Warren, Arkansas I drove to St. Cloud, Minnesota. I drove north from my hometown of Warren to attend a summer National Science Foundation Institute. It was a fascinating experience just being in Minnesota where I studied, fished, and practiced my German on the Minnesota farmers who were fluent in German.

In late August 1967, we returned to Milan, Italy, picked up our automobiles, and then went to pick up our dog Heidi. It so happens that we had found an Italian family who raised Dachshunds, and they had a 14-year-old daughter who fell in love with our dog. She entered Heidi, only about 2 years old, into a Dachshund beauty contest, and won 3 international prizes for beauty.

She was, no doubt, one of the most beautiful Dachshunds my wife and I ever owned. We owned 3 Dachshunds-Suzy, Heidi, and eventually Rusty. Suzy was our second one and this dog was loving, beautiful with reddish brown beautiful long hair and with some black flecks on the ears. What a beauty! The dog got a great taste of Italian during the summer, but she did not forget the regimented German commands barked out by my wife, Brigitte.

The only problem was that the young 14-year-old teen-ager, who was caring for our dog, fell in love with Heidi and did not want to give her back to us. We had to spend money, and a lot of time coaxing her to part with our dog. They lived in Pordenone and we got their names from some neighbors. They were great dog-lovers, entered many into contests, but this was, no doubt one of the loveliest creatures this Italian family had ever come across.

We finally retrieved Heidi, left the teenage girl crying, but departed with a workable solution. We learned one lesson about dogs, and that was to have a firm understanding with the adult in charge, before leaving a dog in the care of someone for a long while, especially for almost 3 months.

We spent only a couple of days around Italy that August and realizing sadly that we would only be returning on visits after departing this duty station permanently. We had had our household goods packed in late June and in storage, then bound for Brunssum, the Netherlands, for the new School Year 1967-68. We spent the couple of days living in hotels, and chose to drive, in our Volkswagen and Valiant, to Pisa, Venice, Florence, and over to the Italian Riviera before returning to Germany and the Netherlands.

We spent the time getting our last glimpses of the lovely ancient cities of Vicenza, and Verona. We traveled on south of Florence and enjoyed lovely restaurants along the Mediterranean coast because we knew it would not be long before we headed back to the Germanic culture to greet Brigitte's relatives again. Brigitte knew then that she would try to keep me near the heart of Deutschland, although she dearly loved the Italian experience. Being apart from the Germanic culture and area was not in her scheme of things.

The many years I have lived since that time, and reflected back on Italy, since leaving it, have left me in a state of remorse because of the potential years I could have remained in Italy. My regret is mostly because I had at my fingertips, the opportunity to lavish in the Adriatic sunshine, dwell in the culture, and steep myself into the beautiful Romance language, Italian. It was a language one wants to learn because its beauty, not even like Spanish, has a charm with the crisp clear cut phrases and words that come quickly and stay with one as your vocabulary builds.

After distancing myself from the beautiful Italian language, and a chance to reattach myself to the German language, I knew I would lose the small Italian vocabulary I had accumulated from my year in Italy.

But one memory I would not forget while living in Italy was that of a beautiful young lady from Villach, Austria. I, along with a couple of buddies would often visit Villach, Austria, only a couple of hours from Pordenone, where Brigitte, I, and Liane lived, a few kilometers from the high school where I taught. I and my guy friends, some married, and some single, would drive up to Villach on weekends, up on Friday evening, return Sunday evening ready for Monday morning teaching.

I met this lovely lady, about 23 years of age, built like a model, who was dating a buddy of mine, a Tech. Rep. for one of the air planc companies servicing the planes on the air base at Aviano. We were all chatting, and swimming in one of the hot pools of Villach, since it was a spa city and had the usual hot baths for various cures. I jokingly stepped on her lovely ass while she was lying, in her bikini, near the edge of the indoor pool. Such "firmness" I have never felt....I thinking, this is one delightful butt and I would like to explore it! Explore it, I did.

Someway I made a rendezvous with her because she was a manager in a nearby Swiss hotel, not far from Aviano. We made our rendezvous, however for a weekend at Lake Como, a considerable drive from Aviano, where I taught. I faked illness so took a long weekend, calling in sick and for a substitute teacher to take my classes one Friday, leaving Friday, Saturday, and a part of Sunday for dining, drinking, and having sex! I picked the young lady up in Locarno, Switzerland, hen drove her to Lake Como on that Friday, starting our long weekend. My wife was off to Germany taking care of the odds and ins of our adoption of our darling daughter, Liane.

She, the lady, I will call her Maria, sadly to say, was killed in an auto accident in Austria after I lived in the Netherlands for a couple of years, probably around 1970ish. So Maria and I drove in my beautiful year old Volkswagen Convertible, Cabriolet, as convertibles are called in German, to Lake Como.

To this day, I cannot remember a more glorious weekend of sex, dining, dancing, and the delights of the beautiful region of Lake Como, Italy. We slept together in a reasonable priced hotel, because she had connections and discounts because she was a manager of one of the nicer hotels in Locarno, Switzerland!

Sex was good, she had a gorgeous body and I was in my 30s so enjoyed touring, eating, "fucking" like crazy and just a wonderful vacation! This lady knew her way around, had no remorse about betraying my buddy, the Tech. Rep, Bob, a great skiing friend and drinking buddy! He, Bob, was the guy she was dating when I stepped on her beautiful ass at the pool in Villach. He never knew she betrayed him, and why should he know that? Not only that, I visited him when visiting Glendale, California where he and his wife, in the 1980s, owned a plate factory so I looked him up, met his lovely wife and we talked and drank beer for hours, talking about our wonderful times in Italy and Austria!

The memories of Italian beauty are reflected, in my mind so often, even today, 2014, as I revisit this book! Of the places I have lived, Italy is like a diamond brilliantly shining in my journey through life. And even today, in social conversations, I can readily say, that of all the cities I have visited or lived in, my number one choice of cities in which to live, I would have to cast my vote for the lovely ancient city of Rome, Italy.

Even with the several two or three day trips I made there, the Coliseum, the beautiful architecture, lovely sights, and great restaurants, and most of all, the mild climate, I still lavish in the memories of its character. Someday I will surely revisit this great city, re-immerse myself in its language, drink its red wine, and simply walk its ancient streets of beauty.

Living in Northern Italy, with surrounding cities such as Venice, Padoa, Verona, Bergamo, Udine, and Trento, one cannot complain, because the access to Rome is so convenient. When one speaks of the Latin based language countries, Italy and Spain, I really favor Italy over Spain. In my opinion, because of the influence of the Roman Empire, magnificent history, its closeness of cities, and its multiplicity of ancient architecture, Italy has the charm seldom found in other European countries.

Italy still ranks as one of my favorite countries in Europe. Even though I was intensely entrenched in the Germanic culture, while abroad, and Germany has multitudes to offer,

Italy ranks at the top for a country for living pleasures. The relative friendship between the two cultures is, in my opinion, is still strong. I found that when I did speak German with my wife, among the Italians, there was never any sign of hostility because of the German language. I was often mistaken for a German citizen because of my frequent use of the German when around my wife, whether in Italy or in Germany.

My future plans to visit Europe should unfold after I retire from my teaching position in San Diego, California, around August 2001. At that time I intend to continue writing, travelling extensively in Eastern Europe, then drift on down to lovely Italy, write more, and lavish the beauties of Rome and its ancient beauty.

I have often conversed with others about my twenty plus years of living in Europe to various friends, and casually interested persons. Each time I mention my profitable years overseas, I am always asked, "What was your favorite country?" I immediately let it be known that my greatest familiarity is with Germany, but my heart has a real love for Italy, and especially Rome and Venice!

Even my 6 months in Libya, a country with much Italian connection due to past colonial possessions, had the exciting and beautiful remnants, not of only ancient Rome, but traces of Italian culture. Many of Tripoli's restaurants even in 1960 were Italian. I also frequented numerous Libyan restaurants that had excellent lamb, chicken and fish dinners. The traditional Cuscus was also excellent. Cuscus is a staple food of Libya, made, I presume from a grain, but was quite delicious and went well with their traditional foods.

Living abroad exposes one to a host of varied restaurants, and I found that in most countries, the indigenous foods are sometimes exciting and tasty to try. Italian food in the United

States was something I often partook of. But North African food was completely out of my realm of experience.

I enjoyed my first artichokes in a lovely restaurant-hotel in the downtown part of Tipoli, a city, of course, with Arabic influence, so their foods include lamb and other fine foods. This happened to have been one of the Italian influenced restaurants with both North African and Italian food. But I tried much of the North African food, especially that found in Tripoli, and enjoyed it, along with the extensive Italian selections.

Italian people, their culture, and their language were predominantly found because of the colonial influence. The Italians left a definite cultural mark on Tripoli, even though it was from the past historical scars of colonialism. The blend between the two countries was satisfying while I lived in Tripoli, because little did I suspect that I would live in Italy as a part of my overseas experiences.

From 1975 through 1982, while back in Germany, I made several trips back to Italy, and visited an old friend who was a teacher Aviano High School. I could not resist the magnetic attraction Italy had imbued me with. My friend was still teaching at the same high school, had spent almost 15 years in Aviano. His Italian had become polished, whereas when I was there in 1966, Earl Hansen spoke very little Italian. But the constant socializing, restaurant visits, and shopping around the Italians must have made learning the language inevitable.

Earl was an excellent skier and hang-glider fanatic. I took him up to the top of the local mountain overlooking some of the areas northwest of Aviano, and watched Earl soar down several hundred feet below to an open area for a safe landing. Earl was in his late forties at that time, but in excellent physical condition. He was definitely the outdoor type with his history of skiing and at that time, hang gliding.

He was previously married to a lovely person, Teresa, who was originally a native of Yugoslavia, but a citizen of Austria. She was a wonderful cook and I experienced my first taste of calf brains prepared (deep-fried) in a way different from the way I ate them in the southern part of the United States. She was a nurse, worked a hospital in Villach, Austria, and we visited her in her modest apartment, before she and Earl were married, in 1967.

Earl married her before we left Aviano in 1967, but lovely Teresa died of cancer in the mid-nineteen-seventies. She was a lovely contact, and my wife and I had the privilege of visiting her and her relatives near Zagreb, capital of, now Bosnia-Herzegovina, and today has a population of 800,000. It was in the early fall of 1966 that Brigitte and I visited Teresa's family, in their farm house near Zagreb, before adopting Liane around Christmas 1966.

I witnessed, what was a most splendid event at the home of her brother, near Zagreb, where we spent the night in a nearby hotel. On a Saturday evening, the Yugoslavian family, Croatian now, would do folk dances for entertainment. Earl, Teresa, my wife, Brigitte, and I sat back and viewed with amazement the dancing by the wife and husband for prime entertainment. The background music was a folk record.

Earl told me that the family had been saving money for ten years, and wanted to purchase a German automobile, but the sister, Teresa, would have to make the purchase, go through all kinds of import processes to get the automobile into Yugoslavia. I presume that this transaction actually took place after we moved from Aviano.

Not only did we visit areas of Croatia but we visited different towns near Sarajevo, which lay farther south and east of Zagreb, now a part of Croatia. The roads only resembled a major highway, smooth enough for the couple of hundred-kilometer drive out of Italy, our home. We always noticed the friendly Yugoslav people ambling along the highways, modestly dressed, and some waving at us as we drove along the somewhat primitive highways.

At the time I was driving into Yugoslavia, 1967-68, the ruler Tito, had a firm grip on the people, and there was a certain air of communism, his brand, about the country. I was often amazed, especially around the coastal area, and in the lovely city of Rijeka, (now a part of Croatia) at the hotel service. The waitresses and waiters were well trained, and served meals of fish and white golden wines, with the most obedient and regimented attention. It was almost "Tito" in its character as the young waiters and waitresses in their appropriate dress and rigid, but respectful manners, proceeded to serve us the finest of foods.

On our Yugoslavia visits we would leave Pordenone on a Friday afternoon, then stay in a nice hotel in Rijeka and visit other parts of Croatia and Bosnia-Herzegovina. One reason we visited Yugoslavia was to enjoy wonderful food and rooms for menial prices, even compared to Austria and Italy. At that time, it was one of the best places to visit and get more food, wine or beer, and service for the money. In 1966 and 67, all these areas I traveled in, around Croatia and Bosnia-Herzegovina, including Slovenia, and Serbia, was all JUST Yugoslavia; Tito made it so easy! The wars from 1991 to 1999, involving Slovenia, Croatia, Bosnia-Herzegovina, and he Serbian-Kosovo conflicts certainly jigsawed all that area which was kept glued together by the special brand communisntic leader Tito, especially during the two years (1966-67) I lived in Italy!

The excitement of being able to purchase an immediate visa at the border areas of Yugoslavia (1966-67) was beyond my belief. On one occasion, we were driving down from Villach, after picking up Teresa, and got to the Austrian-Yugoslavia border at about 7:30 p.m. The border guards proceeded to partake in a liter bottle of Austrian red wine, of which we had several bottles, some as gifts for Teresa's relatives. Teresa, in her Yugoslavian language, began persuading the border guards that we did not, after all, need required visas, or whatever the proper papers were at that time. Not only did she coax them to let us go through free, but got them intoxicated in the process. She, Teresa, and they were talking, singing, and interacting with us in a most congenial way.

This was, without a doubt, one of the most interesting experiences I have ever witnessed, especially if one knows how tight-fisted the iron curtain countries were in the late 1960s! We spent about 45 minutes with them, or maybe a whole hour with the cheerful and tipsy border guards. What an experience! These communist border guards were not nearly as regimented as the border guards of East Germany of the 1960s-1980s. Such a loose social gathering would never have occurred in the other Iron Curtain regions of Eastern Europe!

In summary, I can only say that the opportunities provided by our residence in Italy, opened up the world in the expansion of my experiences, especially the experiences for travel and meeting exotic people. The Adriatic culture, Italy and Yugoslavia were rich in depth and beauty. The people of the area were warm, the locations charming, and food excellent!

My memories will entice me to return to the Adriatic area, revisit the many wonderful locations of Italy, and perhaps Yugoslavia, especially in its new ethnic jigsaw configuration. I shall return with camera in hand, and ready to relive the wonderful years of 1966 and 1967! Italy, with over 60 million people, the Pope, a strong Roman Catholic tradition, and a multi-party Republic, was a most favorable place to live.

Though Italy's citizens profess to be about 85% catholic, there are other denominations found in the country. The air of the people is not fanatically catholic, and the warmth of the families makes associations congenial and pleasant.

I had the opportunity to see the Pope at Easter services in 1967, and the crowds were unbelievable. Though I am not Roman Catholic, the opportunity was a once in a lifetime opportunity, especially if one does not live in or around Rome. The vision of the Pope was a worthwhile experience and the resounding cheering crowds made one know it was a great experience. It was just another opportunity to celebrate and enjoy the beauty of sharing part of a long tradition of the fantastic Italian people.

The people Hitler left behind, in their visits to Italy, still revel in its sunshine and beauty, just as I did while spending an exciting year in this dynamic and historical country. Though the regimentation of Germany is highly contrasted to the casual mannerisms of Italy, it is still exciting for me and the Germans to visit the beaches, lovely ancient cities, and fantastic people of beautiful Italy!

Chapter 5

Return To Germanic Areas

After leaving Italy, in the month of August 1967, I made my journey to Kerkrade, the Netherlands. It was in this city that the American Dependent School was temporarily located, until it was to become a part of the 4 Nation NATO-School in Brunssum, the Netherlands. My wife and I drove to the Netherlands in our two automobiles, after spending some time In Kiel, visiting her mother.

Coming into the Netherlands was quite interesting and different for us because everything was flat, unlike the rolling hills of Pordenone and Aviano, Italy. The houses were sometimes row houses, jammed close together, but neat and clean as one could expect from the historical storybook tales about the fastidious Dutch.

After a few days in the Netherlands, waiting for temporary quarters, our adaptation to the area came quickly and we certainly felt more secure, because of our nearness to Germany, than we had felt on first entering Italy.

Already, I began to develop an ear for the transitional language of Dutch, which I was told by my previous German teachers, progressed from German, then across the English

Channel to the English language. The sounds of the words and their relation to German already caught my ear when stopping to ask people for directions.

When one heard such terms as "Zaterdag" for Saturday, instead of the German "Sammstag", then an American such as I could make the connection. Then there is "Ziekenhuis", the word for German "Krankenhaus", or in English, "hospital", one can certainly make the connection to English,"sick house."

The complexity of the Dutch language was extremely difficult, to me, that I knew my quick acquaintance with German, then Italian, would not come so easily. I did like the pleasant ring of the language, and my daughter, who eventually went to kindergarten in this small and friendly country, was soon singing songs and reciting poetry like a native. She had neighbors with whom she played in the nice town of Schinveld, near the German border, to teach her many words and whole sentences. The excitement and pleasure of watching my beautiful daughter attach herself to the culture, language, and people were most satisfying.

Before we got into our house in Schinveld, we lived in the city of Kerkrade, where we had to stay in temporary quarters for almost two and a half months before we found permanent quarters. But when we finally found our nice 3 bedroom two-story, 1 1/2 baths, newly built house, we were simply delighted. The house was buff brick and sturdily built, as are most European houses.

The people we rented our bedroom and shared kitchen from, in temporary quarters eventually became our friends and remained so until we left the Netherlands in 1971. They were the Family Haas, and were simply delightful people, helping us in every way imaginable. In the true, friendly Dutch fashion, they prepared us breakfasts, which were included in the temporary housing costs, showed us places to shop, and enjoyed it when we supplied them with American coffee, cigarettes, and a bottle of gin now and then.

We finally found the house in Schinveld, only about 3 kilometers from the AFCENT (Allied Forces Central Europe) International School where I was to teach physical science. What a location for us since we were only about 2 kilometers from the border if we drove over to Gangelt, Germany, where I was to eventually meet my hunting friend, Dr. von den Driesch. Gangelt, Germany had a small border crossing, usually closed after about 10 p.m.

We lived in an almost perfect place and my German wife had the tremendous advantage of enjoying a lovely Dutch, quaint two story brick home. She could drive every evening, if she wished, to Germany. But with Liane, just a very young child, she preferred taking care of her and enjoying the quaint and friendly Dutch village.

Aachen, Germany, well known for one of the great battles during the Second World War, was only about 18 kilometers from us, and we shopped there, enjoyed coffee shops or German restaurants, visited museums, and simply lavished in the Germanic atmosphere. It was a historically rich city with a magnificent cathedral and remnants of Charlemagne.

We also began to acquire several tremendous Dutch friends, invited them to our home, and it turn, visited their homes. We also made many friends who were attached to the German Air Force, young officers, and had many social hours with some great career military families.

I was in a great multi-national social maze one could hardly imagine. The school I was assigned to, with Canadian, German, American, and British elements included in the 4 nation make-up, proved to be a source of international contact which one, especially at my age of 38, could only dream about.

My wife and I were in social paradise, rich with dynamic and interesting people.

The interaction of German, Dutch, British, Canadian, and American personnel was to be envied by my counterparts back in the United States. But only one negative element emitted itself into the aura of the halo surrounded Americans in those years, and it was the Vietnam War. Germans and other nationalities were often questioning the American status in Vietnam, and ready to attack, the British and Canadians were always inquisitive and asked why we ever got bogged down in this intolerable conflict?

The stigma followed me through the five years I remained in the Netherlands, and when the war ended in about 1974, Americans no longer had to explain the complex quagmire of Vietnam to our European friends. It was comforting that President Nixon finally made the right historical decision, and helped us get out of a complex American nightmare.

Returning to the Germanic areas made my wife and me quite comfortable as far as the language was concerned. The Dutch language, in its complexity, was a language I began to pick up through everyday exposure, and interaction with my Dutch friends. They, however, because of the nearness of Germany, were happy to utilize German. The German language, because of its broader usage in the world, is a more valuable language than Dutch language. I, however, never felt that German usage was excusable in the Netherlands, so I tried to use Dutch phrases, but never got into a formal study of the language.

I felt that Dutch did not have the international utility I felt German and Italian had, so I never made the all out effort to learn the language to a "high proficiency" level. But I did learn to shop, ask for gasoline and all the necessities in the language. Because of its transitional level, I did not go all out, and admitted, that because I lived in the country, it was inexcusable for my wife, or me, to expect the Dutch to speak German for our convenience. So we often tried our best at a very complex spoken and written language.

The last year of my tour, however, I began to acquire a sincere desire to utilize various sentences and phrases of Dutch. Even today (1987-2001) I try some sentences and niceties with a Dutch lady who teaches at the school where I teach in San Diego. We sometimes speak German also and enjoy the practice of a language we both have common grounds in.

Since I was at a most ambitious age in my career, I was quite assertive in my teaching, always attending conferences in different parts of Europe. I also participated in my teacher's union, and went to various cities of Europe for conferences and they presented a further opportunity to expand my travels. The teacher's union was one activity I was highly active in because I knew it was the only way to improve a profession which needed drastic changes to even begin to elevate itself to the par of the European level of professionalism!

I also liked sporty cars, and even bought a mid-sixties Citroen, a French car, because I was simply enthralled with the front wheel drive of the car, and since I enjoyed hunting in Germany, felt it had some off-road capabilities. Little did I know when buying the automobile second hand, I was literally "one-upped" by my temporary housing land lady's son in the car deal. The disappointing experience was when the car left my wife, Liane, and me, stranded on the autobahn halfway between Aachen and Kiel, Germany during winter holidays in 1972.

I learned a good lesson regarding second hand, high mileage French cars and lost my desire for driving French cars after the episode. From then on it was BMWs, Mercedes until after the U. S. Dollar fell in about 1970, and then I began to drive U. S. automobiles, which I purchased from the PX outlets.

We liked the location of our Netherlands assignment since my wife and I were in the proximity of Northern Germany, and Kiel, my wife's hometown. Kiel was only about four and a half-hour's drive from Brunssum, the Netherlands, where we made Thanksgiving holidays, winter and spring holidays the time to visit family. We most often journeyed to Kiel, Germany to be with Brigitte's mother, her sisters, brothers and the in-laws. If we did not drive to Kiel, we had some of the family come stay with us in our lovely 3-bedroom home in Schinveld. With my newly added office that had a couch and desk, it could also serve as an added sleeping room, especially for the children.

Schinveld was a small town with a couple of thousand friendly Dutch citizens, but with several nice restaurants, so it was a pleasant town for festivals, and getting to know the locals. We even met one unusually interesting Dutch mechanic, "Bruno", who would accommodate the Americans in anyway possible. Any time I had car trouble, I took my car to Bruno. Bruno had a Slavic background, and he was great fun, loved his American whiskey, and had hundreds of American friends.

Bruno worked for a Ford dealership in nearby Heerlen, but ran an auto repair shop out of his own home. He had a big lot, an extraordinary garage, and knew all the proper state tax personnel for clearing American or other European cars through Dutch customs, than any human in the universe.

I spent many fun days at the local Schinveld restaurants drinking beer with Bruno, who also knew many of the American personnel high-ranking officers, attached to NATO. It is a very good thing that Bruno was not a spy for Russia in those days because he knew more personal things about more NATO personnel than any mechanic I have ever known.

On a weekend trip to Mannheim, Germany, I was stranded in one of my American cars, on the autobahn, only about 30 kilometers from Schninveld. I, found a telephone, called Bruno and he brought over my second car he had already repaired and was in his garage, and in less than one hour, he took the problem car back to Schinveld and we were in the good one, then continued the trip.

If a repair price was too high, Bruno was ready to compromise and would adjust the price if we were not satisfied. One thing I will say, the man was a great master mechanic. I visited him, even after I moved away from the Netherlands in 1971, because he knew everything about everybody in Schinveld and NATO, and was exciting and delightful to talk to. He also never seemed to suffer from lack of money since he was making money in his auto management job and also from his booming home repair shop.

The years passed by in the beautiful land of the Dutch. I found myself taking drives up to Rotterdam or Amsterdam, even on Sunday afternoons, just to enjoy cake and coffee in the two wonderful cities by the sea. The drive to either of the two cities was autobahn all the way, and one reached either Amsterdam or Rotterdam in less than 2 hours. Driving along at a hundred miles an hour was no task for me since I had had plenty of practice on the German autobahn.

My daughter was about 3 years old 1969, and was most delightful to take strolls with, or just for a drive to Aachen. Sometimes I would take her for short strolls, or enjoy being with her and my wife on short shopping trips to Aachen, Germany or Maastricht, the Netherlands, or other nearby German or Dutch towns or cities.

Liane took to the Dutch Kindergarten like a native, had several little 3 or 4 year old neighbor friends, and eventually was walking with the neighbor, Sonja, when she was 4 years old, in 1970, to the kindergarten right around the corner from my house.

We had a great landlord in the village of Schinveld. The owner of our house was a 25 year-old lovely Dutch lady, named Leida, who loved our daughter, and our dog, Heidi. We could leave Liane and the dog in our own rented house, and Leida would come over and take care of both of them and we were never concerned for their safety. What a wonderful assignment we had while living in the Netherlands. I paid for the child services, and the care was worth much more than the money Leida received, because of the excellent and responsible care extended to our daughter.

On one trip, when my wife, Liane, and I returned from Mannheim, Germany, I had left a "Toto" type lottery, based on Dutch Soccer, with my landlady, returned, and learned I hit about 9 numbers out of 11. Leida and her brother checked the numbers for us, and they thought we had won about 40,000 Dutch Guilder, but it turned out that there had been more winners that weekend than usually hit, so I ended up winning only about $200. In the Dutch Toto pool, the more people who win, the less the total winners received. Many times those pools brought the 40,000 Guilder, or more, if there were not too many wins. What a disappointment that turned out to be.

Nevertheless, this family turned out to be one of the nicest landlords we ever had in Europe. They took excellent care of our living quarters because they owned the duplex we lived in, and any request we made was usually carried out. I wanted an office added onto a back patio, and within a few weeks, a lovely glassed in area was added, with all the room I needed to do my school work, correspond, and relax if needed. As previously mentioned, it added more sleeping area for visiting family, if needed.

It is interesting to observe the difference in regimentation between the Dutch and the Germans. The Germans move and work like machines. The Dutch, liberal in tradition, even began organizing unions among the military while I lived in their country. The Germans on the other hand were highly structured in schools, work, and daily living. The German military strict and uncompromising compared to the Dutch!

I would socialize with the Germans, drink wine and beer, sometimes until 11:30 or latest 12:30 a.m. on a weekend or holiday evening. But if you were socializing with the Dutch, 3:30 a.m. meant nothing for them on a Friday or Saturday evening. They wanted to get the full benefit out of their leisure time. The generalization might not hold for all families, but when with my Dutch friends, there was no stopping when it came to partying or socializing.

One of the other customs I noticed, while walking, in my little village of Schinveld, and in all the Dutch towns and cities I visited, was that the living room windows never seemed to have the curtains drawn, especially in the day time. This, according to what I heard was that the Dutch liked to show the cleanliness and tidiness of their homes. Everyone walking by had the right to look into the living room admire and observe the very beautiful furniture, or even modest settings. The curtains in the daytime were never closed. This seems to be a ubiquitous custom in the Netherlands!

In Germany, this was not the tradition, and such was not the case. Most German houses or apartments were well protected by being up high, elevated, but certainly not on exhibition for the public passersby. Of course, in the Netherlands, there were many high rises or social type projects, which one could not gaze into, especially in some of the larger cities.

Two of my very good friends, whom I met, while living in Schinveld, the Netherlands, were Martin Reubsat and his wife Tung Fu. They turned out to be lifelong friends, and my ex wife and daughter still visit and receive visits from Martin and his wife. They owned a beautiful small hotel in Sittard, the Netherlands from the middle 1970s through about 1996. Now both are retired and in order to protect their retirement, so I am told, live across the border in Belgium, but very near the Dutch border. The taxation is obviously less in Belgium.

When Tung Fu and Martin bought the hotel, it was rather old, but they renovated the whole project, and the workers, who used some large earth digging equipment to rebuild the hotel, made some archaeological discoveries, which were later displayed in glass cabinets in the hotel. Some of the artifacts were given to the city for the museum because of their primeval value.

When I met Martin, he was an electrician, and we met in 1969, in a bar in Sittard. Martin was single at the time and we began talking, in German, so we bought each other beers, began a conversation and discovered that he also lived in the village of Schinveld.

Through conversation, we learned about each other's work. He, the electrician, and I, the teacher, began to drink beer together, meet each other's families, and even travel together. He set up my stereo set in my living room in Schinveld, then our friendship became closer. Dutch beer, by the way, in the tap form, is almost as good as the German beer, and is consumed by the Dutch quite frequently as in Germany.

A couple of years later, to my sadness, I learned that Martin's younger brother, was killed by an American military personnel, while on foot, near his work at the U. S. Commissary, where he was employed. The family was awarded insurance, but this did not eliminate the sorrow, especially from Martin's mother.

Martin and I, before he was married, even took a trip as far as Copenhagen, Demark one summer. We drove my new British Ford Escort, which had a high rpm engine, with a four speed manual transmission. It was a wonderful compact car, and brand new, in 1969 and burned up the streets in and around Sittard, the Netherlands, and Aachen, Germany. It was a fun car to scat around in, shop, and tour villages. The good gas mileage made it a worthwhile car, and I enjoyed it until I improved my status with the 1970 BMW 2002, 2 door sedan, in 1971, after my move to Karsruhe, Germany.

We spent about a week in Denmark, during our summer 1969 visit, admired the beautiful weather on the beaches, sight seeing, and some expensive restaurants. Fortunately we had beautiful weather in the month of July, so we were relaxed and enjoyed ourselves on a wonderful vacation. We shared costs, and had an inexpensive trip. My wife was home occupied with some of her German relatives who loved visiting the Netherlands.

Sometimes my German in-laws would make visits, and though with intentions of only remaining for 3 or 4 days, extended them into 10 days. My house got a little crowded, so I enjoyed myself by touring different parts of Europe. This gave me the space I needed, and my wife could enjoy the relatives. The close quarters of too many in-laws gave me claustrophobia.

It was interesting, that though the Germans were the conquerors of the Netherlands during the Second World War, the Germans, I believe, enjoyed being in and around the Dutch cities, more than the Dutch enjoyed visiting Germany. With many years passed, some of the scars were healed. I found out, also, that Dutch people along the border, did not mind utilizing the German language, and often shopped in border cities of Germany, especially the larger shopping areas.

Working in the 4-nation school, and having other U. S. Dependent Schools visit us, for competitive sports, from Belgium and Germany, proved to be quite interesting. We had these sports, just like many schools in the United States. I also visited other schools, sometimes to see an American high school type football game. Since soccer was the big sport of Europe, the AFCENT School also had a soccer team, as well as baseball, basketball, tennis, swimming, and even golf.

NATO, since the troops were moved out of France in1967 after President De Gaulle withdrew from the NATO military command structure, selected the Netherlands and Belgium to fill the void left in France. Many of the troops were placed in Belgium and the Netherlands, so the United States had 2 friendly countries in which to reside. Both countries seemed to enjoy hosting the NATO facilities and personnel because they were the victims of the German army during the Second World War, and suffered from obviously weaker military strength during Hitler's march across the lowlands after the beginning of World War II. The Netherlands and Belgium still seem to enjoy having the superior NATO units on its turf, especially since both are small countries.

The receptivity was friendly and they reveled in the military fortification. France did not want the U. S. military, so Belgium and the Netherlands opened their doors and also enjoyed the economic elevation. I always felt our military in those two countries received the best treatment, with extraordinary congeniality from the citizens in both countries.

France was and still is nationalistic, and does not like the interference of other troops on its soil, obviously. The concept of France wanting their property for themselves was brought out in a speech I heard from a foreign office dignitary. He observed, from a French family visiting him in his home, with children, that the French families marked off an area in which their children were to play, and were told by the parents to stay in that section. This somewhat characterizes the French feeling of wanting their territory for themselves. This feeling of interference into France's territory must have been a big motivator for the French pushing the American military out of France in the late 1967.

Another observation related to Vietnam, during the Vietnam War era, was that I felt the protest element of some military high school dependents quite frequently. It was mostly because of our nation's involvement in Vietnam. Even though some of the students were from military families, they were objective enough to sense that our involvement, from what they gleaned from newspapers and television, was not the healthiest mission for the military. The "Hippie Generation" and student protest movement began to permeate the high schools abroad in the 1970s.

But the Dutch, as far as I could determine, were so thrilled about the economic gap filled by NATO, that our existence there was well received. We learned that some of the old mines where coal was profitable, no longer had enough accessible coal to support the industry. Some of the old mines, and others in the vicinity, were converted into NATO administrative offices.

New NATO commissaries, and post exchanges were built around the area, so the troops and the Dutch were pleased. The NATO troops had access to good shopping, and the Dutch increased employment.

We, as Americans, had the convenience of shopping in American facilities and NATO facilities, so this made shopping for needed items very helpful. Even European car dealers were doing well selling their automobiles. Many BMWs, Mercedes,

Opels, Fiats, Renaults, Volvos, and other brands of cars were reasonable in price, and many officers were taking advantage of buying European, tax-free cars.

My exposure to the concept of international education, of which I always enjoyed reading about, so I could be knowledgeable of other countries' schools, was excellent in Brunssum. The school site provided me with an opportunistic situation that any American schoolteacher could dream about!

Working at a 4-nation school brought me in contact with Gymnasium teachers, especially the chemistry and physics teachers, and the opportunity of using the German language. I found the German teachers to be very professional. If I, as Department Chairperson, called a meeting, and did not get the meeting started and ended at the correct time, they got upset. But after a few meetings, and professional interaction, the Germans learned to become more flexible. I liked working with them very much, especially since the school administrators taught classes. This was true of the American school administrators. The American administrators, just as in the United States do not teach their students, and therefore lose all contact with the truest element of education, teaching students.

This is sad, and even today it causes me to lose respect for a system of education gone astray, deteriorating, and missing the rich elements European education provides. These are things I did learn while living among the Europeans, especially in the 4-nation school in Brunnsum, the Netherlands, from 1967 through 1971.

But my task in this book is not to explore education, as I have previously done in another book, but to dwell upon the complexity of the German people after the devastating Second World War, the people Hitler left behind. Also, I am interjecting the experiences gleaned from the other countries I lived in, and those three countries were the Netherlands, Italy, and Libya.

Enjoying the richness of the culture and associations with Dutch citizens were highlights of my many years in Europe, especially observing how they interacted in their association with the Germans. Being closer to the border, I found some animosity, but to my surprise, I found many who had experienced the occupation of the Germans, not be as antagonistic with the Germans as I anticipated.

Where my wife and I found more animosity, was as we wandered more northward, towards Rotterdam and Amsterdam. My wife was rejected more than once when shopping around shops or flea markets in those two cities, especially in Amsterdam that we frequented more often.

My wife was a great collector of antiques and any relics that displayed the touch of other countries so she could mix the items with the already collected, "museum" like element of her household. My ex wife is a "pack rat", in that she never throws away an item, just collects.

If one visits her lovely home in Hargesheim, Germany, near Mainz and Bad Kreuznach, Germany today, one will find valuable pieces of furniture, and antiques, which I would not guess the value of. The house is orderly, but I would almost use the word, "cluttered", except she is too well organized. I think her materialistic attitude comes from the fact that she was a child during World War II and never really had the opportunity to have stability and maintain many materialistic things. Because of the war, her family lost everything they owned in East Prussia.

We were criticized several times when speaking German with some of the people in Amsterdam, because of the vicinity of the city, not being close to the border of Germany, the people would openly come in conflict with Brigitte, who speaks German with everybody in the universe. But she did know some Dutch, immediately switched to what she knew, just to prevent hostility, but to no avail. The merchants, in some instances, in Amsterdam seemingly had rather lose a sale than deal with Germans. This may be a generalization, but we found it to be true on various occasions. I would expect to anti German syndrome in the northern part of the Netherlands to be diminishing presently, but I have not been in that area since the 1970s, so I cannot say.

I had heard of anti German sentiments in conversations with many people who traveled and visited Holland, the northern province of the Netherlands. And why should we impose German or English on the Dutch? However, the use of English was more respected than that of German. And I feel it was the lingering aftermath of the Third Reich.

The five-year stay in the Netherlands was about to come to an end. This was especially true after I got involved, romantically, with a young business female teacher on staff in the American section of the 4-nation school in Brunssum. My wife, with her German dictatorial manner, got angry with the teacher, was on the verge of physical violence, and the director of the school encouraged me to transfer to save my marriage. After Brigitte confronted the teacher about our relationship, the trouble began so I had to make a decision on whether to leave my wife or not. I chose my wife to make a long story short.

Because of an incident at the AFCENT Officer's club, when my wife threw a gin and tonic glass (full) directly in front of the commanding general's wife, at my girl friend, I established a name, "worldwide!"

I finally decided to transfer for my own good. The principal of the American section had no love for the American director of the complete complex of the 4-nation school, and sided with me in the dispute, but encouraged me to transfer because of the emotional distress wrought upon my family and me.

I took his advice, transferred to Karlsruhe, Germany, the headquarters of the European area American Overseas Dependent Schools. I was a personal friend of the director, and he wanted me to be under his tutelage for awhile, I suppose, because it turned out that after about six years, I was promoted to administration.

I truly admired Dr. Joseph Mason, one time worldwide director of all the American Dependent Schools abroad, and had close contact with him while I lived the following 6 years in Karlsruhe, Germany.

After the episode, I decided the time had come to leave the Netherlands. With many good Dutch friends in that splendid and friendly country, I moved back to my to Deutschland, home of my wife. She was happy to be away from the events of the past year at Brunssum, and we both went to Karlsrune in splendid unity, and a desire to maintain our marriage. That we did, after a most interesting stay in the Netherlands.

The teacher I was involved with was transferred also. She was sent to a school in England and I heard, a few years later that she married an officer and seemed to be quite happy.

I sometimes think that if I had stayed in Italy, the Netherlands phase of my life would have been eliminated, especially the last unpleasant year of the 4 nation school experience. But I feel the overall experience was one that richened, and elevated my knowledge of another culture. The beauty of the people, windmills, Dutch social diversity, friendliness, and interaction with a high-density populated country provided me with insights a thousand books could not have given me.

The experiences of the excellent 4 nation school, and the experience of observing Canadian, British, German, and American education working together made my life, especially as a secondary teacher, so much richer than the doldrums so many American teachers, in their provincial setting, must endure. It is not to belittle them for being captive in a caged environment, but to applaud myself, along with the many other teachers from different countries who were willing to accept the challenge of adventure, and expose themselves to the many facets of other countries and cultures!

My living in the rich environment of the friendly Dutch people was an experience I shall forever cherish. To live among such a progressive people and interact with them in the many social settings there will always be a highlight in my multi-cultured prism of life. It goes beyond every day routine living. The fun and excitement of being abroad is making a living in your profession and living in a different country while employed. Working and living abroad is the same as being on an extended vacation with full pay. One of the main goals, I have observed, of the middle class Americans, and up, is the climatic trip to Europe, especially after one has saved enough money.

I had some opportunities to work with corporations, especially in the 1970s, but I turned them down because of the richness of living in other cultures. Being in my late 30s, not as today in my late 60s, provided me with the ability to make the transition out of teaching, but I chose to stay, and only because of the European experience.

If young people, especially those with college or specialty training, miss the opportunity to travel abroad, especially to Europe, I would offer the advice to take the step. Take the step and enter into a world of fascination and exposure to other languages and cultures. It is a chance to expand horizons for inner development, gain the vantage-point of seeing the world from a higher plateau.

The exposure of Dutch society, and contrasting it to German society, and Italian society was a triple run for me. All were countries of delight, when it comes to travel, dining, interacting, and gaining knowledge of other languages. "Why stay at home?" A Chief Petty Officer in the U. S. Navy once told me; "Travel and see the world because you can always come back home."

The petty officer's advice was true, and I will continue to build on these experiences because they are now beginning to lay the beacon in my life I can follow, elicit information from, write about, expand in inner reflections, and utilize to broaden any future horizons of travel.

Maybe there will be another country, perhaps Mexico, the Orient, or a revisit to Italy. Most of all, it will be another culture from which to extract experiences and revelations. The Dutch experience was one of five-years, and one that intensified my desires to see and learn more.

My reflection of the Netherlands, a very small country is predominantly a very positive one. Though the country is small, it is dynamic in character, friendliness, and beauty.

The Netherlands presently has only 15 million people and is a country with a heart. Liberal, in scope, compared to countries like Germany, and entrenched in a Constitutional monarchy, it is a pleasant place to live and visit. The current Queen Beatrix of the House of Orange-Nassau that goes back to 1370 seems to be quite successful in her relationship with the Dutch people and the political structure.

One never tires of the pleasant greetings from its citizens, and its clean villages and cities. Maastricht, Heerlen, Kerkrade, and even border villages of Belgium, were always pleasant to visit. Never would one get bored from living in such a friendly and small country. I learned to love its people, cherished the thought of living in a country that was small enough to visit easily, any location on the map, and even try to speak its transitional language, though very complex!

I dearly loved my tour there, and thankful for the gracious and friendly which its people extended to the NATO forces, especially during the time I lived within its borders. My thanks to the people for the wonderful five years I spend there. For a country with only about 15 million citizens, it has a lot of beautiful tradition.

Of the approximate 15 million people in the Netherlands, their liberal attitudes might be depicted by the statistics on religion in the country. The country is about 1/3 Roman Catholic, 1/3 Protestant, and 1/3 non-affiliated. This sets a middle of the road mode in religious practices and further illuminates the tolerable and somewhat liberal nature of these friendly people.

I was impressed with its people, culture, and many opportunities to mix amidst the friendly, kind, and well-mannered citizens. Any future opportunity I might have to visit in the country would be a pleasure, and a reward I am again awaiting.

Germany and the people Hitler left behind still enjoy visiting the clean, compact and extremely gracious people of the Netherlands. I watched the German tourists visit and they were immersed in the beauty of the tulips, the windmills, the dikes, beautiful clean streets and quaint houses. The relatives of my wife cherished the visits, came frequently, and praised the magnificence of the Netherlands!

Chapter 6

Karlsruhe, Wie Schön!

Karlsruhe, Germany, in 1971, when I arrived, was a city of about 240,000 people. The friendly city is located in the State of Baden-Württemberg. My return to Germany, from the Netherlands was delightful. It was a chance to renew old acquaintances, especially with teachers from the Dependent Schools, in Ramstein, Germany, not too far from Karlsruhe.

In Karlsruhe, I made some of the most interesting German contacts of my overseas career. The city was exciting, had a great opera house, a beautiful zoo, and lovely sights. The location was just south of Heidelberg, and very close to the lovely SPA resort of Baden Baden one of the highlight cities of the Black Forest, just south of Karlsruhe.

When I moved to Karlsruhe, my family and I, had to live in temporary quarters, supplied by the military, before moving to a permanent house on the economy. My wife, I, and Liane had to spend almost two months in temporary quarters. These were officer quarters right near the downtown area when we moved to Karulsruhe, where I taught in the American High School from August 1971 until August 1977.

We actually loved the arrangements because we had two rooms in the BOQ that were near the middle part of downtown Karlsruhe, and close to the school, commissary, P.X. and all the U. S. facilities Americans needed.

There was no problem shopping on the German community because of our previous years of living in the country. Heidelberg, Baden Baden, and other lovely cities, villages and towns were in the nearby vicinity of Karlsruhe. It was an exciting area to live in and Karlsruhe was actually in the heartbeat of Germany because of its central location.

When we finally found a house, one which had about 3,200 square feet of living space, we learned we could not move in until about the second week of October. By that time I had already started teaching at the Karlsruhe American High School, and began to get a feel for what my mission in the school was.

I began to meet new Americans and Germans, so the time I spent living in the officers' quarters proved to be time well spent. I could walk almost anywhere on base, and shop either at the American facilities or downtown. We began to adjust to the community quickly.

By October, however, we were in our large house in Hagenbach, Germany, a neighboring state from the one where I taught school. Our newly rented home was in Rheinland-Pfalz but our school was in the State of Baden-Württemberg. These were two different states and separated by the beautiful Rhine River. The location proved to be a pleasant and beautiful area in which to enjoy everyday living.

My drive each day was about 16 miles to and from work. I had to drive across the Rhein River, which ran north between Karlsrune and Maximilliansau, with Karlsruhe on the east side and Maximilliansau on the west side.

Karlsruhe, a large city, and Maximilliansau, which had a Mercedes plant mostly used as a shipping point for the Mercedes factory, was very small. It was no surprise, that the little town just west of the Rhine, had only a couple of restaurants, and Karlsruhe, a city today with over 260,000 inhabitants, had many bars, hotels, restaurants, an opera house, and a beautiful palace. Karlsruhe is a city with many things to do, and in my opinion, it was an exciting place for my wife, my child, and I to live. We enjoyed the diverse restaurants, the Opera House, and my child enjoyed the zoo, along with many other beautiful sights.

The Karlsruhe Palace was built in 1715 as the residence of Margrave Karl Wilhelm of Baden-Durlach. The building was partly wooden and the architect was lieutenant Jacob von Batzendorf. The castle and the city were renovated in 1746, and the opportunity was taken to rebuild the castle out of stone. The castle served as the seat of government of the Baden dynasty for 200 years. In the third quarter of the 18th Century it was basically rebuilt and the interior was repeatedly changed and re-furnished. Baden revolutionaries threw the Grand Duke Leopold out of the palace in 1849. It finally left the monarchy in the 1918. The archaeological and ethnological collections and holdings of the Applied Arts Museum were united as the Baden State Museum in the former residence in 1921. Karlsruhe Palace, in 1944, was completely destroyed by air raids. In rebuilding it, the latest styles and technologies of museum design could be used.

I always found the area of the palace to be quite splendid and a contributing attraction to the city of Karlsruhe. The city is not always the easiest to drive around in during the time of high traffic, but the vicinity of the downtown area was close to the American facilities so it proved to be rather pleasant for night life, the opera, and restaurants after working hours.

I lived south of Maximilliansau, in a village called Hagenbach, a town with only a few hundred people. Recently I drove through the city, over the Christmas holidays, of 2000. To my surprise, the village, not like many American small towns, had grown in size and numbers. Many towns in the United States, I suspect, after 20 plus years would tend to be stagnant, or constant in size. This town had increased houses, and the streets were improved. It had only become neater in appearance.

Improvement and population increase was also evident in France, just across the border, the small town immediately across from Germany and in Alsace, had grown in size, and was maintained in a beautiful fashion. The small town is known as Lauterbourg, France, and is very neat and well kept.

I return, almost once a year, either in the summer, or during the winter holidays, and visit one of our favorite restaurants, the Bord du Rhin, a French Restaurant, which prepares the French frogs' legs in a style only known to them. These are appetizers, but sometimes one can almost make a complete meal from one-half order of these wonderful garlic flavored dishes.

My time in Hagenbach, Germany, along the Rhine River, was absolute bliss. I rode my Peugeot bicycle each day, enjoyed the terrain, and wonderful flat areas along the Rhine River. I always kept in shape and relieved the stress of high school teaching, enjoying the beautiful Rhine area each day I was there.

Though I had to drive to work each day, I always enjoyed the trip across the Rhine River. I drove a BMW for several years, and had the fun of accelerating around the curves on the way home, in the secure manner my 1970 2002 BMW vehicle would carry me.

What a way to spend my 39th birthday through my 43rd. I was at an age where I was at the top of my career, and really enjoyed teaching physical science in the American Schools abroad. The career of teaching overseas was certainly richer than I would found it had I have been located in the United States. The additive of enjoying Germany and Europe in its magnanimous richness only enhanced each minute I lived.

My profession as a teacher opened many doors into the social realm of Karlsruhe and the vicinity. Through the American Rod and Gun Club, I began to make many contacts with top quality German families in and around Karlsruhe, and across the Rhine River to the west, in the State of Rheinland-Pfalz.

The opportunities that opened up for rich and communicative contact were beyond description. I do not believe Ernest Hemingway had a richer setting in Spain or Italy than I had in social relations with the hunters (most all professionals and business personnel) in Germany.

The teachers, doctors, and business people were fantastic. I got to know their families, visit their businesses, and have many occasions to eat, drink, and celebrate with them. A city the size of Karlsruhe, with about a quarter of million people has such a great Opera House, and the culture one receives in a city that size makes its people that much more alert, music oriented, and pleasant to be around.

Some simple statistics, not just for Karlsruhe, but for the country of Germany are that though the country is mixed-Roman Catholic and Protestant-they celebrate many holidays that have the genesis of both religions. The whole country is almost evenly split between Roman Catholic and Protestant, with 45% being Protestant, 37% Roman Catholic, and 18% unaffiliated. The blend is, today, quite peaceful and I noticed no conflicts between both groups because of religion.

It seems that when the holidays come, all its citizens celebrate. They are always ready to partake in the national religious holidays. While working in the American Dependent Schools, I enjoyed the festivities of both religions and participated with my many German friends, whether they were Protestant or Roman Catholic.

There was one thing different about the Rhine River Valley, and I had never experienced what happened to me there. In 1971, after transferring from the Netherlands to Karlsruhe, I noticed unusual sinus pressures in my head, and finally realized the Rhine River Valley in that area must have had something to do with the variable atmospheric pressures.

I graphed the pressure changes with a mercuric barometer I had in my science class, and also noticed it affected the students' behavior modes. When the varied pressures changed, especially the extreme jumps, I noticed extreme restlessness in the students in my classroom.

But regardless of the varied atmospheric pressure changes, the wooded areas, the Rhine River, and the beautiful farms in the area gave it a definite charm. I enjoyed many days of pheasant, wild boar, hare, partridge, and deer hunting in the two German States of Baden-Württenberg and Rheihland-Pfalz.

In 1971, I placed my daughter in a school in Hagenbach, where we rented the 3,200 square foot beautiful house we lived in for six years. We had plenty of room and enjoyed the new house because it was wonderful for interacting with German and American friends at our many parties.

Liane was in the first grade, at about 5 years of age, and I now realize she started a little early because down the road there would be a need to let her repeat a grade. This was because of the extremely difficult time she had with mathematics, which started to enter into some aspects of abstract mathematics at about the third or fourth grade level of the German school.

We found the German schools, because of their discipline, autocracy, rigidity, and high expectations, were excellent for a foundation in education for our daughter. With some kindergarten exposure in the Dutch school, Liane began to grasp the process of learning under German tutelage, quite well.

With her mother reading to her in German, and I reading to her in English, we found that she was beginning to be a serious student at an early age. I have no regrets at having my daughter in the German schools at an early age. I also had the facility of putting her into the American school if needed. Actually we did this when we found out about the complexity and rigidity the third grade of the German school, because of her starting too early. We started her in the first grade at early five years of age and this was too early for what was to come in the German schools.

I pulled her out of the third grade of the German school at about mid-way, let her finish out the year, then put her back into the German elementary school until she was a little more mature for the steady grind of serious German schooling. I did this at the third grade level, and then again in the fifth grade level, and found out that because of it, Liane was ready to tackle the track to the German Gymnasium (college preparatory track) at age 12 or 13. I did not mind the extra exposure of school for Liane and I think such a philosophy is good, especially if a child enjoys learning, which Liane definitely did.

My association with both German and American educators in Karlsruhe, because I was also a teacher, was excellent. We also provided Liane with a private piano teacher, after purchasing a very heavy upright piano while living in Hagenbach. She got a great teacher from the local village, and we enjoyed watching her take to basic music notes in a lively fashion.

In Karlsruhe and the vicinity, my most important contacts were through my hunting because I met such great people as Max Griesinger, owner of one of the largest bakeries in Germany. He had a bakery in a village just north of Karlsruhe, and I was invited to many large beautiful drive hunts for pheasant.

It was on one of his hunts that I met my life-long friend, Herbert Dietrich, and whom we called a Gastjäger (guest hunter), as was I. He and I were guests on many hunts and Herbert, though he owned his own small hunting Revier (hunting land) in the middle of Karlsruhe, was not a large land owner as were Herman Stultz and Max Griesinger, so he participated in many invitational hunts where there was more game.

As one hunted more often, and I hunted almost every weekend of the fall hunting season, one would meet more and more hunters. Many of them were very serious hunters and hunted every time it was possible. We, as Jägers (hunters), were right at the point of being fanatical about the sport. We wore the forest green clothes, carried the proper weapons with the strap, and some hunters even bought green cars in order to blend with the beautiful green German forests. Hunting in Germany was quite different than hunting in the United States in that when hunting in Germany, one would kill game on 90% of the hunts. This was definitely not always the case in the United States, as many hunters will attest to.

I never remember coming home without game, except for high seat hunting, where one would sit in a little platform in a tree, then wait for wild boar or deer to appear. One always shot game on the drive hunts, but they were purchased from the Pechter, one who leases and controls hunting rights on private hunting land. When hunting on the state controlled lands, one paid the Förster (keeper of the game) on such hunts.

One Oberföster, Herr Glasser, became a rather close social friend of mine between 1973 and 1977 and he controlled a large tract land around the Rhine River. We shot more wild pigs on his hunts than most any area I have hunted in. The special area was in the Hagenbach hunting region. On some of the hunts, always with dogs and drivers, we would shoot 20 wild pigs or more. Herr Glasser was a master at controlling the hunts, smoked excessively, and is now deceased, but well educated, as the Försters of Germany must be, because they are educated as are our degree foresters in the United States.

One of the differences in the United States forestry program, and that in Germany, is that the Försters of Germany integrate wild life studies into the forestry program. All are excellent hunters who are fully educated in the German "Abschuss Plan", a scientific plan of balance of cover, forest, and feeding to attain the optimum quantity of game on given plots of land.

Herr Glasser was the ideal concept of the State Forest Administrator who ran his program with tight control, knew when, and where every shot was fired on any given hunt. His keen knowledge of the population and habitat of wild pigs was simply magnificent. He could almost tell a hunter how many pigs were in each litter around the forest region he controlled.

His magnificent and flawless dress, with boots and Lodenmantel (a heavy woolen coat for hunting) illuminated each step he took on the surrounding dirt roads of the hardwood and pine forests of the area. Never did one make an error, shoot into the drive, which was forbidden. Hunters must wait until a pig is driven out of the forest, so he or she can eye the animal, then turn and shoot as the pig comes blazing out of the forest. Shooting the animal took excellent shooting or the wild pig would be by you in a flash.

On one hunt, I only got part of an animal in the deep swamp like forest, when I and a G. I. shot at about the same time, and I know my shot, with a .12 gauge slug time hit the hind quarter of the 200 pound boar. The G. I. must have been an excellent shot, because just after I saw the pig drop in the rear, then regain his speed, he was hit with a .308 bullet that brought him to the ground. On that day we shot no less than 19 pigs because they were everywhere in those deep woods near the border of France.

This specific hunt turned out to be a great, with the usual horn blowing, warm soups, knockwurst and Brötchen (hard German rolls), and plenty of beer and wine after the hunt. The Strecke (assembled game) was appropriately laid out with the high game descending to the low game. What a magnificent day, with Herr Glasser in all his glory, enjoying the compliments of the Americans and Germans alike.

I do not believe I have ever had such thrills as those I had on Herr Glasser's hunts. He was king in the hunter's world and every American envied any American military or civilian who got invited on such hunts. He was also, from hearsay, one of the most respected administrators in the Federal Ministry of Forestry.

I was going to make sure that this gentleman, Herr Glasser did not forget me, because I had a magnificent rented home, only about 4 kilometers from where he lived. His office was in Hagenbach and only a few blocks from where I lived. I proceeded to extend a written invitation to him and took this one directly to his office so he would be sure to receive it. He accepted the forthcoming invitation after I explained the function and that I was a teacher and hunter wanting to expand my hunting in the area.

My wife and I procured about 40 T-bone steaks, proceeded to grill them, bought a couple of kegs of German beer, a couple of cases of excellent white and red wines, and threw one of the largest Jäger parties ever given in the area. I made sure all the good hunting contacts in the Karlsruhe-Hagenbach area were invited, so nothing but conversation about hunting would take place. Other topics were brought up, but I wanted to keep on the good side of all the best private land owners and Herr Glasser so we kept the main theme that of hunting.

He later became a solid social acquaintance of mine and I made sure my wife and I prepared the best meals for Frau and Herr Glasser. We succeeded in becoming one of his prime candidates for guest hunters when the wild boar season opened. I missed very few of the hunts while living in the area, and even attended a couple after I moved away in 1977.

On a recent visit to Karlsruhe, Germany, in about 1999, my very good hunting friend, Herbert Dietrich sadly informed me that Herr Glasser passed away several years ago, in the early 1990s. This saddened me, as did the other news that Herr Stultz and Herr Griesinger had also passed on.

As sad as it may seem, the high consumption of cigarettes probably had something to do with the deaths of all three of the major hunting friends of mine in that area. I sometimes am awed that Germany, and the rest of Europe have not brought promoted the statistics of deaths related to lung cancer and heart disease as we in the United States have done.

Fortunately I was exposed to the statistics of lung cancer, especially, when living in Tripoli, Libya. Dr. Ochsner, founder of Ochsner Clinic, New Orleans, made a talk at Wheelus U. S. Air Force Medical Clinic in October 1960, Tripoli, Libya.

Because I taught biology at Wheelus High School, I received a personal invitation to the lecture.

From the lecture Dr. Ochsner gave, I learned that the first study of 10,000 deceased veterans regarding the relation between lung cancer and cigarette smoking, was made through this fantastic medical pioneer. He discovered that 1 pack a day for twenty years led to early stages of lung cancer for about 84% of the smokers. About 16 % escaped the tragedy through resistance.

Filters do not reduce the tar factor that in turn gives the carcinogenic effect that causes the lung cancer. The less inhalation causes less cancer effect. If one quits smoking, the positive effect begins immediately. These factors I always related to my science and biology classes while teaching in high school. I also use the statistics for my high school social studies classes today.

If only smokers, and there are so many in Europe, were provided, more generously, these statistics, maybe so many would not hasten their death. One of the reasons I really like about California is that, statistically, it is a state with diminishing smokers, and the education program against smoking is beginning to take effect, with a less percentage of smokers here than any state in the nation.

Nevertheless, Herr Glasser was a magnificent forest administrator, tops in his position, and a great hunter, espousing hunting tradition in its magnificent form on all the hunts conducted by him. He was astute, keen, respected, and knew forest and game control like no individual I have known. I very seldom heard him discuss, too extensively, his past relations with the Third Reich.

Karlsruhe was not only a lovely place to enjoy hunting and the forests, but an area that had fantastic restaurants. My wife and I would get a baby sitter, drive to nearby restaurants in France, Durlach, Baden Baden, Heidelberg, or restaurants along the Rhine River to the west in Rheinland-Pfalz. One of my favorites, and not elite, but a down-to-earth type restaurant, was the Bord du Rhin, located in Lauterbourg, France, only about 13 kilometers or 6.8 miles from our home in Hagenbach.

My ex wife, Brigitte and I still visit, along with Liane, my daughter and her husband, Thomas, the restaurant each time I return to Germany. We have to drive a little farther, since Bad Kreuznach, where they reside, is about 110 kilometers or about 66 miles away. The excellent Province type frogs' legs, prepared in winesauce, sautéed in butter and garlic are beyond description. They are excellent appetizers and always lend themselves to excellent taste when accompanied by some of the great white wines of Alscace, France.

I would even drive down to the Bord du Rhin on a Saturday afternoon, when there were not hunting (though hunting can happen almost 12 months a year in Germany) events taking place. I would have a delicious lunch, come home smelling like garlic, but satisfied with a good meal of frogs' legs, possibly a pork tenderloin for the main dish, from a selection of chicken, filet mignon, or fish. All the meals at the Bord du Rhin were delights.

It was interesting to observe the transitional blend when coming away from Hagenbach, then driving into the small village of Lauterbourg, France. The people were suddenly French and no longer German. The bakeries right across the border did lend themselves to magnificent loaves of crusty French bread, and it was only a 6 mile ride on my Pegeut bike if I wanted to extend myself to the venture on a Sunday morning, especially when the weather was warm and sunny.

Riding a bicycle along the smaller highways was extremely dangerous in those days. The German motorists, in their

Mercedes and BMWs would come whizzing by at speeds of greater than seventy miles per hour, and one was risking one's life when taking to the open roads for the pleasure of riding a bike and getting exercise. My friend, teacher at Karlsruhe American High School, teacher of history, lived in the same village as I, Hagenbach, and would often take evening rides with me.

He was often angered by these fast riders, so we learned a trick, and it was to point to the front of oncoming, speeding cars, as though there were a flat or defect on the car. This would cause them to slow down in most cases. If the driver were to stop, and ask us what the matter was, we would merely say that we though the tire looked low, but guess we made a mistake. We did this for our own protection because the drivers, not like most Americans, had no concern that our 30 pound bicycle could not compete with a 3,000 pound vehicle which had a tremendous potential of momentum had we have been struck.

One day I performed this trick and pointed down at a Mercedes that was traveling almost 90 miles per hour. He slowed down, turned around and pursued me, but I rode my bike into the woods for safety because I know the German driver would have been ready to shoot me, had he have had a gun. I escaped without confrontation or injury, but continued using the trick for my safety. The drivers were violating the top speed of about 70 miles per hour or less on the secondary roads.

The accessibility of the Rhine River, which was only about 300 meters from the village of Hagenbach, made bicycle drives most gorgeous, and we could ride along the river, and even to villages like Berg, and other small villages along the Rhine. We, of course, took the advantage of riding always to Lauterbourg, France. At that time there was a border guard stand or hut on the border crossing between the two countries, France and Germany. When making these bicycle rides, one would usually have to show a passport, and sometimes, if we forgot the passports, then most French border guards would let us go into France with only our military identification, which we always carried with us while working for the Department of Defense.

We would ride to France, especially in the spring and fall, when the weather was quite pleasant. My friend and I would ride along, no helmets, as are required today, no flags on the bicycles, just leisurely riding along, talking, philosophizing, or talking about the wonders of Germany, the Cold War, our coming trips back to the United States, or about students in our school. We enjoyed living in Germany, but my friend was the perfect U. S. super patriot. America exceeded in all, could do no wrong, "Nazis still existed in Germany", and he just did not seem to get along with all Germans because of their dictatorial and dormant and conservative attitudes!

He was a magnificent teacher, resisted learning any German, and the perfect type to preserve the nationalistic attitudes developed in many American teachers (teachers tend to be a conservative group, as a profession) brought up in New England or the mid-west. My friend was from New England, and to my knowledge, never assimilated into German social life, as I pictured myself doing.

But he was a very good social studies teacher who had many excellent activities in his classroom. His wife was attractive, conservative also, and they had two beautiful children, one girl and one boy. They were always nice to have over for coffee, especially if there were no Germans around.

My colleague was the stereotype often found teaching in the American communities. They were patriotic, flew the American flag on the Fourth of July, even in Germany, and ate apple pie and talked about retiring in the good old United States after finishing 25 or 35 years abroad. They seemed to enjoy the insular effect and protection given them by the U. S. Status of Forces agreement set up between the United States and Germany, and always attended American functions on base.

But then there were others like my teacher friend, Matt Olivo, who spoke Italian, German, and had a Roman Catholic education of excellence, steeped in excellent historical and English learning. He attended St. Mary's in Baltimore, Maryland and studied for the priesthood but I do not think he could pass the morale requirements because he was too much like me. He liked wine, women, song, and hunting too much.

We spent many a night in the local Karlsruhe bars, admiring the beauty of the German women, and consuming quality German brews along the main bar areas of downtown Karlsruhe. Matt was a true friend, whom I taught to hunt with the Germans, while he taught me where to find the best Italian Pizza in Karlsruhe, along with the best brands of German tap beer.

I just talked with this magnificent person, who, by the way blended in with the Germans in true continental fashion, speaking their language, mixing with the people, and learning, in depth, all the facets of German political, economic, and educational life. He was a true scholar whom I admired extremely.

I just spoke with Matt Olivo, by telephone, today, April 22, 2001 at 1:47 p.m. and he is retired from the Overseas Dependent Schools and lives in Rhode Island with his lovely Austrian wife. They have two very successful children, female and male, who both have college degrees.

The Olivos were excellent representatives for Americans living abroad. I cannot say too many good things about this outstanding teacher, family person, and scholar. The teachers respected Matt and also the administrators who lived in Karlsruhe, Germany in the 1970s and 1980s because he was like a walking encyclopedia when it came to scholarly knowledge, especially in the realm of World or United States History.

There were other teachers who represented the United States well when teaching for the Overseas Dependent Schools. Another one whom I knew and came to respect was Mr. Boyd Ramsey, a teacher, and graduate of Drake University. He taught chemistry and physics, and had that certain quality that led him out into the community to mix and represent the United States in a positive fashion. He worked on his French, spoke very good German, and was always studying in the realm of German and French areas, whether it was philosophy, science, or their languages.

Boyd was an excellent cook, loved to travel, mix with the Germans, and invited my wife and me to his house near Karlsruhe quite often. I do not know how many years he remained in Karlsruhe, or with the Overseas Dependent Schools, but I presume he is now retired.

I am one of the last teachers of our vintage to retire because I broke up the continuity of a full Civil Service retirement by resigning from the Department of Defense without building the full retirement benefits. I received only a partial retirement package and do not consider the teacher program abroad to be as good as some state systems, especially that of the very wealthy STRS (State Teacher Retirement System) in California.

There were many teachers who lived abroad and well represented the Americans in Germany. Germany is a country that should have the best Americans visiting their soil because they look up to many aspects of American technology and its people. Their cooperation in NATO is to be highly respected because full support of Germany during the Cold War was, no doubt, one of the forces that would have made the USSR think twice had there ever been a global conflict created by the opposing forces during the Cold War.

Having good people abroad certainly was beneficial for the United States during the years we spent abroad. Whether in the past, today, or in the future, exemplary representatives of the United States were and are important. America still has a strong interest in the NATO alignment in keeping peace in Europe, therefore quality representatives abroad can magnify the image of the United States by example!

My stay in Karlsruhe intensified my love for Germany and the German people. I hope to keep a close contact with the country, exercise my German when visiting, and possibly teach again in the German Volkshochschule when I return. My last location for teaching in the German Volkshochschule was in Bad Kreuznach, and I will elaborate on that aspect of my life in the next chapter of this book.

Karlsruhe is a magnificent city, and the beauty and charm of its people cannot be over-emphasized by me. I will always enjoy visiting the city and my many German friends made while living in that area from 1971 to 1977. The Rhine River and vicinity, with its beauty, made living and hunting in the vicinity one of the most exciting and interesting phases of my life. The people Hitler left behind in that area of Germany tend to voice their friendship toward me each time I return, and I found a rare beauty of the land because of my many positive experiences from 1971 through 1977.

Chapter 7

Bad Kreuznach And Nahe Wine

In August, 1977, after returning from a quick trip to Pisa and Florence, Italy, I returned to my home in Hagenbach, and learned I had been offered a position as assistant principal in a small school called Bad Kreuznach American High School. The school is located in the same state I was living in at that time.

I made some inquiries, talked to a few teachers who knew about the school, made a decision that I would leave the classroom and further expand my career aims in education and venture into another phase of American education abroad.

After taking the job as assistant principal, I decided to go up and visit the area so I could visualize the living situation for my wife and daughter. I drove up one weekend, alone, and discovered the area to be just as a German friend described. It was a little "Baden Baden", with the SPA facilities extremely nice, and of high quality. The hotels and SPA area were exquisite.

All I had to do was find a nice house for the wife and child. This proved to be a task since school was to begin the first week of September. I was to report to work during the last two weeks of August and I decided to bring up my trailer and park it on the school grounds, after the principal, Leon Rivers, my boss with Dependent Schools approved it. The Base Commander of the 8th Infantry Division also gave me permission so everything was clear for me to sleep in the trailer during the first two or three weeks of work before I found a house. I was allowed cost of living allowance, so this made things much better.

It turned out that my wife, Liane, and I ended up living in the trailer, from mid-September until the first or second week in November. We finally made an agreement with Herr Laun, a well respected gentlemen of Bad Kreuznach, who was ready to rent his upper floor in a beautiful old house on Weinkauff Strassse, in the middle of the "Kurgebiet", or SPA area of Bad Kreuznach.

We finally came to an agreement of $800 German Marks per month, and I kept this place with no rent increase for about seven years. The actual cost in German money was about $460/month. I was delighted to find such an inexpensive place, and so near my school and the heart of downtown Bad Kreuznach. It was a dream and I was the in the center of the beautiful SPA area.

Not only was the location good, but I could ride my bike, jog along the Nahe River (SPA area) until the day turned into darkness. We were within a couple of hundred meters from the Nahe River, and it was a delightful area in which to reside. The new experiences in my life were invigorating and the lovely city, bustling with excitement and well to do Germans made things even more exciting.

This could have been a school in the backwoods of Hahn Air Base in Germany and I would have loved it. Though I had offers for school administration since 1961, I never really wanted to leave teaching and students in the classroom. But now I was beginning to mellow out and want something else in life, and that was probably the desire to utilize my experience for administrative services and of the teachers for Dependent Schools.

Bad Kreuznach was a lovely city, a town of about 34,000 people at the time I moved there. The military-complex, schools and all agencies were scattered throughout the city of Bad Kreuznach. I do not know if this was a planned scheme of the military, or because the Americans had taken over some World War II facilities used by the Germans, and the placement of facilities was a tactic to prevent centralization and retard bombing raids.

How the Germans set up the military locations such as barracks, administrative buildings, hospitals, and housing during the war was puzzling. These facilities are scattered all over the city and one had to run back and forth from Civilian Personnel to Payroll, then to the Officer's Club, and perhaps to the BOQs just to have papers signed. The base facilities were not as tightly and centrally located as were those on the base in Karlsrue, but were quaint in their interspersed fashion and the military personnel were excellent to work with.

In back of Bad Kreuznach American High School was one of the most beautiful views one could ever imagine. As one looked down, southwest of the school, there was a beautiful view of a SPA area and soccer field that was owned by the city of Bad Krueznach. We were about three hundred feet above the area behind and below us, with the Nahe River winding through, with rapid shoals moving, glittering, toward the Rhine River to the north.

I thought that for a high school teacher or administrator working in such a high school in its beautiful setting, it was heavenly and peaceful. I was in my glory, and was supervising, with the principal, about 30 secondary teachers and about 650 students. It was a perfect setting and I loved every minute of the job, from the time I was assigned, until I was granted a sabbatical to return for postgraduate work in 1983, at San Diego State University.

I had an African American principal for a boss when I was first assigned there in 1977, who was not the best at writing, as many of us are not, but was a skilled administrator who utilized articulation as a substitution for high demands in writing. He had a great secretary so she took care of any spelling errors. After two years at the school he was promoted to a larger school because I think the sensitivity of the very small school began to aggravate him. The Department of Defense was looking for increased numbers in minorities, especially African Americans, during that time, and he was highly skilled in verbosity.

At any rate, we survived my first two years in the high school and my boss was sent to the larger high school in Hanau, Germany, and he was, no doubt, in his glory. There was friction between us in my second year because of my wife's close affiliation with the base commander's wife. The base commander was a general and he exercised the ultimate power around the military and U. S. civilian population. My wife expressed some disdain toward my boss who had a conversation with regarding his relations with me, his assistant. I think there was more friction than Leon related to me.

These are areas of human relations, and I would rather not expand on the ramifications of the conflict. If my ex boss reads this book, he will recall that my description of the incident has merit, and is truthful.

At any rate, I began to involve myself in the community of Bad Kreuznach, both military and civilian. This meant that I exercised my ability to speak German in its essence. I met school directors, doctors, lawyers, dentists, and teachers who were in the area of Bad Kreuznach.

The contacts were invaluable in that I got an insight into the mentality of the German citizens, as I had never before done. We had parties in my apartment that was 3,200 square feet in area (a 2nd floor of a large old, beautiful German home) was absolutely immaculate, elite, and enchanting.

At one party, mixed military high echelon, and leaders of the civilian community of Bad Kreuznach, we had almost 125 guests. I had several baked turkeys, a suckling pig, and a couple of hams. We had every type of drink and a variety of food, with a Puerto Rican bartender, and two German ladies serving. We also had two large kegs of beer and several cases of the best Nahe Wines.

This party was after my African American boss left for Hanau, and my friend Lee Kirsch was appointed as new principal of Bad Kreuznach High School. Lee was a businessperson and absolutely loved the aggressive business modes of my wife Brigitte. Brigitte is an assertive woman who set up a Bed and Breakfast section of my large apartment and started making more money at that than I made as a school administrator.

Lee was a mid-westerner from Minnesota who worked on a dairy farm for his father and was nonsensical when dealing with students. He expected Middle American values from students with no foolishness and carried out his administration in a strict business like fashion. He was unbelievably skilled in school operations, sometimes too skilled because this led to his demotion at a later date. He told me I had the human relation skills he lacked, but we together, made an excellent team.

After I left for the sabbatical in San Diego, my boss informed one of his buddies about the position. He was hired and this later caused his (Lee Kirsch's) demise. His friend got Lee into more complications because of his assertiveness and Lee ended up being assigned to an elementary or junior high school in Heidelberg as an assistant principal. This was definitely a demotion for Lee who was accustomed to calling all the shots.

Several years after he was assigned to Heidelberg, I flew over to Bad Kreuznach, then took my ex wife down to the Bord du Rhin in Lauterbourg, France, where Lee Kirsch, his wife and Brigitte and I met for dinner. We met and had a wonderful meal during the winter holidays. We talked about old times had a fantastic dinner, wine, and discussed the world's problems.

A couple of years after that, Lee and I talked about retirement, while I was visiting him at his home in the Heidelberg area, and he informed he wanted to retire in the Reno or the Lake Tahoe area. He and his family all enjoy skiing, so I know Lake Tahoe would be the right choice for wonderful people like Lee and his family.

While enjoying the stay in Bad Kreuznach from 1977 until 1983, I often enjoyed the company of my landlord, Herr Laun who was a salesperson for Tobler Chocolate. He traveled all over the country before the war and after the war. He walked with a cane, so I imagine he was wounded on the Russian front, as were many German men. He, however, never really told me how he was injured and was always very guarded about the handicap.

Herr Laun was quite interesting and I learned that he had some excellent Third Reich 16-millimeter film that showed many of the German military marches down Salinenstrasse, one of the main thoroughfares in the Bad Kreuznach, and it also ran almost directly in front of our house. The films were taken, in color, with a good 16-mm movie camera, in the late

1930s and the early 1940s. Herr Laun had about 8 rolls and he and I agreed, verbally, that if I could market the film in Hollywood, we would share the profits if the film were sold.

In the summer of 1979, I flew to Hollywood, near where my sister lived in West Los Angeles, and found a company that expressed extreme interest in the property. I found the company in the yellow pages of the phone book and the owner, whose name was Bailey, I believe, expressed a desire to purchase the film if he could view them. I tried to entice Herr Laun to send a sample of the film to the company, but the son, Heinrich Laun Junior, talked Herr Laun into keeping the film for a later sale.

I presume the son wanted to save the film so that some day they would have even a better value. To this day, I do not know if Heinrich Junior still has the film, but I presume he does. We communicated, via the Internet, last year (2000), but I have lost his address so I do not know if they are still available.

Herr Laun, my landlord, was a man whom I socialized with on many occasions. His wife was also one of the very good acquaintances off my wife Brigitte, and we were social friends. Frau Laun enjoyed drinking with us but we soon learned we could not invite her because she had previously abused alcohol and could no longer drink, and for obvious reasons.

The family was fantastic about keeping our dog, Rusty, our third and very beautiful long hair Dachshund that I dearly loved. I would go for long walks with Rusty and had one of those twenty-foot extension leashes so we would run along the beautiful Nahe River each evening after my strenuous days in school.

In the late 1970s Herr Laun passed away and it was one of the saddest days of my life because I become an extremely good friend of this old gentleman. He had diabetes and suffered extreme problems with his circulation and eventually lost on of his legs, living in extreme pain for many months before his death.

On attending his funeral I cried like a baby and was saddened at losing such a dear friend. He was kind, considerate, and very helpful if I had any needs in the city of Bad Kreuznach. He was one gentleman whom I shall never forget because of his extreme generosity and kindness.

This brought me to realize my closeness with the German people. I also realized that there are great similarities between the Germans and Americans. To vision Americans killing Germans or Americans killing Germans as happened in the First and Second World Wars, is to me, sad. That is why the film, "Saving Private Ryan" was almost an unbearable film for me to watch. The depiction of hate and killing in the film was not pleasant for me, but nations seem to soar above the level of personal friendship in time of war.

Maybe, during the Second World War, had I have been old enough to fight, it would have been possible, because of the propaganda, to take a rifle and shoot my enemy and work toward saving the allied nations from the grasp of the dictator, Adolph Hitler.

My brother, Cone Stell, was a World War II pilot of the Martin B-26, a medium fighter-bomber, and allegedly sank a German submarine in the Mediterranean in 1942. It was an act of heroism at the time, and the event was presented in a comic book, Adventure Comics, I believe, and I read and viewed it proudly when it came out. I personally showed it to my brother when he was home on leave. I was in the sixth grade at the time and the month was December 1942.

My brother read it, smiled, and wrote on the comic book, "I made the comics!" We enjoyed discussing it and he, though reluctant to discuss the war, did give me some answers when I asked him about his experiences.

Only a few months later my brother William Cone Stell lost his life flying from Miami, Florida to Lake Charles, Louisiana, on a training mission in the B-26 Marauder which he was in command of. His plane was lost and there was never a trace found of him, the plane, nor the crew. How ironic for someone as brave as he, to return from 50 completed missions around the Mediterranean Sea, then to be lost on a routine training mission.

The warmth, however, I find in the German people, after my many years in Germany, convince me the German people are very intelligent, highly civilized, congenial, and warm people. The extensive social contact with my wife's family and acquaintances over the many years were illuminated by my ability to burrow deeply into intimate and expansive conversations with them because of my knowledge of German.

I found that many doctors, teachers, military officers, and business personnel did not always have the ability to delve into conversations in idiomatic English, as I did in their language. The nearest ones to my German speaking ability were some of the German English teachers whom I knew while teaching at Ramstein Junior High and AFCENT, the 4-Nation NATO school in the Netherlands.

After taking 42 semester hours of German, the grammar still remains complex. One must practice and write frequently, with the conjugation rules nearby and often reviewed to write and speak with perfection. The greatest road to success, with all languages, I believe, is to exercise constant conversations on a day by day basis, as I did for many years in Germany.

I learned to recognize dialects while living in Germany and this takes much skill, even for most Germans, but they do it quite naturally if they travel extensively. Unfortunately

I am losing vocabulary at the present time since I have been out of the country, except for yearly visits, for sixteen years.

It will be sad if I my vocabulary was to diminish extremely, but I feel that with practice it will not. I plan to split my future time between here and Germany after I retire later this year. I also tend reenergize the language because of frequent visits from friends and my daughter and her husband to the United States.

This summer I will be fortunate enough to have two Gymnasium students, both 18 years of age, visit me and stay with me for about 6 weeks. The time frame will be July 21, 2001 until August 31, 2001. Such visits always vitalize my spoken German, but one needs to use the language on a daily basis in order to fully rejuvenate the full mobility of proper verb conjugation, pronunciation, and proper inflection.

While studying German at San Diego State and UCSD, La Jolla, I was continually analyzing, researching, and writing sentences. I hope to have the opportunity to regain fluid usage when I return to Germany to teach English in the German Volkshochschule, in Bad Kreuznach in 2001 and beyond.

As a gauge of my ability to utilize the language while living in Brunssum, the Netherlands, I had the opportunity to apply for work with the Central Intelligence Agency. I took the German test and the test administrator told me he had never seen a score as high as mine for the common military word usage in German. I was proud of my score to say the least. Unfortunately the fact that my wife, Brigitte, was a German citizen, hampered and prevented me from joining up with the agency.

At the apex of my stay in Europe, I was doing quite well in the German language and had full opportunity to utilize German in a daily. I enjoyed the utilization, and above all, I enjoyed having the ability to capture a sociological perspective of Germans in various locations through my speaking ability.

To highlight with my observation of many German colleagues, I must say that there are some aspects of German character which impress me, and some which do not. The frequent quick judgment of Germans about man's status and character is something I feel Germans should be more cautious about. They assume, quickly, that someone if in a magnanimous suit, and has a new Mercedes, is of stature, well educated, and wealthy. This, most people know is not always true. Some of our most successful entrepreneurs sometimes walk about in battered blue jeans! Looks can be deceiving, especially in American culture.

Also, sometimes I would be speaking to some, not too analytical types, and they would assume, that because I am American, I spoke no German. Even when I came back with quick crisp responses in their own language, they would continue speaking in broken English. Some alert person in the conversation group would alert the German, person ignoring my German, that I was speaking distinctly and grammatically correct. Then, if that unobservant person continued speaking broken English to me, I would merely continue speaking German until he or she realized my German was much better than his or her English.

My encounters with different types of German persons spanned the spectrum, and certain types, were especially beneficial in my acquaintances because of my profession. I mixed with many types of German people, and enjoyed the diversity because of the opportunity to intensify my acquisition of knowledge about them.

My professional association with some of the German educators around Bad Kreuznach was great in that I was often chosen, because my ability to speak German, and to attend official trips for educators. We had a group of administrators who fell into the realm of an informal organization for educators and I was always selected as the American representative from the school to accompany them on various expeditions.

We made wine expeditions, traveled to local festivals, and met in social gatherings, of official capacity, in various restaurants or hotels throughout the city of Bad Kreuznach, a city with about 300 restaurants and hotels. The exchanges were always congenial, informative, and the school, and sometimes city, administrators were certainly curious about the American method of education. They were also interested in making visits to our high school and elementary schools, seeking grade levels of students in the same age bracket of their own schools. They knew I had to deal with heterogeneous settings, so were extremely sympathetic with my problems as an administrator. The schools that the Germans were in charge of had more of a homogenous setting since the school system was of a selective nature.

On one expedition, with about 30 educators from the area, the liberal or SPD mayor promoted an expedition composed of German-American educators. This took place on a beautiful Thursday afternoon, and ended on Saturday morning. I was granted two days off for the expedition because it was in the realm of community protocol and encouraged by the Overseas Schools, always. The other mayor was CDU or of the conservative party, and that was Herr Schmidt. The liberal mayor was Herr Schindowski, of the SPD party.

A conflict broke out between the two mayors because of our rather expensive visit to the wine area of Alsace, France. I let the cat slip out of the bag at a social gathering and the conservative mayor learned that Herr Schindowski sponsored the trip and paid for it out of the city's treasury. This caused extreme problems, and I was caught in the middle.

The conservative mayor was a neighbor of mine, had a lovely beautiful wife and I often got together with them socially. Their daughter, Katja Schmidt was a close friend of my daughter, and I saw her quite often visiting with Liane in my own home. Eventually things were healed and the conflict died down, but not before a confrontation at one of the administrative meeting of Bad Kreuznach city officials. I explained the situation to the conservative mayor, Herr Schmidt, and nothing big was made out of the trip with me, but I know the liberal mayor caught hell from the senior mayor, Herr Schmidt, the leader of the majority conservative faction.

I can laugh with Herr Schmidt today and he always bring it up when I visit him in Bad Kreuznach. He still does not find it humorous, but smiles reluctantly when it does come up. Herr Schindowski is now deceased, but he was my contact for teaching in the German Volkshochschule where I taught 2 or 3 hours a night for two nights a week. This was a fun job that I loved and earned some tax-free money on the side. I maintained my classes for the duration of my stay in Bad Kreuznach, after being selected for the job during my first year there.

I hope again teach with the Volkshochschule when I retire because it enhances my German, and gives me a chance to meet wonderful students trying to learn more English. I, in turn, will enhance my German speaking skills and it is a delightful job, especially working with adults of that professional level.

The Volkshochschule is equivalent to our adult education schools in the United States. Sometimes there are Gymnasium Students participating in the class, and they are trying to enhance their idiomatic American English so they can someday travel to the United States.

These opportunities for teaching, provided me with frequent social and professional contact, and came mostly because I was an administrator in the American School. The position carried a high degree of prestige because I, the Konrektor, or assistant principal was in a prestigious position, especially in the eyes of the Germans.

This granted me the opportunity to break into the social structure of the German school administrators in that area of Germany, and I took full advantage of it. I met people whom I would never have met had I still been in the classroom, though I realize that classroom teaching is the most critical aspect of American education, it is not honored as such. And classroom teaching is not honored in American schools as in the German schools.

Americans do not honor teaching in public schools, and, as they should. Here is where our society needs to look at German public school structure and adopt some of its ideas, in the field of American public education. Because of the degrading state of public education in the United States, there needs to be a reevaluation of our public school system.

Sometimes I would even be introduced as the director of the American School, and I began to limit my corrections of this error because whether I was an assistant principal or principal, it made no difference in their eyes. I was the principal or assistant principal, both positions of high honor in the perspective of the German citizen or educator. I was always invited to the German school functions and I loved the prestige I had among the German people

The German-American community affairs structure in the military community was almost a necessity because of protocol in the relationships between the two cultures. The

Community Base Commander of the 8th Infantry Division, Bad Kreuznach, always scheduled many holiday events to which my wife and I were always invited. I got to know the top military personnel and they began to call on my wife and me to act as official interpreters at many of the functions. We greeted people coming into the Nahe Club, the officer's club on these occasions. Whether it was the official Christmas Ball or New Year's Ball we were always there. We received plaques for the participation in events or balls and my wife loved it. Sometimes it was burdensome to me but I loved the status. As I look back on this illumination of being a community educator, and leader, I often wonder how terrible it must be for teachers in the United States to have such little prestige in many community affairs in the United States. Too bad they have not had my experience of being held in high esteem because I am a teacher and educator!

If one were to ask me if such duties as a community representative in the field of education were rewarding, I would be the first to say that they were. After all, we, Americans were building good relations between Americans and the Germans in the Bad Kreuznach area. I would enjoy the evenings because after the official greeting assignment was over, my wife and I would proceed to mix with the guests, dance, drink wine, and have a marvelous time.

Germans are great for ceremonies, enjoying good wine, beer, and food. That is what we did have and the evenings would go on until, sometimes two a.m. in the mornings. We would go home, tired but sober, because everyone was served coffee and desert so that they would get home safely. The base commander ordained these balls, so if one were to be stopped by the military police, it merited only an explanation that we had been to the military ball. Were we to be stopped by the local German police, they were, in those years quite tolerant because they could see from the formal dress that we were dignitaries of the community and would let us pass, no questions asked.

These wonderful experiences and events continued from 1979, until 1983. Then I departed for the United States to study at San Diego State University. I selected my field of studies well. The courses of study, ordained by the Department of Defense Dependent Schools, were viable programs for my sabbatical and enhancement of my administrative needs. I also pursued more German courses that were readily accepted by the Department of Defense as legitimate courses for an administrator.

Before I departed from the Bad Kreuznach area, I went through the spring of 1983, and saw the graduating class of seniors on their way to such schools as Harvard, Purdue, Notre Dame, and Stanford. There were other schools chosen by our outstanding students at Bad Kreuznach High School, but the students all had good intentions and were ready to return to the United States and pursue a field of study at a good community college or a good university in the United States.

There were students who stayed and entered the Sorbonne University, Paris, the University of Paris, Oxford, and other great schools in Europe. Our students at Dependent Schools were ones of good quality, and ended up going to better schools in the world.

My last three months in Bad Kreuznach were endured with great anticipation of my returning to San Diego State University for a year of studies and getting away from the grind of Dependent School administration.

I laid out the plans to live with my brother, Jim Stell in San Diego, wrote to San Diego State and told them I wanted to pursue a study in school administration, computers, and

German. They informed me that there would be no problem for post-graduate students pursuing advanced courses to enhance their professional status, so I was readily accepted.

I moved to San Diego, taking my wife and daughter for the summer to visit friends in the United States. The Department of Defense shipped my car, paid me half salary to live and study in San Diego for the full academic year.

I was, in some way a little reluctant to send my wife and daughter back to Germany after the summer of 1983, and stay alone in San Diego. But my brother was glad to have me so I remained, set up my field of studies, began to meet friends, called my wife and daughter once a week, and pursued the prescribed course of studies.

The return for a whole year and leaving my family hit me hard, and I began to miss them extremely. I had a very devoted wife who was reluctant to let me take this great adventure, but since I left her ample support, and she was a dependent, there was no worry as long as were still married.

I, while living in San Diego, got the full advantage of military support, P.X. exchange, commissary, and even gasoline. There was a technical difficulty, and that was that the I.D. card issued to me in Bad Kreuznach, under the Department of the Army, did suffice here for its validity. I was questioned now and then, but since they, the Navy military personnel, were not familiar with the overseas identification card, I was just waved through the gates, so I continued to utilize the military food, gasoline, and post-exchange items.

The convenience of using the identification card, PX and various facilities such as the commissary helped me with the costs while living with my brother. He was pleased with the food I bought at the commissary since it about 30% cheaper than local food chains.

I spent my one-year in San Diego, but something strange happened to me, and I fell madly in love with a domineering, beautiful American Italian blonde woman, whom I remember vividly, of course, to this day. She broke ties with her husband, who had a respectable position in the City of San Diego, and fell in love with me, as I fell in love with her. She also told me she knew she and her husband were mismatched after the first week of their marriage.

She had a beautiful home in a lovely suburban area of San Diego, was a teacher in the area, as I later became, and we were magnetically attracted to each other. It was a sexual attraction with an explosion of about the highest level of megatons one could expect in a love affair.

My lover's name will be kept anonymous, but this person was delightful, dominating, and the most sexual woman I have ever known. We were compatible, never wanted to be away from each other and when I informed my wife in the spring of 1984, there was extreme sadness from us both in our telephone conversation.

I spent many hours with the woman whom I met in one of my elementary science classes at San Diego State University. I took this class in order to round out my curriculum studies because I wanted to leave secondary education and move into elementary administration. Nevertheless, the whole sabbatical program caused me to depart from my wife, Brigitte, during the School Year 1984-85, and leave her and my lovely daughter alone in Germany.

I never dreamed I was capable of leaving my wife and daughter because of my extreme attachment to my family and Germany. The lovely lady with whom I lived after October 1984, endured my dramatic transition of leaving Germany, a country which I had grown extremely attached to from 1960 until 1983, but suffered psychological turmoil because my frequent reflections of Germany and its people. She would react dramatically whenever I would bring up memories or experiences that were so positive during my years overseas.

It was tragic in some ways, but before I returned to Germany in August of 1984, this woman actually fell on the floor and screamed when I told her I was departing for my newly assigned elementary school in Kitzingen, Germany. I was to become building principal in the American Kitzingen Elementary School, near Würzberg, Germany in early August1984. This was a fantastic location and assignment that I have long regretted leaving.

Never have I seen such behavior on the part of a woman, because she thought she had won me away from my German family. And in the long run, she did win, but the victory was not permanent, because in the end, though I lost my marriage, I elected not to marry her, my newly acquired lover of San Diego. After I returned from Kitzingen, Germany, to San Diego, where I was Building Principal assigned to the K-3 Elementary School of Kitzingen, school year 1984-85, to San Diego, she knew she had won her prize back for four years only.

My wife, distraught, a fighter, and a wonderful mother to Liane, tried to prevent me from leaving Kitzingen, but to no avail she, had to let me go. I returned to San Diego, fully in love with this lovely fanatical woman who also left her husband. We lived together and tried to work it out for 4 years, and though there were many happy times, there were too many conflicting times.

I taught as a substitute around San Diego, missing Germany for the next year, and then landed a 60% position at Mt. Carmel High School, Poway School District, where I taught biology in the spring of 1985. It was an interesting experience, with my constantly missing Germany, with its magnetic culture, and people, my wife, and child. It was a conflicting time of definite mixed feelings.

Could I survive these travesties I suffered because I had been so settled with Liane and Brigitte for the last 22 years? These were confusing times for me. This was also the readjustment time for me living in San Diego because I had lived so long abroad.

I yearned for my family in Germany but was also pulled toward my new found woman, 33 years old, a very good teacher, who was working on her teaching credential at San Diego State University where she and I met.

I shall dwell on the contrast between Germany and the United States in a later chapter. The emotional stress was heavy and the impact of leaving the German culture, after being adjusted so well to it, and leaving the Overseas Schools were costly to my career, as well as to my emotional makeup at the age of 50.

The people Hitler left behind carried on with dynamic events, after I left in 1983. Germany, with its new democratic political trends toward dynamic European unity and progress would leave dramatic nostalgia with me. I chose to return to the United States, leave all of them, sadly, behind, but seek a readjustment to the country I had left some twenty-three years ago.

The sadness was that I still missed the rich and deep friendships I had established in a society that left me with dramatically rich experiences. Now I had to make the challenging readjustment to my own homeland, but with a more challenging experience of relinquishing my prestigious past as a school administrator, and becoming a post graduate student and prepare myself for unknown events to come.

~⁊~

Chapter 8

The German Educator

Working with German educators was one of the rich experiences I recall from my many years abroad, especially those in Germany. There were many opportunities I had in several locations that brought me in contact with the German schools and their educators.

I also had various visitations in German elementary and secondary schools. Also providing me with many opportunities was my daughter's enrollment in the German schools because she is German in nationality and spent most of her kindergarten, elementary, and secondary years in German schools.

The earliest encounter I had with German education was through a visit I set up at Ramstein Junior High School, Ramstein Air Base, Germany, in 1963. A couple of colleagues and I set up exchange visits with a Gymnasium in Landstuhl, Germany in 1963. I was invited into the director's office at that particular school and we had a private conversation regarding education and the Second World War. He was a very kind person, about 40 years of age, and offered me coffee, so we talked for almost 30 minutes.

He was in the German Wehrmacht (Armed Forces), the army, I believe, during the World War II and fortunately was in a support position where he did not have to do the usual dirt and mud warfare. He related to me that he and many other Germans never realized that they were defeated until about early 1944.

During our conversation, this gentleman began to tell me about what he observed while he was on duty on the Western front. This director of the Gymnasium in Landstuhl told me that he could not believe the amount of equipment, materiel, the Americans brought forth in this war.

The tanks, guns, ammunition, fuel, jeeps, cannons, airplanes, and all the support equipment possessed by the Allies to fight a war were unbelievable for him. That is the overwhelming phenomenon of American society, its potential for industrial output that surprises most people about this country. Previous to World War II there was a cultural lag with military production, but the Second World War ignited our potential for a tremendous output of military weapons and armament.

I once heard a comment during the Cold War, regarding the Americans and their production capacity. It was that if we had invited the Russian leaders to the United States just to view our junk yards, they would have been too frightened to start a war with our country.

When this school director told me that he and thousands of other Germans had given up the battle, psychologically, in the late part of 1944, and it was all over for the them. Our massive movement into the Pacific Theatre, before the two atomic bombs were dropped, were, no doubt, beginning to affect Japanese morale also, and all because of our massive weapon output. Our industrial potential had not really been felt until the Second World War, and then the United States became a world leader, along with the USSR in this arena.

At any rate the conservation I had with this school director left a lasting imprint upon my mind regarding how the Americans had gained respect, especially in Germany, for our massive military power.

The only war where all our military potential did not seem to make the difference was the Vietnam War. From 1963 to about 1974, this war lingered on, and the reason was that the military strength did not make the difference, because it was a civilian, politically controlled war that merely supported a strong butter and guns policy.

I had many discussions with German educators regarding our stalemate in Vietnam and the prolonged war that lasted longer than the Second World War. Germans were puzzled and wanted input when we were engrossed in conversation during the late 1960s and early 1970s, regarding the Vietnam War.

I am convinced of two things regarding the Vietnam War and the two major aspects are: 1) We should never become involved in such a ground war in Asia, and should have left Vietnam alone. We should have learned from the French loss at Dien Pien Phu, and withdrawn, or Eisenhower should never have begun the involvement. 2) The Vietnam War was not left to the military or we would have won militarily as the far as the concept of winning goes.

I interject these concepts because I often discussed Vietnam, as well as World War II with Germans and specifically German educators. They were, of course, very interested in both these eras in history.

From that short conversation in the German director's office in the school in Landstuhl, Germany, I was enlightened about the power of the American forces. When summoned to accomplish a mission, the American military can deter or beat any military force on the earth today, if the cause is right and it is left in the hands of the military. I do not know how the American military might will be in the future, or fifty years from now. But during the Second World War and even today, the power and potential is awesome. Much of our military strength will depend on public support, along with political determination out of Washington D. C.

What I observed, during the Second World War, as a youth in Arkansas, was that the unity of Americans, when the cause is right, is that we do have ample strength to utilize our military capability when needed.

Actually, during the Cold War from the end of the Second World War, we probably would have had no problem defeating the Soviet Union, had it ever come to that. We wasted time, money, and progress from the loss of the satellite countries that fell under the wing of Soviet aggression, and should not have let the Soviets rule that area, had it have been possible to prevent it. There were too many years of freedom lost for the eastern half of Europe during the Cold War.

This little conversation with the German school director opened my eyes about the country I was born and raised in. What the future holds for the United States depends on the choices we make as a nation. We should not have chosen the path of the Vietnam War, that I am now convinced of, and some of the leaders, including the then Secretary of Defense, Robert McNamara agreed many years after the fact.

We chose the right path of going after Germany in 1941, when the Japanese attacked Pearl Harbor, and putting our economic and manpower efforts with 100% energy into winning the Second World War, and were successful.

But encounters with the German educator did not end in Landstuhl, Germany because there were many visitations by my classes and me, between 1962 and 1984, to German schools. All these visitations increased my understanding of the German school structure, and the way the Germans run their education system.

Another visit included a couple of my classes, a representative from our district headquarters in Wiesbaden, Germany, and several teachers from Ramstein Junior High at Ramstein Air Base, and the year was 1965. We took a trip to Saarbrücken and visited a Grundschule. This was an elementary school with over 800 students. The director was congenial, walked around showing various rooms and classes. He was delighted to have American visitors because he had made a previous visit to our schools in Ramstein.

He was the debonair and delightful director who walked down the halls smoking a cigarette, and this was the most surprising thing that the American teachers and I could not believe. He actually smoked in front of his pupils. But one astonishing thing was that the director did not have to set an example and was only concerned with the functions of the school. We all laughed about this, including the director who was smoking, in that it was the complete contrast between autocracy in a school setting and a democratic setting. How that principal of a school could actually walk, with no regret, among the 6 to 10 year old children, smoking a cigarette was beyond our belief.

But our visit was rewarding and we spoke with many teachers and students on that day. We were happy to have the contact and I am sure the teachers of that area continued to make the exchanges after I left in 1966.

The next incident exuded a completely autocratic ambiance of a director in the German school setting, as opposed to the somewhat democratic director in the American setting in my own school in Brunssum, the Netherlands in 1969. It involves a conversation I had with the director of the German wing of our 4-nation school in Brunnsum, the Netherlands.

I was visiting the director of the Realschule. That is a level of the German school system that goes only to the tenth grade. It prepares students for the technical colleges, but not for the universities. It seems that when the 4-nation school at Brunssum, the Netherlands was built, the concept was that the best way to set up the school was to select the level of school where the most students would be reached. If any officers or other personnel had children who wished to prepare for the highest level of the secondary school, Gymnasium, they could later pick it up if high grades were maintained, when reassigned to their duty stations in Germany. Or the military personnel were informed about level of school available to their families before the assignment.

The director or principal of the school taught one or two classes per day, as is customary in most German schools. If my memory is correct, the German administrators, when they are selected for administration, must teach at least one class a day in order to stay in contact with the students. This is the basic faltering of our diminishing school programs in the United States and it separates the administration from teaching personnel. Administrators not teaching in American schools is one of the elements that establishes pyramidal structures that are contributing, in my opinion, to the failure of our education system in the United States.

At any rate, the director, congenial, and about 42 years of age, was very friendly toward me because he knew I was chairperson of the science department of the 4-nation school. He invited me in to his office, we sat down, and we began to have a great exchange of ideas. We discussed our teaching backgrounds, locations, and philosophy of education.

To be cordial he opened up the bottom right hand drawer of his desk and pulled out a fifth of Johnny Walker Red Label Scotch. I remember it distinctly because I had never experienced this, especially in an American school setting. American teachers never kept bottles of alcohol in their desks and not even in Dependent Schools, where alcohol is part of the military culture. Or the cocktail scene, especially.

He was so cordial, and I, to this day, if I had ever had a bottle of alcohol in my desk at school, would feel highly unprofessional in the American school system. Oftentimes, in the Overseas Dependent Schools, there might be champagne on a Friday afternoon but no students were around, and this was acceptable.

The German director had red, short cropped hair, wore thick rimmed glasses, and spoke mostly German with me because his English was not as good as my German. We exchanged ideas and continued to be good friends until the day I left the Netherlands. But his demure was typical, with some aspects of autocracy permeating the scene, as is frequently found in German educators.

The next episodes I encountered were in Hagenbach, Germany, where my daughter, Liane, pursued her elementary education. I dealt with the teachers often, because of frequent contacts, parties, conferences, and general visitations parents have when they have children enrolled in school

The teachers I encountered in the elementary schools, especially Hagenbach, Germany, in the state of Rheinland-Pfalz, were always cordial, and always happy for my wife to bring food and drinks, especially when celebrating the birthday of our child.

They were, to my surprise, very receptive to our supporting our daughter and her little friends during the first through the fourth grades. My wife was very generous about providing lots of punch, cookies, cakes, candy, and other snacks the children enjoyed.

Liane reached the third grade and seemed to be having some trouble grasping the rapid and regimented pace of the German elementary or Grundschule (grades 1-4). I took Liane out of the German elementary school after a few weeks and placed her with an American teacher in our Dependent Elementary School in Karlaruhe. Then during the next fall, I again placed her at the third grade level of the German school to complete the third grade over again. Her maturity level was appropriate for the intensified and regimented German processes.

I am a believer in repetition for strength, especially for school reinforcement. She did amazingly well in the American school. This gave her mind and body enough time to mature to an elevated level, then after one year of the American school where she absolutely excelled in her school grades. After she finished the American school year, and was placed in the German school in the village of Hagenbach. She stayed there for the 3rd grade through the 4th grade, and was quite successful.

It was not until the fifth grade in Bad Kreuznach, and in the Gymnasium, that I again held Liane back for a stronger foundation. The fifth year is the first year of Gymnasium, and I knew she would profit by repeating the foundation grade.

After Liane's second trip through the German fifth grade, she was reinforced in the German Gymnasium, the college prep level of the German school that entails grades 5-13. The repetition helped her tremendously, and she sailed on through to the level of the 10th grade, also an honorable level to attain in the German school system.

Reflecting back on Liane's experience in the elementary or Grundschule, in Hagenbach, we had Liane under Fräulein

Dagmar Brandenburg, a beautiful, slender lady about 30 years old. She was the best teacher Liane had encountered in the German schools. I fell in love with this woman because she was the ideal teacher. She gave Liane a solid foundation in fundamentals and I cherished her relationship with my daughter. I shall reflect on this magnificent person later in this chapter because she made learning so positive for my daughter in the early stages of educational development.

After leaving Karlsruhe, and I received a promotion to go to Bad Kreuznach American High School as assistant principal, we searched for, and found a proper school for our daughter, the Lina Hilger Gymnasium in the heart of Bad Kreuznach.

I let my wife, who was magic with German agencies, schools, or businesses, find the proper school for Liane. She found the school, and it was a fantastic Gymnasium, as mentioned above (Lina Hilger Gymnasium) of Bad Krueznach. It was strong in modern languages and was not classical in Latin or ancient studies, as was one of the other Gymnasiums in the city. The city, with only about 40,000 population had three Gymnasiums. Does that tell one something about the value of education with the Germans? One cannot imagine three high schools in an American city of that size.

Lina Hilger Gymnasium had an enrollment of over 900 students, and was only about 10 city blocks from our house. Liane could easily ride the city bus to and from school each day and it was even conceivable that she could walk if necessary.

Since I was assistant principal at the American High School, I began to make contacts with some of the teachers at Lina Hilger Gymnasium. This made it convenient, especially for conferences, because I began to be known by the Gymnasium teachers and this was valuable for dialogue regarding Liane's progress.

I will reemphasize that the selective process of the German schools, especially the Gymnasium, creates an element of no foolishness, and academic rigidity, which I probably could not have endured in my years of secondary school in Arkansas. Liane belonged to the choir, could not sing very well, but with her background in piano, knew the structure of music. Except for the lack of voice range, and no natural voice for singing, my child traveled with the choir to France and other places in Germany. She tried, and that is what pleased her, her mother, and me. She loved this extracurricular activity of music and singing in the Gymnasium. Extracurricular activities were very few, by the way, in German schools.

Liane did quite well up until the age of about sixteen, then she began to fall back some in her academic output, even after the repetition of the fifth grade. I would walk down the street with this beautiful young fifteen-year old German beauty, and I noticed that she was speaking to many of the nice lads around Bad Kreuznach. It was then that I began to get the hint that maybe she was not focusing as intensely as she should in academics.

I would go to various conferences at the school, taking off from work, to see what intensity toward academics my daughter was applying. I soon learned that she again had some academic weaknesses, and they were in mathematics and German, probably the most difficult disciplines of the German Gymnasium. That is probably the same case in American schools, with mathematics and English, the accents of the SATs, being the most difficult American courses for students.

Liane was beginning to falter academically. We had to watch her grades because of the intensity and pressure of the German Gymnasium. But it turns out that she eventually finished the tenth grade, which provides a certificate called the Mittlererreife in German schools and has a level of respect because it was completed at the Gymnasium. We transferred her to the American school in 1983, while I was on sabbatical, where I had been assistant principal. We did this because the rigidity of the German school was very intense and becoming more so. She might have eventually completed Gymnasium, but I would have again sought a repetition of tenth or eleventh grade, and her goals in life were more functional, not those of the university.

After I left for the sabbatical in the United States, we placed her in the American High School in Bad Kreuznach. I could easily short-circuit the educational process of the German system, if needed, and send Liane to a college or university in the United States after her high school diploma. As it ended up, I directed her toward a medical field in physical therapy. This she pursued in Boppard, Germany, a quaint city along the Rhine River. The institute she attended specialized in massage and physical therapy, which she completed in about three years, or four with the internship.

While I was on sabbatical at San Diego State University Liane graduated from Bad Kreuznach American High School in the spring of1984. I returned to Kitzingen, Germany, in August of 1984, but stayed until October 1984, then went back to San Diego to resume teaching in the San Diego City Schools. This was, no doubt, one of the biggest mistakes of my life, because of the diminished quality of public school education in San Diego, and in California.

Liane, with the help of her mother and me, completed her American high school education, then went on to physical therapy college, and now has her own clinic in Bad Kreuznach, Germany, where she and her husband Thomas have a thriving business.

We are happy with Liane's out come, educationally, and feel that because of the diversity of German education, and with reinforcement of the American school abroad, she got the best out of secondary school, and 3 years in the physical therapy school.

I am proud of my daughter's accomplishments, though the German school experience was intensive, she did receive the most from education the German and American school combination could provide. I see her at least twice a year because she and her husband love getting away from the long German winters and returning to San Diego for the pleasant weather.

When I retire, I shall return, to write and relax in my townhouse at Hot Springs Village, Arkansas, a pleasant mountainous resort area. The weather is quite mild there, with the extremes only in July and August, but the Ouachita Mountains make it a very desirable place to live. Expenses are only about half of what they in San Diego and my townhouse there would easily come into the $200,000 price range if located in San Diego.

To focus again on the educator in Germany, I must say that teachers are well educated, always align themselves in suitable schools for their education, and proceed to teach in a society that respects the process of education. Because of selective approach to education, the teacher in Germany is well suited to the level for which he or she is prepared.

As I reflect back to the richest experience I remember, and the relations we had with the elementary level, or Grundschule, in the past, I remember most vividly Hagenbach. It was in the little village of Hagenbach, on the West Side of the Rhine River in and that quaint and clean Dorf (small town or village) in the State of Rheinland-Pfalz, that we had the best interaction between parent and teachers.

It goes back to the delightful teacher whom Liane loved, and did so well because we were interacting at the optimum level parents could achieve between child and the educational process. Liane's positive attitude toward education stems back from, I believe, her exposure to the youthful teacher, Fräulein Brandenburg. Though she had only about eight years experience at that time, she was terrific, and was fond of Liane. Fräulein Brandenburg had a brother who was also a teacher in one of the Karlsruhe area Gymnasiums. He was a biology teacher whom I respected highly because of his fine preparation in biology. Before I went into school administration, I had also taught biology and physical science, so Fräulein Brandenburg's brother and I had an excellent rapport.

My wife and I often stopped by this gifted teacher, bringing a gift from the commissary or to have a cup of coffee with Fräulein Brandenburg, and often invite her to a social or dinner at our house. She accepted the invitations often and we loved having her. She could speak with authority, and was extremely knowledgeable in the realm of pedagogical philosophy. Her classes were delightful to visit.

Fräulein Brandenburg and her brother came from a very nice family, and if I recall correctly, they had lived, previously, in the Berlin area. It could possibly have been in the eastern part of Berlin and the family came to the Karsruhe area after the Second World War.

After leaving Hagenbach and the Karlsruhe area, then reflecting back on the Gymnasium experience, I must emphasize the importance of the interaction I had with the German educator as a critical and influential part of my experience in Germany.

We found the Lina Hilger Gymnasium, in Bad Kreuznach, with Frau Schönborn, director, to be an excellent school. Frau

Schönborn, in her fifties, and appropriately understanding with the task she had in a school with almost a thousand students, was an excellent and understanding director.

Frau Schmidt, Liane's history teacher was also a very sympathetic and excellent teacher. We saw her often, with Liane maintaining C and B level work in her class, Bs in art and music and a satisfactory C in mathematics and sometimes Bs in chemistry and biology.

At any rate, Liane, with the intensive academic regimen of the German school, scored in the top national exams administered by the Overseas Dependent Schools, when she moved into the 11th and 12th grades at the U. S. School, from the Gymnasium. We attribute Liane's strong academic performance, especially in the American School, to the rigid processes and discipline a student must acquire to survive in the Gymnasium.

The parent conferences I had, always in German, proved to be most gratifying because I expressed complete sympathy with the German teachers since I myself am an educator, and at that time I was an administrator. I received the utmost respect and found out what Liane was and was not doing.

It is interesting that in the German schools, the students, especially in the Gymnasium, spend 3 to 5 hours studying after school each day. Liane would bury herself in her room at about 1:30 p.m., after she got home, and sometimes not come out until 5:00 p.m. or later. I would sometimes try to help her with a dimensional analysis approach to some of the mathematics problems, but Liane had intuitive ability in mathematics that I myself had never acquired, so I could not help her often. She could hammer it out alone.

With Liane's exposure to the German school, and I feel she has been exposed to both worlds, certainly helps her see both sides of the coin when she reflects on the years she had in the German schools.

Fortunately the American Overseas Dependent Schools were about as good as American school systems get so I was glad to have her at the Bad Kreuznach American High School, where I served as assistant principal from 1977 through 1983. I check the school out on the Internet now and then and have recently learned that the school, with over 700 students when I came, now has only about 238 students.

Liane often articulates the differences between the two school systems to me, and has good things to say about both systems. I was glad to have her gain the "democratic" approach as compared to a very rigid and rigorous school system as portrayed in the classical German "Gymnasium". I know that someday, especially when she has children, she will at least be able to counter arguments for both educational philosophies.

If the time she needs to expose her child or children to elementary and secondary education, she might too have a choice because of my residence in the United States. A year in the United States might be possible so that here, her child or children can have both experiences.

I laud the German and European school system because of the selective process and feel that European schools are more diverse in providing students with schools and education that is tailored to their needs. The stringent selective process, and placing a student into the Realschule (grades 5-10), Gymnasium (5-13), or Hauptschule (5-9), all have their advantages because they are tailored to academic ability through testing. The German process of allowing students to change from one type of school when high level ability is exhibited is becoming more frequent in Germany from what I have read. I also have a nephew (by marriage to my ex wife,

Brigitte) who tested out at about the 11th grade and shifted from the Realschule to the Gymnasium, and he seems to be doing quite well.

There is no doubt that there is rigidity in the German schools, but that is what is supposed to happen in schools. In our American education, in many settings, inner-city schools, and poor tax based school in the United States have become ridiculous. Teachers are afraid, parents, and students are afraid, classes are too large, and the learning curve has seemingly diminished since the 1950s.

I laud the German schools and their no foolishness and strict learning processes certainly receive my respect. I only wish that American schools could pick up some of the methods and move to a selective type school.

I will, later, in this book, relate the concept that the intense level of autocracy imbedded in the German school setting may permeate through the society of Germany. Because of the undying obedience to the authority figure in Germany, void of much of the democratic activities in U. S. Schools, and perhaps British Schools, strong dictatorial processes seem to still be prevalent in the German system. This strong highly focused autocratic element that still exists in German society, and could possibly lead to a return to a new Nationalism in Germany.

The autocratic methods I have observed in German Schools though with some liberalization since the end of the Second World War still seem to be detected in the final products of the students themselves. I have seen dictatorial overtones by teachers in various schools, but they were not always obvious in my visits and the teachers seemed to have some of the same congenial relations American teachers have, especially when the students are themselves amiable and high lever performers.

What I observe more often is the end product, the student, or the citizen in Germany who lauds, and I appreciate the respect, **the teacher** as the **infinite ruler** and **controller**. This has been depicted, not only by high school students I have observed, but also by many parents whom I have met in German society.

So the underlying concept of complete obedience to teacher, director of the corporation, leader of groups, or the military officer still exists in Germany. I think autocracy, even though the processes have been somewhat lessened since the Second World War, is still **an underlying element** ingrained in the educational processes of German society.

The comradeship often developed in the university or college level in the United States, developed by many American professors is not attained in German or European universities, from my conversations with European students. The concept of the "Doktor Vater" or Doctor Father (head professor) and the highly specialized level of respect can be admired, but could be one of the **extreme differences between** the two higher education systems.

When the time for strong national leadership evolves in a society, and the universities and secondary schools fall into line with the strong leader, the country could fall into blind obedience. This, I feel, could still happen in Germany, as it did during World War II. The schools and universities had to follow the regime during the Third Reich or those not following were certainly punished, and most likely eliminated in order to promote the state goals.

I have sat in many Gymnasium classrooms in Germany and the freedom of exchange is not as integrated into the flow of educational processes. This may be good in many respects, but the idea of student interjection with, sometimes creative ideas, is, no doubt, more prominent in the American education system.

Though there are many flaws in the American education system and I think the structure does not meet the needs of all the students in our society, the processes of liberal an creative thinking, is a strong element in American society. If only the structure of the schools were improved and tailored to meet the needs of our many high school dropouts, our society would profit.

The Germans, however, are on the right path when it comes to fitting their students into a school matching their ability. This has positive effects in that it prepares students to go out into society after an education and be productive and attain an income.

The people Hitler left behind, especially in the educator, are undying in their ability to keep education in the authoritative mode. It is a great process, but the creative element found in the liberal approach in better American schools, and they better American schools seem to be diminishing, might be the element missing in German schools. The German schools are definitely better structured, but the liberal thinking and open exchange between educator and student might be the element which has led the United States in world high tech and industrial achievement!

Chapter 9

Northern Germany, Kalt (Cold)

In 1963, when I drove my new green Volkswagen Beetle the 500 kilometers or so, from Ramstein Air Base to Kiel, Germany, to pick up my wife to be, I got my first vision of the cold streets of Kiel, Germany. It was Thanksgiving so I had a couple of days free from school. This is a city, of about a quarter of million citizens, and very beautiful, but ice cold and windy during the winter months, November is well into the winter season in that area and one can imagine what my impression was for my first visit.

Kiel is only a couple of hundred kilometers from Copenhagen and the opportunities for exploring the Scandinavian countries are great. Since my first visit, I have visited Denmark, Norway, and Sweden, and used Kiel as my stepping stone. I have visited all the Scandinavian countries except Finland. Kiel has a flavor similar to the Scandinavian countries, and if you visit the area in the summer, it is most delightful. The city is modern, and is surrounded by small Nordic villages with the traditional thatched roofs.

Though Kiel is a city of about 250,000 inhabitants, it is the capital of Schleswig-Holstein, the northernmost state of the Federal Republic of Germany. The modern city is located on the Baltic Sea and is known for its international sailing regattas attracting thousands of sailors and spectators each year. The weather is surprisingly mild in September with temperatures of about 15 to 20 degrees Celcius and typical refreshing breezes. Late November, however, begins to bring in the start of the long winter months.

National air flights connect Frankfurt, Cologne, and Berlin with Kiel. The nearest international airport, however, is Hamburg and is directly connected with Kiel by the airport bus "Kelius".

I have spent many weeks there around Thanksgiving, Christmas, Easter, and also the months of July and August. The strands are lovely in the summer, with bathers sometimes as thick as on the Italian Riviera. Though there is about a five hour drive from the Frankfurt or Bad Kreuznach area, one can make it quicker on the German Autobahn if you find a time when there is not too much traffic. I have made it in my 1980 Chevrolet V-8 Camaro in about 4 hours and that was in 1980 to 1983. My cruising speed was about 180 to 190 kilometers/hour and this converts to about 112 to 120 miles/hour.

While living in Bad Kreuznach in 1979, my wife and I purchased a lovely small condominium, in Timmendorfer Strand, Germany. Condominiums are called Eigentumwohnungen in German and they are privately owned apartments. This one had only about 650 square feet, or roughly 65 square meters of area. It had a living room with no bedroom, so it was really an efficiency apartment. It also had a nice kitchen, bathroom, and a nice balcony. We utilized a small storeroom in the basement as an extra bedroom with a pull out double bed that made the apartment big enough to house my wife, Liane, me, and even a guest or two. We had one of those drop double beds (I believe they are called

Murphy beds in the U. S.) that one could pull down from the wall so it was ample for weekend or vacation living.

We rented the apartment when we were not there and received enough income to make the payments on the apartment. We purchased the apartment through my brother-in-law, Otto Stöben, a very successful realtor and a wonderful person, who was married to my wife's oldest sister, Christiana. When Otto approached us about the possibility of an investment, my wife was immediately interested, and looked at me when Otto told us we needed about 5,000 German Marks (about $2,800 at that time) to pay down on the apartment. At that time my wife did not have that much money, but I had just sold a Hasselblad camera which brought a considerable amount of money, so I had that, and a substantial sum of money in the bank.

She looked at me and I told her I thought we should make the investment so I gave her the money. Later, when her bed and breakfast business plus her real estate business expanded, she bought me the new Chevrolet Camaro for my 50th birthday. That is the kind of German wife I had. She was frugal, saved money, was hard working, and very generous to me, as I was also to her.

We made many trips to the apartment in Timmendorfer Strand. This was probably the loveliest SPA resort on the East Sea, or Baltic Sea and has several thousand people. It also has unusually good restaurants and hotels. It was a joy and delight to take a long weekend, with or without family, get in my new Camaro, that was always kept in a rented garage and make the trip. I kept the shiny new car in the garage except for weekend trips or other excursions, and would cruise up toward Hamburg, then veer east and come into this quaint and lovely SPA resort.

Timmendorfer Strand is, beyond, a doubt, one of the most delightful homes away from home I have ever experienced. It was sad to learn that after I had been living in San Diego about 6 years, my ex wife, Brigitte had sold our lovely spot on the Baltic. But that is part of what happens when one hands over a power of attorney to a wife, then gets a divorce. We decided to do that just so my wife would retain a certain amount of security before my sabbatical that was planned for the academic year of 1983-84.

Before I left for the United States in 1983 to return for my sabbatical leave, I signed over the power of attorney to her to do what she liked with the Timmendorfer, along with the furniture which had thousands of dollars worth of antiques and hand woven Oriental carpets, I, on the other hand kept my several acres of land in Northern California but also sold that property in the mid-1980s. We had always dreamed of building a nice home on the property near Redding, California, but the divorce nullified this venture.

My reflections, as far as Northern Germany go are that it was a delightful place to go to in the summer, and only in the summer. Timmendorfer Strand is one of the most popular SPA areas in Germany. It is only in summer months that the sun comes out to extend the sunlight hours for beach walking, socializing, sun bathing, and enjoying a Riviera like location in Germany!

I used to enjoy jogging along the beach, watch the nude bathers, exercising, photographing the scenic Baltic Sea, or eating extremely delicious dinners of fish in delightful seafood restaurants, of which there are plenty of in Timmendorfer Strand. There was also the lovely, and larger city of Travemünde, which had an exclusive gambling casino, and provided an air of international flavor.

The delightful row of towns and villages such as Lübeck, Sharbeuty, Sierksdorf, Neustadt, and Gromitz were all lined sleepily along the lovely coast of the Ostsee. The sea air was healthy, invigorating, and provided one with an atmosphere of relaxation and leisure.

I am a great fan of seafood restaurants, and eat seafood about twice weekly here in San Diego, but never have I found a restaurant that prepares Scholle (flounder) like the Northern Germans prepare it. They would grill the fish, filet or whole, in butter and garlic. Enjoying that deliciously prepared meal with a delightful bottle of white Rhine or Mosel Wine simply cannot be duplicated in the United States. If a restaurant in the United States can duplicate the preparation of fish as is done in Northern Germany I have yet to find it.

We would also do local shopping, especially when my wife and Liane would accompany me, and cook in the apartment. My wife is about as good as they come in German cooking, unless it would be my daughter, Liane, who is also an excellent cook.

My reminiscing over the beautiful times I enjoyed in Northern Germany makes me think of the many experiences I had around Kiel, Hamburg, and Timmendorfer Strand. There are many great cities of the northern part of Germany, and now with the East opened up, I am sure there are other ones east of Hamburg.

On one visit, during the Christmas holidays, I received an invitation to hunt the European hare or the Hase, as it is called in German. I was introduced to a most congenial farmer who owned his own hunting Revier and we had a terrific hunt in the snow. The European Hare attains a weight of about 11 or 12 lbs. and is a delightful dish if prepared properly. My brother-in-law set up the hunt and I enjoyed every minute of it. We shot several of the animals and I even brought one to my mother-in-law who prepared it, using a superb East Prussian recipe.

When one speaks of Northern Germans being cool like the weather, I think back on a time I received an unfriendly retort from two German gentlemen talking in a bar. I thought I overheard two hunters talking so, in my friendly way, I interrupted to ask if they were hunters. I was told immediately that this was a private conversation and I shut up immediately, excusing myself telling them I was a hunter and was trying to make contacts. No more was said, and I, disappointed and rejected by the cold winds of the north, got up and went to another location.

It was at this specific at 33 years of age, in Kiel and about 1965, that I found that Northern Germans are a little cold in their nature. They are, seemingly formal, and not nearly as receptive as the Germans of the Ramstein, Kaiserslautern, and other cities of the southern region of Germany. I too became a little more formal and guarded when interacting with citizens of the North. It seems that one should use a little more caution in that area of Germany because the people are a little cooler than the ones in the southern part of Germany,

However, as I learned more German, and could extend the depth of my conversations, I could usually gauge the receptivity of most Germans, whether it was in Munich, Frankfurt, Heidelberg, or most any city of West Germany, and even Kiel.

I actually traveled back and forth, from Ramstein, Karlsruhe, Bad Kreuznach, Italy, or the Netherlands, to Kiel from 1963 until 1984, so I knew my away around Northern Germany about as well as I knew the middle part of the country. It was because of my hunting partners, and many friends around Karlsruhe and Hagenbach, that I felt a little more at home when traveling about southern or middle Germany.

But at the time my wife and I bought the apartment in Timmendorfer Strand, I thought we had some ownership, and we did, of that beautiful area of Northern Germany. The trips were relaxing, always great for sightseeing, and visiting relatives. If we did not stay in Timmendorfer Strand, we could always spend a couple of nights with Brigitte's East Preussian mother, who was a native of the pre-World War II German area known as East Prussia. That specific area presently is no longer a possession of Germany, but of Poland.

Brigitte, my ex wife's mother was an extraordinary woman who had profited by her husband's success, as a merchant in the late 1930s, when Adolph Hitler was gaining control of Europe. It was my understanding, from Brigitte that Walter Jagow, her father, was always venturing into some type of business, and I vaguely remember that he sold different products which aided the expansion of the German military in the late 1930s. He was involved in collecting scrap metal on a large scale and putting it into the war effort.

Her father was a member of the Nazi party and gained influence and even property because of his allegiance to the party. It was also my understanding that in Elbing, East Prussia, Walter Jagow, Brigitte's father had a nice home in which to rear the eight children of the Jagow family. There were 5 girls and three boys, with Brigitte's twin sister being scalded to death when she was only about a year of age. This was done through the carelessness of a Polish servant, teenage girl, who put the child in a bath hot enough to kill the young child.

The family, with their mother and grandmother escaped from the Russians in about 1944. They were coming west away from the Russians, and ended up in Kiel, Germany to settle in an area that was somewhat like Elbing, East Prussia, their previous home. They were to have a driver of the family car help them escape the Russians, but he ended up fleeing from the Russians with the car alone and left the family to fend for themselves.

I remember my ex wife telling me about their trek from Elbing toward the west, walking, hitching rides, and even seeing ships blown up in the bay. It was a trying time, where they had to steal food, sleep in barns or chicken-coops, and had machine guns shooting over their heads by Russian soldiers, and enduring the inclement weather with the few clothes they had.

The visits I had to Kiel, Germany between 1962, the time I married Brigitte, and 1983, when I returned to the United States were most interesting. Brigitte's mother was one who cared for her children, and was fortunate enough to have her oldest daughter marry a millionaire. Brigitte's mother, was put into a precarious position because she did not have much more than a social security pension so it was difficult for her to provide, especially for the two youngest sons, Götz and Roland.

When I first married Brigitte and made my wedding trip to Kiel, Götz, the next to the youngest son borrowed my brand new Volkswagen to run some errands after the wedding ceremony. He ended up blowing one of the pistons in the car. This could have been done only with over straining the engine with extremely high rpms on a turn so he was, no doubt, mistreating the auto. The brother was only about 17 years of age when this happened, and I, so in love with Brigitte, trusted him because he was now part of my family too.

Interesting though, the son of this brother visited me last summer and was approaching 18 years of age, and is without a doubt, one of the nicest German youngsters I have ever known. His name is Matthias Jagow and was one of the youngest German Bundesligue (National German Hockey

League) hockey players in Germany. The kid looks like Sean Penn, and is as charming as they come.

He visited the school where I was teaching summer school, Lincoln High School, and charmed all the young girls, guys, and teachers on the staff. He will be returning this summer and bringing a friend, a colleague attending the same Gymnasium as Matthias.

I am looking forward to the visit and know the two lads will visit Lincoln High School with me again, because I anticipate teaching summer school, hopefully the last venture in secondary teaching before I retire in July of 2001.

The other brother, also from Kiel, Germany, Roland Jagow, is in business in Bad Kreuznach, Germany, where my ex wife set him up in a hauling business. She also provided him with a house and business storage facility that she and her older brother, Detlev purchased as a business venture in 1995.

The family of Brigitte became very close with me and they all seem to be very successful. The mother, when the youngest two boys were quite young, would cater too much to their whims and sometimes sacrifice a great percentage of her retirement check, each month to meet their needs. German mothers are, often, from my observations, very attached to the sons. It seems, as is in the United States and in Germany, the females of the family usually attain independence rather quickly, obtaining the needed education to find a career, or they find a husband and speedily get out of the house at a rather young age.

My ex wife, Brigitte, was well prepared for life because she had training as a dental assistant and seemed to do quite well when I met her before we were married. She did much better once we got married because of the differential between German and American wages in the 1960s. My income readily supported her and me and was ample for us at this stage of our lives.

The ventures into Northern Germany proved to be very interesting, with visits to various family members but limited socializing outside the family. Now and then I would meet friends of the Stöben family, Brigitte's oldest sister, Christians's husband who was and is still quite successful and rich, as previously mentioned. They had us over for all the holidays, especially Christmas. The Stöben family had a farm with horses, a lovely house in the suburbs of Kiel, about 8 kilometers from the city. There was a beautiful 2,000 square foot home, a farm with a barn and about 15 exquisite horses.

Otto Stöben bred jumping horses and had all the facilities to practice his beloved hobby of raising the horses. He also saw to it that his three sons had riding lessons, so all became great riders and competed in jumping exhibitions.

I would visit him often and he loved showing me his farm. One day we drove from Kiel out to his farm in Eckenförde and I was driving my brother's XKE Jaguar which was left in my care in 1962 and Otto was delighted to race with me on the way to the farm. He was driving the most powerful and expensive Mercedes sedan built in the 1960s and we had fun showing off the cars. He was difficult to keep up with, even in the 150 mile per hour XKE Jaguar which had just been out for about a year.

Otto is a wonderful person, caring for his family and the greatest host one could have in a family. We got into some intimate conversations and he was extremely conservative, as many of the German businessmen are in Germany. He always lauded me for my rather good income as a teacher for the Dependent Schools, because relative to the Germans in the 1960s, the income was quite adequate.

Actually my in-laws were very fine people. My closeness with Brigitte's family increased as my German improved. All of her family, except the two youngest brothers, during the

1960s had very good jobs or were married to spouses who were professional and did quite well financially.

The visits to Northern Germany were frequent and many from 1963, when I married my ex wife until I left the country in 1983. A trip with Brigitte and Liane usually meant a car full of PX and commissary merchandise, especially cigarettes, alcohol and food. Brigitte always felt that because of her mother having a menial income, and we ate and sometimes slept with her in the small apartment in Kiel, we should bring ample food for us, and also relatives. This I did gladly because I loved the East Prussian cooking.

The trips, before we bought the Timmendorfer Strand apartment, would sometimes mean stops overnight, especially if the weather was bad, as it often was during Christmas or Thanksgiving. We got to know the cities between Frankfurt and Kiel quite well. Sometimes we would stay in a nice hotel in Kassel, Hanover, or Hamburg. We enjoyed the relaxation of remaining overnight, getting up leisurely, then having breakfast brought up to the room before driving on to Kiel.

We explored Hamburg sometimes because it is a very large city with its beautiful Alster Lake, the biggest lake inside a city in Europe. We visited the Baroque Church of St. Michael, the Town Hall with its distinctive green roof, and the Alster Arcades. Shopping was excellent and restaurants of most sorts in this very cosmopolitan city. Actually we visited the city for a couple of days on our short honeymoon in May of 1963.

Hamburg is endowed with theatres including the Hamburg State Opera (Hamburgishe Staatsoper), the German Theatre (Deutsches Schauspielhaus and the Ohnsorgtheater, which plays in the Low German dialect called "Plattdeutsch."

During our honeymoon we visited the Planten un Blomen park near the Congress Centrum Hamburg, which is renowned for its fountain displays during the summer; in the evenings at 2200 (10:00 p.m.) the display is accompanied by a sound and light show. During the daytime, the Television Tower should not be missed. For a small fee visitors can take the lift to the top platform and enjoy a view of the city, the harbor, the northern districts and the surrounding countryside. Just below is a restaurant that completes the full circle within an hour enabling every vantage for the diners' pleasure.

Then there is the famous Reeperbahn for which there is a German song written. I have visited this area many times, with the most interesting scenes at night. After a long night revelers congregate at the Fischmarkt, which opens at about 6:30 a.m. where one can purchase freshly caught fish, fruit and vegetables. The harbor has numerous tours. It has been so many years since I was there that this tour seems to blend with the many harbor tours I have taken in Kiel.

There are numerous shopping facilities with pedestrian shopping streets, elegant arcades, beautiful department stores and street cafes concentrated in the area near the main train station (Hauptbahnhof). On Sundays one can take a stroll along the River Elbe, which I have driven over and under during my numerous trips to Kiel.

Hamburg is the second largest city in the Federal Republic of Germany with a population of 1.8 million people. It is, of course many times larger than Kiel, with numerous places to visit, but because of its size, it takes a lot of time driving through it, if not driving by autobahn. So if one wants to visit this metropolis, then one needs to spend a night or two for the full flavor of this lovely city. Actually Hamburg is a city-state, and is counted as one of the 16 states of Germany. From research I found that it is one of the four cities forming the ancient Hanseatic League of ports and Hamburgers have always of their independence. The other three cities are LYbeck (the Y has the umlaut above it), Bremen and Rostock.

One of the most interesting relatives to visit lived in a lovely town that lay west of Kiel on the Kiel Canal connecting the Baltic and the North Sea. The small city, is Rendsburg. It is here where my sister-in-law and brother-in-law lived. The drive was only about 45 minutes from Kiel and I spent many Sunday afternoons visiting these two and their two children.

This was the Feil family and they were Ingeborg and Helmut with their two children, Heliana and Helgred (both now grown and married). Helmut is an engineer but now retired and he worked for the City of Rendsburg. Ingeborg is the charming and loving wife who endured many interesting episodes with her husband when they visited me in Hagenbach (near Karlsruhe), the Netherlands, and Bad Kreuznach.

Helmut told me that he had experienced many hair-raising experiences in the Bundeswehr uniform of the Führer during the Second World War. And to be very honest, I think Helmut was shell shocked or suffered extreme psychological damage from the war. He was, and most likely still is, very dependent upon his wife Ingeborg. He would often suffer temporary nervous breakdowns if things did not go right for him. It was "co-dependency" in its essence!

This family visited me quite often and they always welcomed us when we drove to visit them in Rendsburg. Coffee was served, and as usual, the best German coffee money could buy. We would buy a dozen or so beautiful assortments of Kuchen (pastries, cakes, or tarts) at the local Conditorei (a coffee place with a bakery) and enjoy the delights of a truly intimate family get-together.

I had extensive talks with Helmut regarding his experience in the German army and he told me that he saw hundreds of dead German soldiers and this was, of course on the Eastern front. He also told me he endured long periods of time without proper food from about 1943 through 1945.

One very impressionable experience he told me about during the Second World War was when he was on leave and visited the German occupied country of Denmark. He said that he saw whipped cream for the first time in many months and the soldiers ate cakes with whipped cream everyday because it had been a year or more since they had had such wonderful treats.

Another interested thing about this well educated man who showed me some of the extensive and detailed work he had done, from his notebooks, while in technical college, was his skill as a precise and successful student in technical college. He is an engineer and really knows mathematics quite well. I looked through these notebooks and the work was beautiful in detail with extensive complex functional problems solved through integral or differential calculus.

Another fascinating thing about Helmut was that he told me he would never get into an airplane. I think he had flown to various duty stations during the war, but he refused to fly in an airplane because of the structure and the possibility of the planes crashing or not being able to support the passengers.

He was very nervous when riding with me because I usually had a BMW, Mercedes, or the Camaro, all very fast vehicles. This man was nervous and would shake from fright when I would speed along the autobahn.

Helmut owned a Volkswagen for many years but eventually graduated to a German Ford in the 1970s. When he took a trip from Kiel to Ramstein Air Base Helmut would need about 10 hours because of his slow speed and the several stops he made along the way to do exercises and not become too fatigued.

I was sometimes as aggressive as the Dutch or German drivers and would get excited at pokey or slow non-responsive drivers in Schinveld, the Netherlands or in Germany. Helmut would chastise me vividly if I would honk or get pushy with some of the Dutch or German drivers. "Larry, you are not a policeman!" he exclaimed.

He was, however, an extraordinary woman watcher, as I too was, and still am, and we would have fun times in the bars in the Netherlands or in Germany, going to the different locations for good German beer and even dancing. Sometimes we would have our wives or many times we would go out alone for a couple of hours and really enjoy ourselves. Helmut also had very short arms when it came to paying bills. This did not bother me too much, except for the concept of fairness, so I would often pick up the checks. In fact most of the times I would pick up the checks. He rationalized his own reluctance to pay because he knew I made much more money than he at that time.

Again, when it came to paying the bills, I was very fast with the pocket book because I did earn a very good salary because of my employment with the U. S. Department of Defense. The thing that gave me the advantage was the tax-free housing and the very good reductions on food and gasoline from the post exchanges.

I remember on one visit of Ingeborg and Helmut to my house in Bad Kreuznach, and it was to be a week visit. It turned out that they were both so comfortable, they remained much longer than I had been told they would stay by my wife. They really had about 20 days vacation and I did not know this. It ended up that they both spent about two-and-a half weeks with me before leaving. I thought this was rather rude and things got a little intense around the house. Although we had three large bedrooms and an office with a fold out bed, and the family visitors were not too many, it is just that I had begun to lose my independence. I had the double responsibility of taking care of my family and of them, so this got to be too much and overbearing.

It often seemed to be one-sided with some of my German in-laws in that I always had the larger houses and the most room. From my wife's point of view, she wanted to show her family how nice it was to live in the luxury we had because of my very good job and substantial income. She was and still is one of the most generous persons I have ever known. If she is doing quite well in business she is most generous, especially when it comes to thinking of me.

She is on the one hand very conservative with money but on the other hand is extremely kind when it comes to our daughter or to me. I, too, am generous with her in that I set her up with part of my annuity from my retirement and she also will receive Social Security from the United States because of our twenty-four years of marriage.

To give an overall evaluation of my German in-laws, and most of them are from Northern Germany, I would say that they are well educated, provided tremendous hospitality when we, as a family, visited Rendsburg or Kiel. They always provided the best and most excellent meals when we visited and we had warm, enduring, friendly, and extensive conversations that warmed our souls!

Northern Germany has many fascinating areas to visit, and is absolutely beautiful in the months of June, July, August, and September. I highly recommend this part of Germany because of its many restaurants, beautiful sights, and though many Germans also think the people of North Germany are very cool, I believe there is a warmth to them, especially if you have friendly relaitves in the area. The Northern Germans may seemingly be distant to strangers but to be honest, once I learned a little Plattdeutsch (low German), things began to become a little friendlier.

The language, in almost any country of Europe, and I presume of the world, really opens up the thoroughfares and the interrelationships between people unravel. I love the family of my ex wife because they are still relatives in my view. I host them when they come over to the United States just as though they are still my relatives.

One of the cautions I might mention to travelers who use Kiel or Hamburg as a stepping stone to Scandinavia is to be cautious when traveling in Sweden, Denmark, or Norway. I found the prices to be more exorbitant than in Germany. I feel much more secure in Germany than in Scandinavia and I am sure is from the many years of language seasoning. I feel very secure and at home in all parts of Germany.

The beautiful areas along the North and Baltic Sea, the lovely beaches, and the quaint towns are charming in their beauty. The fresh sea air, the wonderful fish restaurants are so inviting that I again look forward to visits in the future. But I really intend to make those visits about the time of Kieler Woche, Kiel Week, when the weather is beautiful or in the warm summer months. This is a part of Germany that has much to offer and with just a little use of Plattdeutsch I am sure it is not difficult to find conversation with most any person around the lovely cities in the area of Northern Germany.

These people, in Northern Germany, left behind by Hitler, have much to offer. Still conservative in their views, they are quite ambitious, and the various seaports are beautiful to visit. Though Hamburg was bombed extensively during the Second World War, it is a city, along with Kiel, and other lovely places in that area, most charming to visit. My memories are still dominantly positive and developing an understanding of the region and people of Northern Germany warms the coolness of the area!

Chapter 10

─❦─

Germany's Social Behavior,
1945 And After

It is difficult to say that Germany, though 55 years after the end of World War II has gone through a complete metamorphosis and is completely democratized. Actually, Germany, as a nation that implemented the annihilation 6 million Jews during the costly and destructive Second World War, has made tremendous inroads toward becoming one of the great leaders of Europe, and with a democratic predominance. Its overtones of a democratic nation seem to ring quite clear, especially since post World War II.

With the tremendous success of the Marshall Plan after the end of World War II, one can say that West Germany utilized its aid to the greatest extent. Via the Marshall Plan, from 1948 through 1952 the United States loaned or gave $13 billion to the countries taking part in the plan. As a result, by about 1952, Western Europe was economically healthy. The Marshall Plan also provided a large market for American goods, and it held back the spread of Soviet influence.

From my Internet research, I learned that most countries, with the exception of Spain under the leadership of Fascist Franco, took part in the Marshall Plan partnership of Western Europe. Countries participating were: the Netherlands, France, Great Britain, Austria, Germany, Portugal, Italy, Turkey, Belgium, Sweden, Ireland, Luxembourg, Greece, Iceland, Denmark, and Norway. With the supporting strength of the United States and the participating countries the plan provided the springboard for, especially, West Germany, to get back on its feet economically. East Germany had to suffer the economic deprivation brought on by the Soviet Union. We can all be thankful that the fall of the Berlin Wall came in 1989. An earlier escape by East Germany and the other satellites from the shackles of communism would have benefited Europe even more.

By the time I arrived in 1961, Germany was beginning to don the characteristics of quite an independent Germany. Its people were beginning to drop off the cult of the Third Reich, Hitler's indoctrination, and become economically alive. Owners of businesses, especially the hotels, restaurants, wine cellars, and beer halls manifested the characteristics of people with a definitive direction. Economic stimulation manifested itself distinctly during the 1960s and from what I was told by my military friends, they were quite spirited prior to my arrival.

In the development of the postwar social behavior, Germans actually lauded the American military, for their ubiquitous existence in the country. Bases like Wiesbaden, Sembach, Ramstein, Rhein-Main, Kaiserslautern, and the many others provided a great economic opportunity for many Germans to receive spurred incomes provided by the U. S. military. They were seemingly happy to have the Americans, as well as the British, Canadians, and the French manning the military facilities.

And then the creation of North Atlantic Treaty Organization (NATO) in 1949 gave all of Western Europe a more secure feeling for its deterrence to the great Soviet threat. Many Germans, in their conversations would often express their fear and respect for the military might of the Soviets. I often heard the expression, "Wenn der Ivan rüber kommt," or in English, "When Ivan comes over," from various Germans, especially the ex military. The feeling was predominant because they remembered the great defeat of Hitler's forces at the battle of Stalingrad, and the powerful resistance of the Russian military on the Eastern front.

Actually, Dean Acheson, who succeeded George Marshall as Secretary of State of the United States in 1949, was the primary architect of the mighty NATO. According to my history book, he presided over the negotiations that led to the signing of the North Atlantic Treaty Organization in Washington D. C. on April 4, 1949. The United States signed with Canada and ten European nations in this broad defense pact. It was a significant achievement toward solidifying post-war Western Europe.

So, with the infusion of the Marshall Plan and NATO, the Germans were on their way to psychological stabilization. These things seemed to enhance the confidence of the German social behavior because they felt that after the havoc wrought by of allied forces bombing and destruction from World War II, things were beginning to stabilize socially and economically.

It was a great feeling coming into Germany after living in North Africa for six months. Seeing green trees, drinking great beer, and eating excellent food was invigorating to me, especially after my college years of dreaming of Germany.

Food and beer were of course inexpensive for me, earning American wages in Germany in the 1960s. I quickly grasped the spirit of a lively and spirited West Germany.

For explorative adventure, I remember driving my little Volkswagen Beetle, about 10 years old when I bought it only one week after arriving at my duty station in Ramstein. I could drive around after school and on weekends and I was like a bird let out of a cage. During such vacations as the Thanksgiving and winter holidays I had the opportunity to venture out from Ramstein to other villages and cities and measure the pulse of the average German citizen.

I, in my then broken German, half mixed with English, begin to go through the routine questions of: "Wie geht es Ihnen," meaning how are you, in the formal usage, or "Wo wohnen Sie?" and "Wie heissen Sie?" (Where do you live? and What is your name?) I was getting into the spirit of the social interaction among our past enemies.

My desire to build on the German language in order to gain a true sociological insight into the German character and his feelings was very strong. With a previous curiosity and desire to someday visit this magnificent country my explorations began to pay of in multitudes of rewards. The visions were even more gratifying than I had imagined.

I would see the smile come across the German faces as I tried to structure my sentences as dictated and taught me by my Berlitz teachers. Then later I took the courses at the University of Maryland extension courses at Kaiserslautern American High School or Ramstein Junior High School in the evenings. I began accumulating college credits in the language, and also began to accumulate a better understanding of the target language.

Taking the university courses after bombardment of the functional Berlitz language teachers was tremendous reinforcement, so my German began to come through with a massive payoff. My German teacher, University of Maryland, immediately told me, to acquire a German girl friend in order to enhance my German speaking ability.

I think she really had a scheme, and that was to marry off as many Americans to the German Fräuleins as possible. The scheme certainly worked on me because, after May of 1962 I was married to Brigitte von Jagow, my newly acquired German bride.

But in my desire to communicate, before marriage, I acquired several German girl friends, and especially liked those unfamiliar with English. I knew that I would force myself to build on my German language if the girl friends spoke less English than I spoke German. It worked because some of them were so beautiful that I forced myself to acquire more German in order to increase my friendships. I immediately added their names to my address book and built a social base of lovely German ladies prior to my marriage.

Some of the most interesting moments were driving from my home base to towns and cities as far as Rosenheim, Munich, Heidelberg, Stuttgart, Nuremberg, Frankfurt, Wiesbaden, and Worms, not to mention the many other cities I visited. The little hotels and guesthouses were absolutely immaculate, clean, comfortable and those with restaurants had excellent food.

The infusion of my curiosity and neophyte approaches to German language utilization led me down paths that were absolutely magnificent. Since I was only about 31 years of age, I had the appearance of someone in his twenties and I had no trouble breaking into the student set around Heidelberg.

Another teacher and I would spend many weekends around Heidelberg on Friday and Saturday evenings especially. We could always stay in a nice German hotel or for the convenience of reading the Stars and Stripes news, we could stay at the military officer hotels around Mannheim, Frankfurt, Heidelberg, and others such as Wiesbaden and Rhein-Main. We also liked the American breakfasts now and then, just for a change of pace, getting back into the bacon and egg routine of our home country.

But to this day, I have always loved the German breakfasts, and especially the dark, finely ground coffee and numerous selections of dark firm breads. The way Germans prepare breakfast is a divine experience because its appeal and beauty. The Brötchen (hard German rolls) are magnificent. They usually have soft-boiled eggs along with various choices of cold cuts, cheeses, and excellent jellies or jams to go along with a beautifully laid out table. My greatest fear each time I return to Germany and indulge in breakfast, is my fear of over indulgence because I do not want to leave the beautifully prepared meal.

We began to visit such places, especially around the student locations in Heidelberg, as the "Rote Ochse" (Red Ox Inn) which was the setting of the old classical film, "The Student Prince," with Mario Lanza and Anne Blythe. The students of Heidelberg, however, were better prepared, in most cases to speak English than my early stages of their language at that time. But I continued to plow into the German language, asking questions about the Heidelberg University admittance processes, "What are you studying?" "How long do you have to study?" or "What are your professors like?" It did not take long to learn that the structure of the German University was not as tightly focused on the college or university credits as it was on a total program of study under a certain professor. The guidelines of the American University with the accumulation process of units tended to be somewhat more credit oriented and the time processes for graduation more defined.

The attitudes of the students at Heidelberg, and later I met many in the 1970s around Karlsruhe University, were quite receptive toward Americans until the era of the Vietnam War. They always seemed to be quite receptive to me as a teacher associated with the American Dependent Schools and had numerous questions to ask about American teaching processes.

I learned a great deal about students and their attitudes while living around Ramstein. At that time, because of the Allied Forces status in Germany, there was always a portrayal of gratitude and respect for the "victor's" (Americans) about the students. Most of the students had a profound respect for Americans at that time.

It was not until the Vietnam War that I began to get bombarded by philosophical questions about why we were in Vietnam. To this day, as I have mentioned previously, that question was always difficult to answer. The fact that I had mixed emotions about Vietnam and our involvement is no wonder, especially after the confessions of some of our past leaders about the mistakes of that war since the late 1990s. Recently, when Robert McNamara made his confessions about the doubts of our expanded involvement in Vietnam, it continues to add to my doubts about American involvement in that war. The loss of about 58,000 Americans and injuries of 300,000 cast a veil of doubt about our involvement in Vietnam. Its tremendous cost to the taxpayers in the United States certainly leave many question marks to Americans, especially in the eyes of the gallant military involved in the war.

It was during the time of the Vietnam War, as a matter of a fact, that many of my German friends began to come out with dire criticism of the Americans being involved in such a conflict. The Germans began to voice their opinions about our investment there and were a little more outspoken regarding their past ventures of the Third Reich. I often caught these remarks at parties, and in some cases I enjoyed the Germans not being quite as apologetic for their blind following of the "Fuhrer." Military duties as a clarification regarding the German Third Reich era became more prevalent as a form of retort.

More vivid descriptions of the Germans' battlefield experiences began to surface in my social conversations. The concept of conservatism not being such a bad philosophy was often expressed. Also, the expression: "The Hitler experience happened because we were looking for a way out of the serious depression in the 1930s, inflation problems, and my parents did not know which way to turn but to follow Hitler and his National Socialist Party." The frank expressions of the Germans definitely evolved after we were caught with our pants down in the great Vietnam tragedy.

The Vietnam War mistake by our country was their chance to get back at the Americans, to some degree, except they still enjoyed the idea of the protective military umbrella spread by the ever watchful eyes of NATO. With the American military bases as the source of protection, the U. S. Air Force exhibitions around Sembach, Ramstein, Berlin, and Rhein-Main, still had the full support and curiosity of the German citizens. I was always amazed at the turnout of so many Germans on those open base exhibitions put on by the American military. There would be thousands of Germans participating in the viewing of planes, tanks, marching soldiers, helicopters and other displays of American strength. The Germans loved them. Germans generally seem to have an innate attraction for military hardware and the newest mechanisms of war.

I often reflect back on my early days of 1961-1966 and the days the U. S. dollar was so strong. I had many unique experiences just shopping, eating in great restaurants, and getting out among the German people.

One experience I remember vividly, and on my first serious shopping spree, in the fall of 1961 in downtown Kaiserslautern, I visited a department store and looked for a to coat because winter was on its way. The department stores, on that Friday afternoon were quite full and I found a topcoat I liked. It looked black and white, somewhat mixed in a tweed sort of way. I purchased the in my size and thought it was smart. Later, when I got it in the daylight, I found that it was not black and white, but green and white. The dark threads running through out looked black but were dark-green. I only paid about $39 equivalent our money, and about 160 German Marks. Merchandise was plentiful, the salespersons friendly, and very eager to sell merchandise to the Americans.

Just being in their stores, with the dynamic work force then going full blast in West Germany was exciting. I always enjoyed buying the German clothes. Their shoes in the 1960s were quite opposed to American styles because most of them were extremely pointed. I did buy a couple of pairs of shoes, but tried to keep my shoes more in line with the American styles which were still semi-square toed or round toed. As a matter of fact, the German styles were quite suitable, and I bought many of the German clothes because the merchandise was excellent quality and I enjoyed wearing them. I seemed to attain somewhat of a continental look, not the loud plaid look, as some of the American military so often wore. I often bought more Italian cut suits, a couple of them tailored by the American PX concessions, and they were plenty sharp. Nice styles, at that time were rather difficult to find in the PX so I selected a more continental wardrobe.

As a young teacher in the early 1960s I had very dark hair and met my wife-to-be, Brigitte while wearing a black, Italian rather fast fitting suit. I always wore a suit or coat and tie while making my weekend visits to Heidelberg and Mannheim because I wanted to look my best, especially if out to attract a lovely German lady. Sure enough, on one of weekend trips, I saw two very nicely dressed ladies window shopping on the main street of Mannheim after I had just left two exciting nights in Heidelberg. This was a Sunday afternoon at about 3:00 p.m. and one of these ladies was just what I had envisioned as the Bridget Bardot type and absolutely gorgeous. As fate would have it, this was the woman of my future, and wife to be.

Brigitte's cousin spoke German when I asked them if they knew a nice coffee shop, and sure enough they told me they could show me one. I invited them both for coffee and cake, a national Sunday afternoon custom of all Germans throughout East and West Germany. We proceeded to go into the establishment, have conversation and enjoy coffee, then later a glass of wine. I stumbled through some German phrases, utilized Brigitte's cousin, Evelene, as an interpreter, and made contact plans for forthcoming weekends.

I made my plans, exchanging phone numbers, and a possible time for a rendezvous in the future. As it turned out, Brigitte visited me in her friend's car and even came on base at Ramstein Air Base, knocked on my BOQ room, but I was out to dinner.

When I contacted her at her aunt and uncle's house in Mannheim on a Friday afternoon the following weekend after she visited me, I was invited in, given the third degree by the aunt and uncle. They told me when she would return, so I came back and asked her out to dinner and a visit to Heidelberg. This is the way I met my German wife, Brigitte.

I had previously asked a student in Heidelberg how one goes about meeting a nice German lady and I was informed that one could meet German ladies on Sunday afternoon walks, just like I did. Since most Americans did not have a solid ground base of social acquaintances during the first few months of living in the host country, this was about the best way, unless it was in a wine locale, or restaurant. Most of the time the ladies were escorted, so it was not always easy to find nice German women in various clubs. There were some dance locales, especially on Sunday afternoons, and this is still a custom in Germany.

Many coffee locales or Konditoreis have music and it is a time one can ask ladies to dance. I have done it many times, though it is not the usual custom of Americans to dance on Sunday afternoons in the United States. Also, the SPA parks have excellent full orchestras just for the purpose of socializing, drinking coffee, wine, or beer on Sunday afternoons. Sunday is definitely a time of leisure for the Germans.

As I began to explore more cities, I began to visit such places as Luxembourg, a neighboring country, not too far from Worms. I also visited Switzerland, Austria, and France. It was no task for me to jump into my old Volkswagen, drive to these nearby countries and get a taste of their wine, beer, and food. It was easy for Americans to do at that time because of the employment with the American Forces, or for the military themselves to take these excursions. Money was very good and went a long way in the 1960s. The value of the American dollar being equivalent to four German Marks was a tremendous exchange rate and I doubt that Americans will ever see that again because of our trade balance status.

To be centered in a location such as Ramstein Air Base, with over 10,000 military and civilians was a great luxury in the 1960s. The only questionable thing about living here was the fact that one large Soviet missile could have wiped us all out in a couple of minutes. We actually had feelings of insecurity in those days, but with the young and eager pilots, many of whom I met while at the Ramstein Officer's Club, we felt a little more secure. These fellows had been taught to scramble in their fighter jets at a moment's notice so this somewhat relieved our anxieties.

The base itself provided us with three theatres, and the latest American movies, two large PX facilities, several restaurants, and a German post office, along with two U. S. post offices. This was indeed the place to be stationed. Why I ever wanted to leave such a fine base, except to see new territory, was puzzling to my fellow teachers at the school on base. I did eventually make the move, in 1966, to Aviano Air Base, Italy. My wanderlust got the best of me and I wanted some sunshine plus a third language. After five years in one duty station, I became restless and wanted to explore new areas.

The opportunity to travel, not only in Germany, but all over Europe was at hand and I was in paradise as far as the location was concerned, while at Ramstein Air Base. The years I spent were some of the most pleasant times one could ever expect in a home away from home. Actually, Germany was becoming my home, and with a German wife, and later a child, I was beginning to become a fully integrated European, and especially one with a tremendous admiration for the German culture and language. I loved the people, their work ethic, their modern techniques, relative to the rest of Europe, their wonderful machinery, especially automobiles, and their fantastic mode of life. It seems the Germans were especially embedded into the work ethic, but they seemed to have a better facility for enjoying festivals, parties, celebrations, and free time, day or night, than I knew as an American.

My stay in Aviano Italy was for only one year, and my opportunity to leave that beautiful assignment came because of the tremendous opportunity at the four-nation school in Brunssum, the Netherlands. The ramifications of that experience have been dwelled on, so the focus is now on Germany and its magnetic attractions for me while in Europe.

After leaving Brunnsum, the Netherlands, in 1971, I fell into the explorative beauty of the city of Karlsruhe since I only lived across the Rhine River, a distance of about 13 kilometers from Karlsruhe. This was about 7.3 miles and a quick drive in my BMW or Mercedes. We were fortunate enough to still afford driving German cars at that time, although the German Mark had begun to rise against the American Dollar. In the early 1970s the dollar was equivalent to about 3.30 German Marks, if I remember correctly. It might have gotten below the 3 Mark level during my stay in Karlsruhe.

There were many disappointed Americans when we began to realize that the beautiful days of the 1960s had given way to a very productive Germany and the balance of payments had begun to pull down the value of the American Dollar. No longer could one hand a German taxi driver a dollar and expect to receive four German Marks for it.

Karlsruhe enabled me to enjoy the hunting that had been an endearing sport of mine as a high school and college student in Arkansas. Along the Rhine River on the Rheinland-Pfalz side (west-side) and in Baden-Würtemberg (east side) I had begun to access the best hunting areas one could imagine. Through the American Rod and Gun Club, I met many elegant and elitist families that provided me with the opportunity to hunt on their private Reviers (hunting areas). Not only, as mentioned previously in this book, did I get to hunt, with land-owners but also I had the opportunity to socialize with them, and gain insight into how very wealthy, but also often conservative German families lived.

Several of the younger hunters or Jung Jägers as they were referred to in Germany were in their early thirties, spoiled, drove Porsches and Mercedes, the newest and most expensive models, but were very generous when it came to parties after the hunts. If there was a private dinner party, the best food and drinks were served, with the Revier owners showing the Americans how the wealthy hunters of Europe lived.

I think that one sees some of the same traits in rich young Americans, but the generosity of the parents often seems to be more constrained among Germans. The Germans, especially in the 1970s tended to be conservative, especially if they were in the early or late fifties, and not quite as generous with money as the youth were. I remember a hunter by the name of Karl Heinz Hötzel as one of the very generous young hunters, with a most gorgeous wife, and he drove a green Porsche to all the hunts. Many of the hunters drove the green automobiles, symbolizing the green forests of Germany. Many might think this is a little far fetched, but it was the truth. The German hunters were passionately into their hobby.

I even bought one of my American cars, which was a Gremlin made by American Motors at that time, in green, specifically because its color was appropriate for hunting. Actually it was not such a great hunting car because it was real wheel drive and the front drive vehicles are much better for the many muddy back roads in the German forests. The car was economical and as long as I stayed on the hard surfaced roads, it was fine. But it was adequate for two persons only but one could squeeze an extra passenger or two in the back. Compared to European cars at that time it was quite adequate in size and horsepower.

I was still inquiring into the German mind of my hunting friends and into the social kaleidoscope I had created east and west of the Rhein River. I had made so many friends who owned hunting Reviers that some would even become jealous when I would not show up for a Saturday or Sunday hunt. I was edging closer to the confidence level I sought in the business families around the periphery of Karlsruhe and to the west, across the Rhine River.

The most compatible friends I had near Karlsruhe were the Griesingers (large bakery firm) and the Hötzel Family in one of the suburbs only about 3 kilometers outside of Karlsruhe. Both families were quite well off, and the wives of each owned magnificent fox coats, ankle length, which were made from the fox shot off their Reviers. It seemed that this was the style, especially for the wealthier hunters in the middle 1970s. They were the beautiful red fox furs and it took twenty or so to complete the beautiful masterpiece put together by their private Gerbers (tanners or one who tans hides).

It did not seem that my being American was any barrier to the social interaction I experienced as a hunter. Strangely enough, the passion was in the hunting, and the hunters were focused mostly on the customs that had been handed down in their families. As far as the social and economic background from which I came, other than being a teacher, and I was highly respected in the German hunting and social community because of my profession, the German hunters were not too curious about my background in the United States.

There were casual questions about the university or colleges I had attended. All they knew was that I was a teacher from the American High School, and this was quite a prestigious position from the German point of view.

Sometimes we would get into conversations about the Second World War and how Hitler gained the political advantage he had to turn Germany into a worldwide power in the 1930s and early 1940s. The pasts of some of these friends were casually revealed in that some had been on the Russian front, and had some hair-raising experiences there, but other than that, there was not too much in the realm of political revelation.

One thing that did come out was that most of the landowners and business owners were definitely not from the SPD (Social Democratic Party) but mostly from the CDU (Christian Democratic Union) Conservative Party. They did not want the government cutting too much into their business profits by higher taxation for more social benefits, but wanted as much hands-off government as could be allowed.

There would be gestures and suggestions that except for the attempted annihilation of the Jews, Hitler was an excellent socialist leader who provided many benefits for the German people. The acquisition of land from Poland, Czechoslovakia, the Sudetenland, France, and other countries, was merely a gesture of good will in providing for the needs of the German Empire and its people. They were cautious in their words and I am sure that when among themselves, the conversations might have been more slanted toward what the rewards would have been had German not encountered the power of the Allied forces to counter this man's schemes of European domination.

When talking with more liberal friends, who were not hunters, but engineers, teachers, and perhaps Social Democrats in various trades or professions, there would be a more disdainful view of Adolf Hitler. Sometimes there would be bitterness for the tremendously treacherous road this leader had led the nation of Germany down. There would be regretful overtones that Germany fell into the claws of a strong leader who hoaxed the German people, and the revelation of Jewish directed Holocaust evolved later in the war and the preponderance of a highly secret society veiled the injustices that emanated from the German State.

So many people actually told me that it was dangerous to question too much as far as the direction of the political elite and plan for Jewish destruction was concerned. The political leadership and Gestapo were so forceful that common citizens could not inquire too much or they themselves would be in jeopardy, and could be easily eliminated.

I had a Jewish student in one of my evening science classes at Ramstein who was vociferous in his feelings that the Jewish atrocities were well known by the German people. He insisted the citizens had to have known the Jews were being killed or burned in the concentration camps because places like Dachau were right in the middle of the town. Daniel Jonah Goldhagen's book, <u>Hitler's</u> <u>Willing</u> <u>Executioners</u> would seemingly support the idea that the Jewish executions were so blatant and predominant, they had to be known.

For the sake of embarrassment, I would often temper my questions about the persecution of the Jews and question the Germans in a round about way with such questions as, "What was your military assignment?" or "What was your rank in the military?" I think that the populous of Germany knew what was going on but with the economic elevation in the late 1930s through the military upgrading and tremendous siphoning off other countries, the jobs and income emergence encouraged them to turn their heads from Jewish persecution and persecution of non Germans.

Acquisition of property and wealth from the Jews and other political enemies of the **Third Reich** elevated the German populous to a level that was comfortable, so the majority must have questioned very little once the economic benefits began to benefit the citizens economically. Germany began to become a leader of Europe with its blatant military might, and the following of Hitler began to spread with a dynamic explosion, once the little man with the mustache began to control most of Europe. It was, no doubt, uplifting for Germans to actually be a citizen of a country that could potentially rule the world. There were many benefits, such as property, houses, businesses, and even monetary rewards that helped Germans economically. The stripping of property and personal goods alone from Jews and enemies of the Third Reich benefited the Nazi State and its followers.

The fact that 6,000,000 Jews were eliminated from Europe only made it easier for the Germans to accept property and economic opportunities because of the displacement of Jews and non Germans. When one has the opportunity to advance because of someone else's misfortune, it is human nature for citizens who are in fear of questioning, to accept the rewards of others misfortunes. This might be especially true if the people in society think they will never be caught by a just world. From a morale standpoint, the German Reich and its people were eventually confronted by the brutal persecutions in the eyes of the world. The Nuremberg trials brought some of the foes before judgement but many no doubt escaped punishment.

I had the good fortune to meet Alfons Heck, author of the book, <u>A Child of Hitler</u>, while enjoying coffee at Starbucks in Mission Valley, here in San Diego, about 7 years ago. I had already read his book when I came upon him and his lovely Dachshund sitting at a table next to me. Mr. Heck lectures and writes for our very conservative Union-Tribune in San Diego. He and I have discussed Germany and the German people, especially since I lived in the country over twenty years. I made him aware of it in our conversation in German.

Mr. Heck was propagandized and brainwashed as a child and became a "Hitler Jugend," or a Hitler Youth. He describes, vividly, his childhood and the tremendous pressures wrought upon him by the Nazis during the Second World War. He was "democratized" after the war, and now is a citizen of the United States. He is an official translator and interpreter for people coming here from Germany as tourists. He is often sought to help these citizens when they have automobile wrecks or other problems.

I enjoy his company because of my positive experience in Germany. I got his attention in one article I wrote regarding the contrast of the German jurisprudence system compared to ours, and especially of the judges in both countries. The German system that abides by a codified law, as contrasted to a law of precedence, is ironically, sometimes very just, especially with the reigning judges in some cases. I received more democratic treatment in Germany when in court than under some of our extremely dictatorial judges. That was the instance I relayed in the article, telling about the kind and fair treatment, plus the temperament with which I was treated while appearing in court in Northern Germany.

Alfons liked the article because I cast some glowing compliments on the German system, and still feel that way. But I do not know how the German society would react if it again rendered the strong political control that existed under Nazi Germany. The concept of "Go with the flow," or adhere to the political direction is the guiding light of contemporary German society.

When you have politically strong conservatives in power, the thrust can go far to the right. Get a dynamic leader like John F. Kennedy, with the political persuasion and magnanimous presence he had, and you might find yourself being more liberal. John F. Kennedy had the persona that tends to be very persuasive. I know that after Kennedy got into power, I liked many of the things he did, and his definitive manner in exerting leadership.

I voted for Richard Nixon because I was an active young Republican in the 1960s, but today I have more middle of the road leanings. At the time of Kennedy's election, I thought he would be a tyrant, with Roman Catholic direction, and potentially a leader with too much clout.

As it turned out, I really admired the direction John F. Kennedy was going. With a couple of exceptions such as the Bay of Pigs blunder, most of the things he did were revelations of one who had great aspirations for this country. His world visions with such innovations of the Peace Corp are amenable to inspiration in positive processes in moving toward improving less fortunate counties.

In reference to Alfons Heck, and his great support of Germany, even now, though he is an American citizen, is a very bright and intelligent person and has great insights into the contrasting personalities of the two great nations, the United States and Germany. He was brought up under the extreme dictatorial leadership of Adolf Hitler and even met him at a rally. I am sure Alfons Heck is the most qualified person to depict the dynamic tidal wave brought upon the country of Germany in the late1930s. He is one of the most qualified to tell of the persuasiveness of a dynamic leader like Adolf Hitler. He did this in his book and in his current editorials is magnificent in his revelations of the mood of the Nazi Era.

From what I have read, regarding **Adolf Hitler**, he had a dynamic, spell binding ability to almost hypnotize his audiences at the tremendous rallies throughout Germany. The people were enthralled by the charisma of this dynamic speaker. But the key to all this, in the 1930s, was that Germany was economically down to its lowest ebb and in an economic stagflation setting that welcomed such a leader as **Adolf Hitler.**

The people I met in the 1960s and the 1970s in Germany were Germans who had been beaten down and disillusioned from the defeats of the war. They were people who were again revitalized by such programs as the Marshall Plan, and the insurgence of NATO to again give Europe and Germany a true concept of European political and military participation.

The people I saw, got to know and began to have faith in, were just like you and me. The **basic difference between Americans and Germans**, in my opinion, is their approach to education and constraints of families on children who are growing up, and that is the strength of discipline, a somewhat higher respect for the family as a unit, propagated by the tradition of the family. It is quite cohesive in Germany, whereas I feel some of the family disintegration propensities in American society are tending to diminish the strength of the family unit. In Germany it is loosening, but tends to have a more solid thread binding the family unit. In German society there is still the element of cohesiveness because the country does not have the intensity of multiple ethnic diversity found in this country.

Americans, on the other hand, are brought up in a more democratic and weaker overall structure of the education system. Democratic insurgence has weakened our direction in education and it must be fixed, repaired, maybe even more in line with the processes and structure practiced in Germany, but perhaps with a little more creativity.

The creativity of the American school system that was once structured to meet the needs of our students might one day regain its now flailing direction. We could gain from the German concepts in types of schooling that are meeting the needs of the students, because Americans no longer have a structure to meet student needs. The American system of education is so diverse and multi-faceted in direction that it is losing an overall centrally needed cohesiveness.

The German social development since the Second World War has evolved to a state of professed democratization, but it could someday deteriorate if the economic structure does not maintain its stability. The 10% unemployment in Germany, with 81 million citizens is not drastically high, but in contrast to that in the United States of 4.5%, both 2001 figures, the U. S. figures are more workable. There is something very dynamic taking place in both countries. Let us hope that Germany, in its political and social development will surge ahead and provide the technological structure it can so well provide for the rest of Europe. With the infusion of the new generations now coming up in Germany, and their desire for more democratic institutions, one can only hope that their social development will lead Germany into the twenty-first century with the highest level of astuteness.

The influx of American ingenuity in medicine, business, and space achievements can only influence the general population of Germany. Their behavior, socially, since the end of World War II, has been magnanimous because they are politically sensitive to the degradations brought on by the leadership of Nazi Germany. No longer can one use the word Nazi as an integral part of Germany. Except for the radical isolated spots, found most frequently in the eastern half of the country, is probably only misdirection brought on by the degrading and demoralization through the fifty years of flagrant communist influence.

The general attitudes and social development of Germany, especially what I saw during the time span of 1960 through 1983 was excellent. The experiences after that and after the fall of the Berlin Wall in 1989 have also been enlightening. The linkage between the eastern half of Germany and the western half will only provide a dynamic renaissance of new creations by a new society that is ready to lead Europe to great achievements!

The vitality and economic aspirations of the people Hitler left behind since the post World War II are seemingly strong enough to continue to give the German people the drive that is needed to keep Germany modern, forthright, and at the forefront of a revitalized Europe. With the oncoming European unity in the twenty-first century Germany has the capability of blending in with dynamic serge of leadership with its ingenious industrial and scientific propensity!

Chapter 11

Returning To CONUS
(Continental United States)

After returning to the United States in 1983 to acquire more courses for school administration, German, and computer science, I was amazed at how I had become so Europeanized. The contrast between Europe and the United States was amazing. Having lived over twenty-years abroad, with visits over the summer vacations only, I was in for the culture shock of my life.

The shock was profound because of the difference in life style and the pace of Californians. They, Californians, seemed very regimented in one sense, and somewhat egocentric in another way. To Californians it did not make a difference if I had lived in Europe or China, these people are in their own world. I was told by my newly acquired wife-to-be, that San Diego was the place everyone in the world wants to be, including most Europeans. I immediately told her that I did not think that to be the case and that I had just as soon be living in Niece, France or on the Italian Riviera because it was just as charming, if not more, because it was Europe.

I had acquired the warm secure feeling of the continental living where one could visit another culture and a country with another language within only a few hours. I had the hunting, camping, travel, fishing, and all the things I previously had in the United States, and even more while living in Europe. All the tremendous conveniences, car washes, fast food restaurants, K-Marts, and modern movie theatres did not make any difference because I missed the warmth and personal acquaintances I had acquired in Germany. My friend resented the fact that I talked about Germany, missed it, and could not get the intensely imbedded German culture off my mind. I even sang German songs in the shower, especially when I wanted to irritate her.

It took me about four or five years to shake off the bonds of congeniality, intensive warmth, family love, and the fabulous European restaurants I had left 6,000 plus miles behind. My dreams were still in German, along with the memories of my wife and daughter I had left behind. The reality of being away from the warmth of Europe, which I had digested for twenty years into my psychic, remained intact in my soul, mind, and body.

There were sometimes nightmares, phone calls to Brigitte and Liane, and sincere sadness that I suffered during the months before I met my girl friend at San Diego State. Even with the beauty of the fantastic California sunshine, and the nearness of my brother Jim, I still missed my family in Germany. I had grown so attached to the solid family structure I had built between my wife, my daughter, and me. The void created by their absence was difficult to endure, but I knew I would return to my home in Germany during the winter vacation from San Diego State University.

It was not until about mid-October that I met my friend in one of the elementary science curriculum classes and found the tremendous fascination for this beautiful 36 year-old woman. She was sexual, could hardly bare being around her husband, and was falling in love with me, as I was falling in love with her. The physical contact was dynamic, and on a scale of 1 to 10, we both reached 9.5s in the sexual pleasure and physical love mutually acquired through our personal contact. Chemistry was high and our mutual feelings for each other positive.

I was invited to her house one Sunday afternoon, in the fall of 1983, to watch a Charger football game and we knew after that meeting that both of us would break up our marriages. She did not falter about our getting together. We were together about as often as possible while studying, and that was almost everyday of the week.

Her grade point fell from a 4.0 to about a 3.4 at San Diego State University. We were both serious students, but I was full time and she was completing her requirements for the California teaching credential. I insured my future in California by taking the C-Best test, the requirement to teach in the State of California. I had all the necessary courses for a secondary teaching credential, and was completing the California administrative requirements.

I continued to maintain about a 3.6 grade-point average, and before the year was over, with a full academic year, and an additional summer, I had about 45 plus units from that institution. I was working hard, but was on sabbatical leave, and therefore I had half salary from my job with the Department of Defense.

My wife was maintaining her real estate business, along with rentals she found for the American civilians and military. She was fantastic in her care and concern for Liane and overseeing our daughter's education at the Gymnasium, and later at the American High School where I had previously been assistant principal. I truly missed them and loved them, but this thing I found, this love affair, hit me like a bomb and I was head over heels in love with this fascinating blonde American-Italian but dominating woman. Her elegance, with perfect height and weight, made her absolutely the sexiest creature God had ever placed in my path, and she sent me completely into orbit. Our differences after I returned from Germany in the fall of 1984, I realized, were cultural. I could not shake off the deeply embedded German traces of acquired mannerisms, customs, love of the language, and intrigue of the pleasant German environment.

This element of residual love for the German way of life, language, people, and intensely deep human interaction was something I did not find in California. There was something I missed about Europe and could not refrain from continually talking about this aura of rich culture and its paragon of beauty and fascination of beautiful old and antiquated architectural settings in Germany and other parts of Europe. It is difficult to express unless one has the almost expatriate inculcation I had endured.

If Hemingway talked about the expatriates living abroad in Spain, Portugal, or Italy back in the 1930s, I certainly had a strong shot of it with the plus twenty years abroad, and living in Italy, Germany, and the Netherlands. Even with the weather, continental living was magnanimous. The six-month experience in North Africa, teaching for the Overseas Dependent Schools, only supplemented the intensity of exotic living I gained living abroad!

Problems began to arise however, when I, in May of 1984, began to anticipate leaving my lady friend behind. She had begun to extract promises from me that I could hardly believe I was making. There were instances of her asking me for assurance that I would return to be with her. Even shortly, after returning to my new location in Kitzingen, Germany, mid-August, 1984, where I attained a position as building principal, with the Department of Defense Overseas Dependent Schools the phone calls began. This was my professional dream, a school of my own, and one I could run with effortless ease, especially after the grueling years as assistant principal at Bad Kreuznach, Germany.

The traumatic crunch for me came about two weeks before the spring semester came to an end at San Diego State, in May of 1984, and I had to visit a psychiatrist. The problem for me was not that I did not want to return to Germany, it was that I could not bear the loss of the contact I had with my friend. She had planted the seed, of what I thought was eternal, love. At this point, I was drawn between the two domains-my family and Germany and my friend. She would not give up. By this time she had me sexually wrapped around her finger, and I am convinced, my complete devotion and sexual attraction also captivated her. Mid-life crisis was about to engulf me for the challenge of a lifetime!

I was a psychological wreck, went on medication prescribed by the psychiatrist I sought at the student clinic at San Diego State. He immediately inquired about my insurance coverage for further treatment, but we found out I was not covered. I wanted to go on a therapeutic Odyssey with this man, and mainly for an opening of the Pandora box of my mind. I wanted to understand myself better. After all, how could anyone with the overseas position I had, have remained in San Diego. Not because San Diego is not a fascinating place to live, but because I am in the field of education and I had been warned about the degradation of the education system, and especially in California.

Why would anyone want to leave the Overseas Dependent Schools for the surprising disappointment of teaching in these schools that was to come to me? I made the mistake and have paid the price. Not only did I eventually lose a beautiful woman and all because of her complete dominance of my mind and soul but also I ended up teaching in the San Diego City Schools for about 16 years, from 1984 to 2001. This was the tragic mistake of my life. This June and July are my last two months of California teaching in the year of 2001, and it is a summer school assignment, or one last shot of a somewhat disappointing sixteen years of secondary education.

In late August of 1984, I went back to Kitzingen Elementary School, was assigned to the K-3, 500 student school, and endured telephone calls every day for three months from the woman I thought I loved. She would not let go. There was a phenomenon about her, because not only did she want to possess me, but also she wanted to extract the acquired German culture, which was so deeply embedded in my very existence, from me. She resented anything I reminicessed about from the cultural German acquisitions built into my psychic.

Her character was strong, she was a good mother, not a faithful wife, but neither was I a faithful husband, she was an excellent teacher, and she knew she wanted to take me from the heart of Germany and Europe. She did not let go until I resigned my position overseas and returned to her. This happened in late October 1984.

When I announced to my director that I was going to give up my position, after he assigned me my own school, he thought I had gone completely out of my mind. He asked me if I was sure I wanted to do this thing, resign, and I said "Yes, I do!" He just shook his head and assured me I could come back, but only as a teacher. This was devastating to my career because I lost a lot, especially in the field of education.

I guess, at that time, because of the sexual persuasion of this woman, I would still have done what I did, but after years of reflecting, I sometimes think it was one big mistake, especially career wise. She always had a rightist attitude in a truly feminine and liberated mode, thinking I had made a mistake by getting side tracked to Europe, and wanted to re-Americanize me. She wanted to re-indoctrinate me and get me back on the right path, to again become the American I should have been all along. I am convinced that this woman had a conviction that I must be saved from my deviance in becoming Germanized.

I even had a guaranteed job at my elementary school in the field of special education at Kitzingen for her as a teacher, but she had another problem. She had a fear of flying. In late September of 1984 she bought a ticket to come over to live with me, but when she went to the airport at Lindberg Field, and approached the plane to fly to Germany, she could not get on the aircraft. She froze, turned around, went back to the terminal and cancelled the flight. I only hope it was a refundable ticket, and feel it must have been, because of her uncertainty of sincerely wanting to fly to Germany, so she, no doubt, insured herself by buying a refundable ticket and taking no risk.

With her provincial make-up, and San Diego "good living" exposure for twenty years, I can almost understand her prejudices. I often wonder how it would have been had she have made that trip. Maybe the situation would have been reversed had I have gotten her the teaching job in Germany. I could have been in command of the relationship or at least in a position of more control. She could have brought the children over for Christmas, then later on have them permanently live with her and me. She had two boys, and was actually going to leave them with the father that fall, but just could not go through with the adventure.

As sad as it may seem, I had to eventually giver her up because of the traumatic situation, and I also gave up my wife. But I succumbed to her constant brainwashing and gave up my position as principal in the K-3 school. When I actually returned to San Diego that late October of 1984, she joyfully met me at Lindberg Field. The heat of passion and excitement of seeing her again illuminated my anticipation so that my flight was seemingly short and one the most satisfying I had ever had.

The myriad of lights along the coast flying down from Los Angeles on the evening flight, after the port of entry in Los Angeles amplified my desire and elevated my passion for again being with one of the most dynamic companions I had ever known.

We lived together for about 4 years then I had to leave her because I could never make the commitment, even after my divorce in 1987. Because of her dominance I had begun to develop a great fear that I would never again know the freedom I had known all my life. She told me that because I had procrastinated, and was never sure we could make the marriage work, she rejected me when I finally did ask her to marry me. She said I waited too long without the commitment. I guess this is that part of the strong and liberated woman, or her uncertainty of me after 4 years of observing my modes that convinced her she needed a less independent type person.

I, in the long run, never wanted to give up my freedom, and wanted to explore the United States in more depth, along with other parts of the world. I did drive back east with her, visited my home in Hot Springs Village, Arkansas, in the summer of 1985. When she walked into my townhouse and saw pictures of my wife and child, she broke glass frames for

20 minutes. I knew this woman was extremely jealous and wanted no reminders of my past.

We had her 11 year-old son with us and I know he was frightened of the temper and irrationality displayed by his mother. He often resented me for displacing his father, but he did not dislike me, and I had begun to grow fond of him, the younger of the two lads. He was a nice child, and I am sure he has turned out to be a successful young man. But I often wonder how he feels about the trip we made back to Arkansas, and the one stormy night we endured because he had never experienced such weather in beautiful San Diego!

The year of studies at San Diego State University and the relations I had with the professors were very rich. I studied German, computers, education supervision, and curriculum. It was a profitable year for me building my skills, as an administrator for the Overseas Dependent Schools. I, unfortunately, never had the opportunity to put the administrative skills to use. There were the short 2 months during the school year of 1983-84 where I served as principal of the small elementary school in Kitzingen, Germany. I did, however get to teach German in 3 of the high schools for about 7 years in the San Diego City Schools, so that was profitable.

The possibility of education administration in the San Diego City Schools was an impossibility because of the control by some of the conforming robot like supervisors who have the power over any "outside the system" recruits, experience, or not. The system in San Diego is imbedded with political dominance and is as conservative as any Deep South school system in existence!

During my sabbatical I gained some great friendships with a couple of the professors at San Diego State and enjoyed my schooling there. It was fantastic to go to classes where I was respected, as an administrator in the Overseas Dependent

Schools because I had traveled, and seen numerous countries, and lived in exotic locations these gentlemen definitely envied me for. I know this to be true, because they often expressed it to me. I made all As in the administration courses and mostly Bs in the German classes, with A in a couple of them. German is definitely a difficult course, grammatically, but I loved the challenge of utilizing and assessing my own speaking and writing ability.

Some of the things I actually enjoyed in California and in the United States, were doing certain things I could not do in Germany. I loved going to a movie and eating popcorn, shopping at K-Mart, going into a Vons, attending Padre games, and also Charger games. These things I could not do in Germany. But one thing I did miss seeing was the European soccer, and especially the soccer of the better teams in Germany.

I remember a soccer game in Mönchengladbach that showed me finesse I had never before seen in sports. It was on a Saturday afternoon in November 1970 or 1971. I feel that the beauty and timing displayed by a great professional soccer team is rarely achieved in our professional American football. I watched many games of soccer while in Europe, and I feel the sport far surpasses our football for timing, precision, and endurance. I love the game of soccer and have a lot of respect for it. I hope it will someday achieve the same level of respect and popularity, in the United States, that American football has here.

Another thing I enjoy about the United States is the beautiful simplicity of traveling and seeing the wide open spaces of the West, the fantastic cotton fields of the South, the rolling low mountains such as the Ozarks in Missouri and Arkansas, or the Smokey Mountains in Tennessee. The beautiful plains of the Southwest, the green and giant

Redwoods and Sequoias of California are paragons of beauty and pleasure. Even the beautiful deserts located in Arizona and New Mexico thrill me. The Grand Canyon, I would say, is a must for all visitors to the United States!

The Northwest, with its majestic beauty, and the beautiful shores of Washington State, Oregon, and California invigorate my fondness and intense love of nature. I have traveled in all of our states except Hawaii, Alaska, and North Dakota. It is sad that I have not, at least made a token visit to the beautiful State of Hawaii, but I usually spend all my travel money returning to my second homeland of Germany. I have returned every year, and sometimes twice, since I came back to San Diego to live in 1984. Some would say I am over focusing on Europe but its richness is its calling card.

At one time I acquired a $400 ticket from American Airlines because of a delayed trip out of Frankfurt one Christmas and we sat on the tarmac for 6 hours before remaining overnight at the Frankfurt Airport, in one of the nearby hotels. I ended up giving my ex wife, Brigitte the monetary credit so she could make the trip to Hawaii, when she was visiting me in San Diego, in the summer of 1988.

On her visit to Hawaii, she saw what I hope to someday see, and she enjoyed it and never forgot the gesture of my giving her the ticket. Fortunately she visited when my brother and his wife were there, so my older brother, David, and his wife, Carol, escorted her around the island of Maui. They have made numerous trips to Hawaii and know the area well. They rented a jeep and saw all the interesting sights. This made my lovely German wife happy and helped heal some of the wounds of the divorce we went reluctantly through in 1987.

Brigitte was loved by most of my family, as I was by her family. We had almost the perfect marriage, with only the exception of physical attraction, and that was the element that made make me break away from her while attending San Diego State, getting side-tracked by a woman who had been waiting for some fool like me!

The differences in Europe and the United States are simple to verbalize, and I find that if one has an attachment for both areas, then one should do as I now do, and spend some time in each place. I find living in the United States somewhat easier as far as conveniences because here one has the accessibility of convenient auto travel which Europe does not seem to provide. But the warmth and intricate beauty afforded by such places as Germany, Italy, Switzerland, and Austria are more difficult to attain when traveling in the United States. The Gemütlichkeit (cozy, warmth, and sanguinity in feelings), provided in German homes and cities, is almost impossible to replicate in the United States. I have, however, found some German wives who moved to the United States who seem to import this quality of Gemütlichkeit right into their homes.

What can be found here in the United States and not in Europe, is the freedom of the vastness and wide-open spaces. I am firmly convinced that I really need to have access to both European culture and that of the United States for the fulfillment of life I need. People who have not experienced what I have, spending 25 years in Europe, and the 44 years in the United States, not quite half and half, but a solid part of my life was spent abroad, and mostly in Europe, do not miss the contrast. The two domains I have experienced, and one could say three, considering the time I spent in North Africa, but not the full experience of the whole of Africa, have provided me with the ability to compare, reflect, and evaluate those three domains of my past. All have their strengths and weaknesses.

Because of the beautiful experiences my years abroad brought me, I did have some trouble readjusting to the different society that the United States provided after I returned. But after the re-indoctrination, I found that, probably the most ideal situation for me is to do exactly what I plan to do in my remaining years, and that is to share, as explicitly stated, the two domains, Europe and the United States. It might even be possible to spend 50% of my time here, in the United States, and 50 % of my time in Europe, especially Germany.

Fortunately I have an understanding with the German Volkshochschule, Bad Kreuznach, Evening Adult Education system, that I am welcome to teach for them, with about three or four months notice. I can then be placed in their catalogue, as a visiting English teacher. The Volkshochschule personnel praised my seven years of teaching from 1977 through 1983 and vociferously request me each time I visit the Bad Kreuznach Volkshochschule administration center to again teach for them upon my return to Deutschland.

It is quite interesting to meet persons who actually do spend half their time in Europe and half their time in the United States because they always have the nostalgic desire to split their time in each arena. I met a gentleman in the Netherlands in 1970, and found that he shared his time between Europe and the United States. He told me that after about 6 months in the Netherlands, he yearns for the United States. Then when he returns to the United States for about six months, he misses the Netherlands and other parts of Europe.

I found this, already, to be true. After awhile here, and especially a year of teaching, I am ready for an August or December trip back to Germany and other parts of Europe. It is no wonder that film stars and business executives, who have the money, maintain several residences. They exercise the freedom of movement provided by their riches, then travel back and forth.

Fortunately, from 1960 to 1984, while teaching for the Department of Defense Dependent Schools allowed me this freedom, because I was traveling back to the CONUS at least once a year. I made one Christmas trip back in 1972, just to be with my family in Arkansas so I could get a rejuvenation of Christmas with some of them in order to relive the past experiences I had had as a child in Arkansas. That trip was actually somewhat of a disappointment because I did not grasp the nostalgic feelings I had as a child. Too much from the past was missing. My father died in 1957, and my mother was living with my sister in Midland, Texas, though I saw her and my sisters and brothers while on that trip around the United States.

I made the whole United States swing. I got a ticket that allowed me to visit almost any city I wanted, and those were Seattle, San Diego, Midland, Texas, Little Rock, Arkansas, then return, via New York City, to Frankfurt, Germany before school started in January of 1973.

The stop in New York involved a visit with a long time friend whom I attended Vanderbilt Peabody University with in the late 1950s. He had a beautiful large apartment on Park Avenue South, near Central Park. Rose Kennedy, mother of John F. Kennedy lived a couple of floors above him so the place was very expensive.

Dennis is the name of my friend and he never forgot our friendship in our college days because I would loan him money, feed him, and chase ladies with him when I was 26 years old and he was only 19. I also visited him at his home in West Palm Beach, Florida between quarters in 1958 and got to meet his very nice mother who was also a teacher. I think she wanted Dennis to become a teacher with his music major from the very fine music and education institution, George Peabody College for Teachers, as it was called then. It is my understanding that Vanderbilt and Peabody are now a combined institution now.

Dennis, however, married a lovely lady, whose father was a retired admiral, so Dennis, with strong in-law support and prestige, became a stockbroker in the Big Apple. He later became president of one of the branches of American Express, and was very successful in the big city.

Before Dennis got married, he visited me in Germany but he had another very wealthy lady on the trip, that entailed a 30-day swing through Western Europe. This was, about 1964 or 1965, and they spent a few days with me in my apartment on Ramstein Airbase. I had the rather large officer's quarter on-base apartment. The lady was about 20 years older than Dennis, who was about 26 years old and she was over 55, but could put away more scotch than any youngster I have ever known.

I jokingly called my friend a gigolo, and he never denied it. Dennis was invited to accompany the lady on the trip and she had made many trips abroad, so it was not a new experience for them. They sailed from New York, picked up a car in London, then after a few days with me and Brigitte, they drove on down to the French Riviera, then on to Italy for a few weeks. They were to return, eventually, to London, and sail back to New York.

Such a trip for Dennis was a must so he could keep up his social appearances in New York and strut with the Madison Avenue group. He was one of the best friends I ever had, and if I ever landed in New York, he insisted that I either stay in his elaborate apartment or in the St. Moritz Hotel, only a few meters from his apartment on Park Avenue South near Central Park. I got to know a lot about New York and went to several plays when visiting Dennis. Before he married he lived in an apartment downtown but it was very convenient, and I spent a couple of nights with him while traveling through with Liane and Brigitte.

After he married the admiral's daughter is when he started his social climb and even became a member of the Metropolitan Opera advisory board. I presume he is still active in his association with the Met. He was a music-major, and in numerous musicals at Peabody College for Teachers in Nashville, when I first met him.

One interesting experience I had was when I was invited to dinner with Dennis, and I was flying back to the United States. I spent three days with him and he invited me to luncheon where he had two ladies, also members of the advisory board of the New York Metropolitan Opera. I, with my fluent German, conversed with one of the elderly ladies who was in her mid-sixties, and she thought I was an extraordinary human because I could carry on a fluent conversation in German. She was an immigrant, and had never lost her accent, and most definitely never lost her fortune. We were having lunch in one of those stuffed shirt New York businessmen's club somewhere in downtown New York, and the whole thing was absolutely fantastic because Dennis loved to make impressions and he did that day.

I think that today I would not have been so impressed with the gala, and exquisite mixture of socialites. One thing for sure, though, is that the element I mixed with in New York City certainly is many levels above the phony sets one meets in California. There is something very rich about the social setting in New York City. They are not too detached from the rich element of social genre one encounters in Europe. San Diego has its super conservative black tie and tuxedo set, but I have only had one exposure. The millionaire lady with whom I attended one of those balls is no longer one of my dating mates.

The opera, symphonies, plays, and truly rich setting of New York are not phony. California, on the other hand, has provided me the opportunity to meet the most disappointing elements in society. It seems here that the whole social stratum is tinny, phony, and insincere. I have never encountered such pretenders as one finds in this state. If one really wants to find these elements, one can merely look at the educators around San Diego, and I am referring, especially to the administrative structure in San Diego. There is also a conservative atmosphere that permeates the whole structure of San Diego. I thought I left that element when I left the Deep South but someway conservatism radiates in San Diego. One only has to read the Union-Tribune and one picks up the flavor quickly.

I imagine the reason our airport is still "bush league" and cannot be compared with Pittsburgh, Chicago, or Denver, is because of the tendency for the powers running this city not wanting the convenience of our little unique Lindberg Field being displaced. The insufficient airport is too convenient for the small town thinkers who dwell in this area, even if the population is over 2,000,000. The logical place to have put the airport would have been through negotiations with the U. S. Navy and share the field at Miramar. Minute brains of the city are also stifling the proposed ballpark, which San Diego is trying to build.

But, again, look at the San Diego City Schools. They are one large fiasco, and I attribute the lack of a progressive and a meaningful education program to the conservative top-down management, and lack of bringing in innovative educators to run it. Their mathematics and science programs are disgraceful, and the classes are so overloaded. There has only recently been an effort to reduce the pupil-teacher ratio so kids will have a chance to learn. Programs are not set up to meet the needs of the students, and I expect things to become terrible before they improve in San Diego and the rest of California.

Not only did I fall into a provincial setting when I came to San Diego, but I found that the people living in this area do not care what an individual knows or has qualifications to do if the person does not have a political inroad into the system. The system being the schools, corporations, or city structure. This is one far-out in left-field, Provincial City.

One of the saving graces this city provided me when I came, in its small town atmosphere, was a lucky break when I met a young Polish gentleman whose name is Lech Piecyk. It was like a dream being sent from heaven when I met this young man, ex soccer player from Germany, and a business owner in downtown San Diego. His parties are absolutely "Continental!" Lech owns a travel agency and at one of his parties there will be no less than 5 languages spoken.

When one is invited to his beautiful large condo in La Jolla, there will never be less than 15 to 25 people. Just listen and you hear the following languages being spoken: English, German (Lech, his wife, Frances, and I speak German together), Spanish, Polish, Mandarin, Italian, Flemish, Japanese, Togalog, and often French. If this strikes my reader in an odd manner, folks, that is just what happens in such an international setting.

Thank God for the attractive weather in San Diego because that is what brings foreigners here by the hordes. This is like another French Riviera, only without the French and its inviting culture. I would be hesitant to bring some of the editors of the Union-Tribune to such a party because they would think they were being taken over by foreigners or there was a conspiracy to overthrow the founding fathers of San Diego.

It is not difficult to see that my associations are primarily founded upon these social-strata which I have found through this very energetic, athletic, and cosmopolitan young friend. Lech loves to practice his German, which he learned while studying and playing soccer in Germany in the mid-1980s.

His children, one boy, the youngest, and the daughter, the older, speak English, Mandarin, Polish, and I think they have a facility in Spanish because of their past nanny from Central America. This is the only element of European culture, that I enjoyed so much while living in Germany, the Netherlands, and Italy.

Comparatively speaking, when one is in Europe, there is no air of Provincialism when one is entertaining guests. I so dearly loved the European setting because of the expansive processes of multi-linguialism, continental flair, and just down-to-earth sincere people who want to improve in the intellectual processes of everyday life. That is the flair and element Europe provides!

These are the things I sincerely miss about Germany and the rest of Europe. The multi-cultured setting, multi-linguistic processes, and richness in the arts, architecture, and sincere people. With many complaints of Californians about Mexico and Spanish speaking persons living in this area, I must say that might be the element San Diego needs. I cannot understand how the conservative base has held on as long as it has, especially with the influx of multi-nationals.

But I do predict that with the Asian, Spanish, and European insurgence into this society and its beautiful location, things might change. The extreme conservative sees this as a detriment and displacement of the good old solid Americans, but I see it as an extension of the multi-cultural richness that could turn the conservatism in this area around in the near future.

The only thing that keeps me interested in living in this area, except for the fantastic weather, are the contacts I have with my European friends. These multi-lingual friends have certainly stimulated my social experience in San Diego. At each party or gathering I find the conversation related to recent travels to China, Japan, Europe, the Middle East, or Russia. These acquaintances never sit still and spend about 25% of their time traveling. I cannot travel this often but do make one or two trips a year abroad.

The shocking experience of returning to San Diego was ameliorated by the embellishment of a continental and cosmopolitan flare provided by Lech, his wife, Frances, and also the many friends they have from all over the world. The culture shock of returning to the CONUS (Continental United States) in 1983 proved not to be so extremely frightening because of the richness propagated by these fantastic Europeans and Asians acquaintances. They could have been Africans or Middle Easterners, but my need was for a group of people who did not impinge on my already stagnant view of some of the local and conservative natives and elements of San Diego.

The "international" setting that I fell into through Lech Piecyk's acquaintance brought on new experiences that were quite similar to what my mind had expanded to while living in Europe. The richness in growth I had attained through the many years of living abroad gave me a thirst for going beyond the local "small town" setting which permeates San Diego's hub and cocky conservative clan of subtle, almost Nazi like conservatism. This may strike people in an odd way to think that such an atmosphere exists.

Actually, super conservative elements one can be found past the east side of La Mesa, and citizens who live in San Diego can name the areas. Some of the conservative aura permeates, in my opinion, the inner-heart of this city. These elements are only more polished, subtle, underlying, and propagate the conservative flair that holds San Diego down from becoming a vibrant international city. Its threshold of becoming a truly cosmopolitan area might someday, however, engulf many of the die-hard conservative tendencies which, in my opinion, prevail in San Diego.

I am aware of these elements from the school district and other associations I have encountered are in all strata of the city. One begins to feel these vibrations only a few days after arriving in San Diego. The city is not nearly as progressive as it should be. San Diego's conservatism is a mode I do not like to see bestowed upon such a beautiful city, but the elements I have encountered through the school system, experienced through reading the Union-Tribune, and through day-by-day associations have convinced me of its almost ultraconservatism. There is much to be desired for a city with such a high potential. Improvements need to be made in attitudes, and someday they will come, but not in the near future I am afraid.

The return to the United States and my 16 years apart from Germany have been interesting, my job with the youth in the secondary schools made it more interesting, especially teaching German in three of the high schools here. But the overall experience does not compare with the richness I encountered from 1960 to 1983 while living in Africa, Germany, Italy, and the Netherlands!

The people left behind by Hitler have also expanded their horizons by extensive travel, and thousands have visited the United States since post World War II events. The many Germans I have met in Germany and traveling in the United States only laud the vast freedom and unique variety of weather and life modes offered by the United States. Their praise of the ability to travel from coast to coast, whether by air, train, auto, or bus, with conveniences and reasonable prices cannot quite be duplicated in Germany or Europe. It is only the richness and depth of culture embedded in past elements of architecture, antiquity, multiple languages, and the multiplicity diverse nations of the European past that cannot be duplicated in the United States.

Chapter 12

Contrasting Richness of Europe To The United States

When one spends twenty years abroad, one must realize that there is a metamorphosis that transpires in the psychic of that individual. This definitely happened to me. My twenty years abroad, beginning with my 6 month stay in Tripoli, Libya, was an experience that was, without a doubt, one of excitement, adventure, love, and enlightenment. My military service and years abroad extracted me from the protected, provincial setting of my youth. This was from the time I entered the U. S. Navy, graduated from the University of Arkansas, then attained my master's degree at Vanderbilt-Peabody University in Nashville, Tennessee, when I was 26 years of age.

My early years as a child through college years in Arkansas led me to believe that if I ever had the opportunity to escape from the small state and venture out into the world, I would at least begin to have a basis for comparison. When I entered the United States Navy, after activation of my Navy unit in Camden, Arkansas in 1952, Korea War, it began my metamorphosis, or evolvement into a person with a broader international perspective.

I got on the train as a recruit headed toward Great Lakes Training Center during the Korean conflict between North and South Korea in February 1952. I was only 19 years old and about to become 20 years of age a few days after leaving Little Rock, Arkansas, bound for boot camp at Great Lakes, Illinois. What enlightenment this was for me. The young men on the train, from different parts of Arkansas, began drinking Manhattans, Vodka Tonics, and Bourbon and Coke. Many must have been 21 years of age, because I was not yet old enough to order alcohol. Some of the recruits were rough, raw products who had tried for exemption from their colleges such as Magnolia State College, Henderson College, or other colleges in the Arkansas area, but to no avail. I too failed to receive an exemption, suitable grades or not. They were celebrating their departure from home and were looking forward to becoming young adults!

I, still innocent and alcohol free, enjoyed the ride and the sleeping quarters paid for by the United States Navy. I made the train ride, not knowing, and wondering what would happen to me in the next few weeks. It did not take long for me to find out when the others, about 30 recruits or more, and I, reached the Great Lakes Training Center greeting center and began our adventure with the United States Navy.

It was a cold 3 months or so for our boot camp that we endured, drilling, training, and suffering the cold marches from the mess hall to the training halls of the Great Lakes Training Center. We marched everywhere we went. I never knew my ears could get so cold as they did with the cold wind whistling from the north to freeze me each day I marched around the training center.

Letters from home seemed to be the only thing that provided the solitude of knowing I had friends and family back in a normal everyday society. I awaited the mail calls with an anticipation of a child awaiting Santa's presents on a Christmas morning. All the letters I wrote brothers, sisters, and girl friends began to pay off. I received so many letters at each mail call that I was the envy of the others in my company. I was not lazy about writing letters.

After the 12 weeks of intense training, and our company not winning one flag for outstanding performance, I began to wonder why or Chief Petty Officer Tague could not outperform the First Class Petty Officer in the barracks next door. About 30 years later I heard that college students who are inducted are the most difficult ones to drill into the blind obedience the military demands of them. I did not realize that it was not because of our inability to learn, but because we had the ability to think and question the brain washing commands of the military. Maybe we were all void of a desire for team cooperation because we never did become an outstanding company.

Nevertheless, after my three months or so, and completion of basic training I was selected, because of my mechanical aptitude, to attend the mechanics school in Norman, Oklahoma. I realized that this was not too bad since I was denied my first choice as an Air Control person, then Weatherman school for my second choice. I rationalized my status and realized that I was not the highest I.Q. of the lot, so accepted my appointment for the 3 month school in Norman, Oklahoma. After that I was accepted to the advanced Aviation Mechanic School that lasted until about November 1952.

After the general preparation course and completing the Aviation Mechanic program at Norman, Oklahoma, I was assigned to a squadron called VC-11 at North Island in San

Diego, California. I spent the remainder of my time there and was discharged in late December 1953. I was just short of two years in the United States Navy because of early release, since the Korean conflict had ended. Ironically the conflict is still ongoing and one wonders if it really ended because of the present status of the two countries. Friction between North Korea and South Korea seems to be a constant problem.

After my discharge in December, it was back to college, undergraduate at the Monticello A & M College, which is today the University of Arkansas, Monticello, Arkansas. In June 1957 I finished undergraduate school, taught at Woodlawn High School, Woodlawn, Arkansas, near Pine Bluff, Arkansas. After one year there, being utterly disgusted with provincial rural high school teaching, I was hired at a preparatory school in Metairie, near the city of my dreams, New Orleans, Louisiana. It was near New Orleans that I taught at Ridgewood Preparatory School that was owned by a wonderful man by the name of O. O. Stuckey. This was an adventure that could be compared, in some ways, to living in Europe. New Orleans is a city of excellent food, a constant bustle of continental people, and a city I shall never forget because of its magnetic charm.

The year was 1958-59 in New Orleans and how the time did fly by. I loved every minute of it, except for teaching spoiled 7th and 8th grade students in the lovely suburb of Metairie, Louisiana. These children's parents were the backbone of many of the businesses in New Orleans. Today I would compare the uniqueness of New Orleans with some of the cities of Europe. This is mostly because of its unending selection of excellent restaurants and exciting places to see, with a spirit of excitement almost every day and night.

After this venture I continued working on my master's degree at Peabody College in Nashville, Tennessee. I completed the degree in December, 1959, then proceeded to California, and left Toni Moon, one of the loveliest women I have ever dated, crying and asking me when I would return. I told her that it would not be too long, but lied, because I never returned for her, but did return to study in the 1960s. She was a charming lady and I often wonder what happened to this beautiful person.

In December 1959 I proceeded to San Diego, California where I lived with my brother Jim in San Diego for a month, then went to Glendale, California and lived in my brother Max's house where my brother David resided. I then proceeded to substitute teach in Glendale, California and found out that in the early 1960s California had very decent schools, at least in that area. California, at that time had much better schools and teacher prestige than today. Glendale, as I recall was the home of George Lincoln Rockwell, leader of the American Neo-Nazi Party. I also recall there were few Black students at this time in the area.

It is very interesting that I was rejected for a job in Pasadena after interviewing with the school board there. At that time their reasoning for not giving me a contract was because of my Southern accent, I was told, and would not fit in with the inner-city environment which had a large population of Black students. I wonder how such an explanation of non-hiring would fit into our society in the year 2001?

It was in January 1960 that my brother David and I interviewed with the U. S. Air Force, under the Department of Defense Overseas Schools and I was accepted to go to Iceland but turned them down. After the second offer, which was Tripoli, Libya, I looked at the map in a world atlas, saw its location directly on the Mediterranean Sea. I made my choice and was off that August of 1960 to Tripoli, Libya. I flew from Los Angeles, California, to Charleston, South Carolina, then departed after one night in Charleston, to the beautiful exotic city of Tripoli, Libya. It was a city full of Arabs, camels, date palms, and a beautiful Mediterranean Sea with beautiful clear blue-green water. I remember it vividly.

While flying to Charleston, a lady sitting next to me told me to write all my impressions down when I arrived in the distant and exotic city of Tripoli, Libya. This I did, and submitted the article in to my local newspaper, the Eagle Democrat, Warren, Arkansas. They gladly published the article of one of their citizens and my extensive and unending impressions of the encounter were printed, word for word, with very little editing. I, to this day, do not know where I left the article, although it might still be among the collections of my ex wife, Brigitte Stell, in Hargesheim, Germany.

The difference in the culture of North Africa and the United States was almost traumatic! I could not believe what I saw. The fantastic Libyan Desert, camels, veiled women, men with white long robes, beautiful shores of the Mediterranean, hordes of people speaking Arabic, and strange customs made me wonder if I was still Larry B. Stell. This was a sight to behold, and I was astonished at the difference in this culture and my native existence while living in the United States.

One thing in particular I noticed was that I, as a foreigner, stood out among the Libyan culture and was constantly being watched and scrutinized by these Arabic women and men. I was the one who was different and unusual for these Moslems who wondered just what I was doing in their land.

On base I discovered that the money we used was script. It was funny money and something one had to live with. I think we were paid in U. S. Dollars, but we could purchase items, eat at the officer's club, and do our general shopping with only script. There was too much danger of black market to use Greenbacks. We would purchase Libyan Lira when we went to town and ate in restaurants or shopped at stores. There was some kind of black market going on there but I never really caught the full picture and only lived there for 6 months so never grasped just what corrupt processes really existed between base personnel and the locals.

While living in Libya, I fell in love with a blonde British young lady, was sexually satisfied with her fantastic charms, and she remained with me for the whole semester I was there. She cried and made all kinds of protests when she learned that I was to transfer to Germany in January 1961. But she was great company and was employed as a secretary for a British company and the tour of duty was two years. She had been there only about 3 months when I met her.

Her name was Gloria and she had blue eyes, was attractive, and was British all the way. I never had another girl friend while I was in Tripoli, and was with her constantly. She was rather formal and often criticized my informal and nonchalant American ways. I was not completely in love with her but became accustom to her ways.

I also met some lovely Italian ladies who were just about the most charming ladies I had yet encountered in my young life, but were only casual acquaintances. I danced with them, took them out, was picked up for having two of them in my 1952 MG sports car, which was a two-seater, but since we had 3 people in the car, was given a ticket by a Libyan policeman. The two Italian beauties were adorable and I had met them at a private party where they were dancing up a rhythmic storm to which I could, at that time, not keep up with. I had not yet gotten into my Latin dancing, which I am now almost an expert at, but at that time knew nothing about.

In December of 1960 I met with a local American/British group of actors and was selected as a member the cast of a play which was to be put on by the American/British Embassy in

March. I was selected for a part in the play, and I am no actor, so the talent must have been scarce in that far outpost. To this day I do not remember which play we were scheduled to put on. I presume I was replaced since I got word in early January 1961 of my transfer to Ramstein, Germany, so I could not carry out my obligation as an actor in the American/British Embassy production.

The beauty of Africa was, in my opinion, exotic and fascinating. I would drive along the coast of the Mediterranean and enjoy the ancient Roman ruins of Sabratha, 45 minutes to the west of Tripoli, and Leptis Magna, 90 miles to the east of Tripoli. These were fantastic Roman ruins. These beautiful ruins, set against an azure Mediterranean Sea, are inviting to any tourist who wants to see an example of architectural antiquity along this beautiful coastline.

Only about three years ago Libya established a Ministry of Tourism. Since 1995, Libyan officials say they have counted over 85,000 visitors. About one-third as many arrive in neighboring Egypt in an average month, so Libya is still striving to get back into the world arena as far as tourist trade goes.

Sabratha, the ancient ruins 45 minutes west of Tripoli, the capital of Libya, was first inhabited by the Phoenicians in the sixth century BC and also boasts a Roman theater restored in the 1920s by Italian experts. I have seen it and it is quite an architectural sight.

When I lived in Libya, King Idris who was overthrown several years after I left controlled the country. In 1961, Colonel Moammar Gadhafi, the Libyan leader who in the past, has been unfriendly toward the United States and drove our military out of the country overthrew the King and has been in power ever since.

One effect of the UN sanctions, imposed since 1992 because of Libya's refusal to surrender suspects accused in the

1988 bombing of a Pan American airliner, has been to ground most of the country's domestic air fleet. This has really limited many tourists in their bid to travel in this interesting country.

The largest collection of ruins, at Leptis Magna, which lay on Tripoli's eastern shore, are the remains of what was once a city of 100,000 people, and are listed by the United Nations as a World Heritage Site. I have walked about these fantastic ruins and they are a sight to behold in its antiquated beauty. I would be very cautious, however, today, about visiting Libya, especially with the attitude Gadhafi still has toward Americans.

My departure from Libya, was, in one way joyful, but in another way sad because the transfer came so suddenly in January of 1961 that I ran about the city trying to shoot pictures with a new camera I had purchased at the post exchange. I knew little about ASA settings of a camera so did not match the ASA settings properly with the speed of the film. Many of my slides turned out under exposed, and this was very disappointing because of my practice of capturing photos in all areas of the world I have traveled or lived in.

I was soon to leave the beautiful desert sands and Mediterranean Sea. I was about to go on a 20-year plus adventure of living in Europe. Libya actually had much more to see, but fate took me away, and it was to my advantage in one way. My desire to venture into Germany was soon to be fulfilled.

The 1,100 mile-mile Mediterranean coast, which contains Greek, Phoenician, and Roman ruins, provides some of the region's most beautiful archaeological treasures. Libya has much to offer and it is a country that earns 96 percent of its income from oil.

Libya has pronounced tourism to be "the industry of the 21st century." If the psychological barriers could be removed, the potential for tourism in the future is absolutely fantastic. I would love to return to the country in the future, if the attitudes of the leaders ever become positive enough to make the visits pleasant for Americans.

As I look back on my experiences in Libya, I feel that the country had some Southern European transitional value for me in acquiring European and especially Italian tastes because of the 1911 occupation of the country by the Italians. Some of the disdain toward the Italians by the Libyans was manifested in everyday experiences because I witnessed this in the Arabic Libyan citizens at various times. There were many businesspersons of Italian heritage that I dealt with for various reasons. They spoke Italian, Arabic, and English so they were excellent salespersons for the Americans and the British residing there, and were also able to communicate well in Arabic.

Libya, with its oil discovery in 1959, elevated its economic status to a level the Libyans had never known in this century. By the 1960s Libya was among the world's largest suppliers of oil.

In the 1969 coup under Colonel Muammar al-Qaddafi overthrew King Idris and established the Libyan Arab Republic. The military bases of the USA and the British, however, after that were not renewed.

From the Pan African News Agency (Dakar) in a news release for the web on October 27, 2000, the Italian government accepted to pay 260 million US dollars as damages of its occupation of Libya in 1911. This process might assuage some of the disdainful feelings manifested by the Libyans toward the Italians while I was there in 1960.

From the news release, I quote: "The agency said that Italy also undertook to compensate the Libyan people for the ills they suffered during the colonial period.

The signing of the agreement Thursday coincided with the day of remembrance of thousands of Libyans where were deported in October 1911 to the barren islands in southern Italy, where thousands of them died from diseases, famine, and bad weather.

Tripoli had asked Rome to explain what happened to all the deportees. Since the 1999 July apology, relations between the two countries have markedly improved."

Maybe the relations will continue to improve between the Italians and the Libyans, but I also hope the country of Libya which was known, before the discovery of oil in 1959, as the "sand box" but this chastisement ceased after the great oil discovery. After the oil economically propelled Libya to higher status, with its nearness to the main markets of Europe, the Libyans could economically take pride in their world status as an oil producer.

I include the experiences in Libya as transitional to European living because of Tripoli's partial European culture with its Italian influence. Much of this was, of course, because of the Italian's colonial possession. After the end of the Second World War, and brief British and French rule, then the United Nations oversight, Libya became independent in 1951. My experience living there from1960-1961 was while oil money was being thrown around, but it did not appear to be well distributed among the many poor citizens I saw in the area. Under King Idris, with a strong monarchy, it is no wonder people remained poor and deprived. Beggars were behind every rock, crevice, and in every alley.

Nevertheless, the experiences in North Africa would have to be considered in my comparisons between the United States, Europe, and North Africa. That is why I have included my experiences in the, now oil rich, Libya, which lies along the beautiful Mediterranean Sea and is a country I hope to again visit. It is also an area where the great German Field Marshal Rommel spent time during the Second World War.

It was in February of 1941 that Erwin Rommel took his Afrika Korps into Libya. For his successes there he made field marshal and was named "the desert fox." In 1942 he pressed almost into Alexandria, Egypt, but was stalled by fierce British resistance and lack of supplies. A British offensive overwhelmed (October-November 1942) the German forces at Alamein. Rommel was recalled to Germany before the Afrika Korp's final defeat. He was commander of Northern France when the Allies invaded Normandy in June 1944. Allied success led Rommel, who had lost his respect for Hitler, to agree to a plot to remove Hitler from office. Wounded in an air raid in July of 1944, he had just recovered when he was forced to take poison because of his part in the attempt on Hitler's life in July 1944.

While roaming the desert caves and hills south of Libya, one can still see signs and traces left by Allied forces on various stones and walls. I drove south and looped back to the Mediterranean Sea on sunny day in late October of 1960 I was driving a new 1960 Volkswagen which was well built for the Libyan Desert. One does not have a radiator in this little jewel of an auto so is delightful for such expositions.

Then, in January of 1961, came my reassignment to my target country, and that was Germany. Most of my twenty plus years abroad were spent in Germany, with one year in Italy, and five years in the Netherlands. I have a solid basis of experience for comparing the United States to Europe and parts of North Africa. I also find the topic of contrasted cultures to be one of extreme interest. This, no doubt, stems from my past years pursuing sociology and human anthropology in graduate school.

My years in Germany, after landing in Wiesbaden, on an Air Force DC-4, the four engine reciprocating, propeller driven aircraft utilized in World War II, were to be the most exciting, pleasant years of my life. My immediate attraction to the German people, even with their postwar economic disadvantages in the 1960s, was overwhelming.

I immediately loved the attitudes, mentality, culture, architecture, work ethic, language, and friendliness of the German people. The years spent in Germany between 1961 and 1983 were to become an inert part of my being and psychic.

It is quite easy for a tourist who spends 10 days highlighting the major cities of Europe, such as London, Paris, Rome, Berlin, Prague, Budapest, and cities in Scandinavia, to make a comparison to his or her homeland in the United States. But because of the short exposure, the comparison is, of course, somewhat superficial. Twenty years plus seems to taint the soul in a manner that gratifies one's being if the environment is pleasant and it was.

It is most challenging for me to expound, especially on the sociological psychic of the German people, and also significant to delve in the general aspects of much of Europe in general. The beautiful memories and dominantly positive exposure of my years abroad elevate my soul and inner being.

As a youngster who was brought up in Little Rock, Arkansas, and one who dreamed about visits to Europe, it was to be almost a quarter of century of residing in Germany and Western Europe. Because of my reading about the area during the Second World War, and studying European History in college, I had dreams about possibly visiting Europe someday but never imagined making the extended partial life's journey I was to take from 1960 through 1984.

When making comparisons, one must have traveled in both settings, and I have traveled, extensively, in the United States, with the exception of Alaska, Hawaii, and North Dakota. But as far as the heart and feelings of the United States and those of Europe, I feel quite qualified to render my heartfelt opinion of the contrast between the two continents. Because of the multitude of interactions with Europeans and Germans for the many years of a delightful odyssey in that part of the world, delving into the their existence stimulates my overall psychic.

When one thinks of the greatest things in the United States, one thinks about freedom of travel, expression, earning a living, and freedom of the wide-open spaces. All things are quite wonderful but the comparison ends when one is looking for antiquated things of beauty, architecture, developed societies found in the magnificent historical medieval settings. In most of Europe and Germany, the centuries and multitudes of varied cultures intensify the curiosity of one's mind.

One cannot sell short, the beauty of the fall and spring seasons in many places in the United States. The variety of foods, festivals, and friendliness of our people to each other and strangers is characteristic of Americans, making this country a pleasure to visit.

If I were to select a city that I considered to have some of the characteristics of those features I loved most in Europe, I would select New Orleans. I first heard about New Orleans, as a child living in Warren, Arkansas, where I spend the first 8 years of my life. I heard it was a great place to visit but never got the true flavor until I had the good fortune to teach in a private school, in Metairie, Louisiana, from 1958 to 1959.

A friend of mine whom I remember with fondness, Jimmy Hopson, New Edingburg, Arkansas, was a college friend of mine from the University of Arkansas, Monticello campus. He told me his uncle had a private school in Metairie, Louisana, just on the outskirts of New Orleans.

In July of 1958, I took a trip with Jimmy to spend a charming weekend with his uncle, O. O. Stuckey, and go through an interview with the Headmaster of Ridgewood Preparatory School. I went through the interview and was awarded a contract for the school year 1958-59.

My time in New Oleans, where I lived on St. Charles Avenue, heart of the beautiful Garden District, was story book. The beautiful restaurants, friendly people with their charming New Orleans speech, the Mardi Gras, exquisite French Quarters, and the beautiful port of New Orleans sent me into orbit as a young man all of 26 years old. This is one year of my life that had deep, rich impressions and I will never forget this intensely impressive experience.

It was the only part of the United States I ever lived in, left for a weekend, and could not wait to return. In fact I still feel that way about the city. I return at least every two years and try to recapture some of the quaint feelings that enraptured my life at such a young age.

As previously alluded to, my private school experience was fascinating and I taught students whose parents were many of the business leaders of the city. Many such families were department store owners, and one I vividly remember by the name of Labiche. Marcus was the son and this particular family I remember, especially after the conference with the very elegant father trying to shed light on why his son was a spoiled child who needed understanding. What the hell did I, as a new teacher of 26, know about true understanding of adolescence, but what I had studied in college? Marcus was a persistent and dynamically demanding student among his class peers. I finally worked it out and he passed my class, but not without constant vigilance of his pranks.

I remember others, and particularly one Jewish family that invited me to dinner, showered me with gifts at Christmas, and had three lovely children. One of the young men I looked up and called about 4 years ago while visiting New Orleans invited me to dinner on my next trip. His name is Michael Berger and they owned Berger's Jewelry store on Canal Street while I was living there. I visited them once or twice in the late 1960s on returning from Germany. During that visit the jewelry store was still in the same location.

Michael told me he has now moved the store to Metairie where it is safer and more profitable to run. He also told me his brother, Larry, the same name as mine, is doing well. I asked about the sister, who was also in my class rode the bus I drove each day to pick them up or drop them off, to and from school. Loraine, I believe is the name of the sister, and was quite mature and definitive about life at her young age. The bus driving supplemented my salary so I could make a decent living as a teacher.

When making overall comparisons between the United States and Europe, I can readily say that both places excite me. Europe in its richness of history depth, and beautiful ancient Roman remnants, such as SPA cities, aqueducts, medieval cities, beautiful medieval cathedrals and Gothic designs, and the touch of antiquity, outweigh the United States because of the hundreds of years in its continuum. Europe is too rich in the historical arena for one not to choose it for its unending beauty in a historical sense. The openness and free feelings I get while living in the United States also intensify my desire of insatiable craving for endless expansion in spatial movement!

My satisfaction scale of living from 1960 through 1983, while in North Africa and Europe attained levels of 9.5 to 10 just because of the newness and potential for exploring the magnificence and beauty in numerous cities and countries. The charm and beauty of Europe is essentially the formula that matched my curiosity from the age of 28, when I first flew to Africa, until I was 51 years of age in 1983, and returned to the United States.

Sometimes I think the intensity of savoring wine as an integral part of European living, with it supplemental enhancement of exquisite meals is enough to capture one's spirit of enjoyment. As a young person, at the age of 26, and living in New Orleans, then later spending time around Los Angeles in 1959 and 1960, I began to experience the satisfaction and charm of consuming better meals with wine. However, the frequency of wine consumption in its beauty during most meals is more prevalent in Europe, and intensifies expression and a release of tension while transcending the multiplicity of European experiences.

The times in Germany and Europe that I would feel the surge of finding new adventure would occur mostly when I would drive my beat up old Volkswagen, and later other vehicles, still dependable, even with its ten year longevity, but exploring every nook and cranny of my new home. I reveled at the opportunity to go out and explore the green forests, mountains, and villages of this enchanting country and neighboring countries.

My European locations gave me the opportunity to visit Spain, France, or Italy, while living abroad. These magnificent opportunities were right at my doorstep. I remember one Christmas vacation and I wanted to try out my new 1961 Volkswagen, taking my future bride to be along with me, with our sights set on visiting Barcelona. I, with proper passport and she, Brigitte, only carrying an Ausweiss, (National ID) for citizens of Germany, got to the corridor of Spain. The ID was not a proper passport for visiting some countries, and Spain, with its strong ruler, Franco, was restricted from use of any pass except the passport.

We tried to sneak through, with my wife to be pretending not to understand the guards. But the border guards in an authoritative but friendly manner stopped us, turned us around and back we drove to France. I learned one lesson from that day on and that was that one should take his or her passport when traveling outside of Germany. Even when crossing the border to neighboring France. I saw to it that my fiancée, Brigitte von Jagow obtained a passport and no embarrassment would ever again occur.

We did make the best of it however and drove to some nice areas during our winter holidays of 1961, including Marseilles, and other points of interest in the lovely country of Southwestern France. At that time the cost of hotels and food in France were as ridiculously low as in Germany. We ventured back to Germany, after about five days in France, then visited Brigitte's sister, Edith, near Baden Baden, where she and her husband, Gilbert resided in officer's quarters. Gilbert was a captain in the French army and by the time he retired was to become a general.

These adventures and many more like them, except with the unpleasant experience of having no passport during that year merely added to the multi-adventure life I was having in Germany and other parts of Europe. Europe's beauty and charm are heightened by the outstanding friendliness of people one meets while traveling in the various countries within its boundaries. While costs were menial at that time, the quaintness of experiencing quality hotels and guesthouses made travel tasteful and fun.

After my marriage, the fun of living in Europe did not stop. The added convenience of having Brigitte's family living in

France and Northern Germany made the experiences more delightful because the utility of speaking German, sometimes broken French made the visits richer. The multiplicity of experiences gained by added German vocabulary was, no doubt, the component that made my search for enhancing my own German vocabulary more intense.

Not only did I want to learn German for the sake of knowing the target or host country's language, but I wanted to have the added element of interacting with my in-laws in a way that gave insight into my own wife's past and make her family more meaningful. The family, after the end of the Second World War, had been pieced back together, as I suppose many had after the Germans surrendered in 1945. Thousands of residents from various parts of East Germany drifted back to the various towns in West Germany. Those from East Germany drifted back west during the immediate months after the war, but because of the Iron Curtain, it later became more difficult to cross over to the West.

For communication purposes, my pursuit of language study started with Berlitz for spoken German and I went after the language with an intensity of focus I had never known in past college experiences. This was because I wanted to march through the unopened doors to gain fulfillment by knowing shades of meaning, dialect, and often used German expressions I did not understand in my embryonic stage of German. Then when I did started grasping the ability for conversation; my ability to gain insights into the depths of the German mind had begun.

My formal study of German gave me the fortification I needed to readily speak and communicate with Germans so my activities would revel not as those of a tourist, but as one who was sincerely interested in exchanging ideas in a language that was previously unknown to me.

Then those shades of meaning, which I think I gained, even in, sometimes dialect, and idiomatic terms, began to glow in a more magnanimous way. My insights into German, because of my formal studies, however, were deeper and broader than those ever gained by my ex wife, Brigitte, in English. I was in her country and had it have been the reverse, she would have, no doubt, become the more avid learner.

Even though I sent Brigitte to the University of Maryland to study English and history, she never became as functional in English as I did in German, and she would be the first to admit it. Although she had an innate ability to interpret simultaneously, going from German to English, she never got into the depths of idiomatic English as she would have, had she have lived continuously in the United States, as I did in Germany.

I dwell on concepts related to basic communication in order to emphasize the necessity of speaking a language in the country one is a guest of. I also wish to drive home the idea that to gain full insight into the depth of a country's sociological setting and personal interaction, one must grasp the language. Language utilization is basic in breaking down fundamental barriers and I cannot stress it enough in my past and present relations with the German people.

Once I hurdled over the barrier, after about two years of continuous speaking, things improved even more. Then, with the sixth year and then on down the road to about twenty years, things really leveled out. The sad thing today is, that I communicate via writing and speaking in German only occasionally, but the day to day practices are not there and some of the foundation begins to fall, with loss of necessary vocabulary. I still read, from time to time, various books and magazines that are available. The tools I gained at the apex of my stay in Germany could probably only be regained upon my return, and that is definitely a possibility after retirement. Comparatively speaking, the whole adventure is one I would not have missed for any amount of money.

The basic differences between the two continents, Europe and the United States, involve, of course, contrasts between languages, history, geography, and the people. Both places I have love for and see my future as one where I shall share time in both continents. Both the United States and Europe have their beauty and charm, with each possessing a multiplicity of differences.

I shall, probably in the future be financially restricted from enjoying both locations readily, but if so, it will be only because of lack of sufficient income. For life's fulfillment, and if I had my wishes, I would own condominiums in Niece, France, Rome, Italy, Bad Kreuznach, Germany, San Diego, California, and New Orleans, Louisiana. The only place I left out is Hot Springs, Arkansas, and I, with the bank, already own a townhouse there.

The people Hitler left behind, and now a country united, with over 80 million citizens, have developed a strong curiosity about the United States. I meet German travelers each year, who have experienced the vastness of the United States, and all reports I have so far heard, are positive. Those who are flying over to the Vereinigten Staaten (the United States in German), and have never visited them, only express great expectations because of what they have read, seen in the movies, television, or travel brochures. When they do come here, their dreams will be fulfilled because their attitudes toward us are already positive!

Chapter 13

Visions Of Eastern Europe

I have selected this chapter of my journey through this writing because I feel there is an excitement emanating from the newly evolved freshness in Eastern Europe. Countries I wish to explore would include Eastern Germany, Poland, The Czech Republic, and Hungary, which now, through their new freedom from the Iron Curtain, are rich with potential for tourists. There are others but these are the ones I wish to focus on for my future travel. I have not had the good fortune to visit Poland but hope to visit it soon. Since I have met many Polish people, even while living in the United States, I am developing an intense curiosity about the land.

After the chains of communism, and the wasted years after 1945 until the fall of the Berlin Wall in 1989, the potential for these and other areas of Eastern Europe opens a new door for travel, business, and expansion.

After 1989, and the dramatic fall of the Berlin Wall, my appetite for travel to East Germany, previously the Eastern Block under the USSR, was whetted. In the summer of 1992, I traveled back to Bad Kreuznach, where my daughter, Liane, lives, and enticed her and my ex wife, Brigitte to take a drive to Erfurt, located in the State of Thüringen. It is only a couple of hours by Autobahn since were driving Brigitte's new 190S Mercedes so we cruised at about 160 kilometers per hour, or 100 miles per hour in order to reach our destination in good time.

We stayed for a couple of nights in the lovely city of Erfurt with a population of about 217,000 inhabitants. It had already been a couple of years since the Iron Curtain collapsed and the East Germans were trying to align themselves with their newly integrated existence with the main part of Germany, where they should have been since 1945, things were becoming energized in that area.

It is an interesting city and I looked up some significant data on the Internet and made some discoveries. In quoting some of the historical aspects, I found out something about this area that is characterized by diverse highlands, lively cities and romantic towns in the State of Thüringen. I pinpointed some awakening data located to this previous East German State.

"The Wasserkuppe is the birth place of hang gliding. On this highest elevation of the Rhon, even today many original gliders can be admired. Further east, and separated only by the Werra river, runs the long stretch of the Thuringian forest, characterized by gently rolling hills, mountains and steep valleys. The forests are traversed by a famous hiking trail, the 104 mile long Rennsteig, running from the Werra in the west to the Saale river in the southeast. Where the Sasle breaks through the Frankinwald, the "Forest of the Franks", a particularly romantic scene, enhanced by castles and palaces, bursts into view.

At the foot of the mountains, important cities with magnificent buildings were founded. In Eisenach, Johann Sebastian Bach was born. High above the city, in the Wartburg, one of Germany's most famous castles, Martin Luther found refuge from persecution. In Weimar, Goethe, Schiller, Herder and Wieland lived and created literary masterpieces. There are many sigts to delight the visitor in Weimar, the superbly restored city of the "German Classics". Erfurt, the city of flowers, boasts a large historic section where you will find a cathedral, and St. Severin's church, old residential buildings and the medieval "Kramerbrücke", or tradesmen's bridge, which is lined on both sides by old houses." These places we saw with a great deal of enthusiasm since they had been so difficult to visit prior to the fall of the infamous Wall.

It was a pleasure to also visit Eisenach, Weimar, and Erfurt because all three cities have a flair of a sort of buried treasure atmosphere because they were encapsulated by the stench of the secret police during the years of 1945 through 1989. Now the breath of freedom permeates all these lovely cities and the flow of freedom, free markets, and free, almost free, expression is the rule. When I say almost free, at the time I visited in 1992, there was still an awakening of the people and one could tell they were just becoming accustomed to the vivacity that freedom brings! I detected some reluctance of the people, at that time, to expound freely about life under the Russian iron hand.

Further research, on the Internet, enlightened me a little more about the lovely capital of the State of Thüringen, and its capital, Erfurt which has a population of 217,000, was founded in the eighth century and is proud to be called a "garden city". The old part of the city has a large number of Patrician houses, churches and monasteries thmake it a kind of architectural museum.

"Johann Sebastian Bach was born in Eisenach in 1685, and was one of a ramified family of musicians. He died in Leipzig in 1750. Martin Luther hid in the nearby Wartburg in 1521-1522. There he translated the New Testament into German-a major step in the development of modern written German. And at the same place in 1817 students called for a united Germany.

During this time there was much territorial fragmentation of culture and barbarity. Thuringia was particularly affected by Germany's much lamented fragmentation. But culturally this proved to be a good thing since the rulers of even small territories were keen patrons of the arts. By far the most prominent among them was Duke Karl August of Saxony-Weimar (1757-1828). He brought to his court the romantic poet and translator of Shakespear Christoph Martin Wieland (1733-1813), the poet and philologist Johan Gottfried Herder (1744-1803), and above all Johann Wolfgang von Goethe (1749-1832)"

Since I studied Goethe while learning German at the University of Maryland, Kaiserslautern, in 1962 through 1966, I found the area of extreme interest. I personally feel the opening of the eastern part of Germany is a needed process in making the whole of Germany one nation again. I think, all Germans should be shouting about the evolving processes, even with the costs of bringing them from the downtrodden state they were left in by the Soviet Union.

I learned from an Internet site that Carl Zeiss, the mechanic, made the city of Jena famous for world tools and precision optical instruments, giving an impetus to these branches of the economy. The world famous automobiles, the "Wartburg" have been manufactured in Eisenach for many years under the GDR (German Democratic Republic), the name of East Germany under the USSR, but since German unification the firm of Opel has been operating there.

Since I lived so many years, in West Germany, and could only visit West Berlin and East Berlin with special paperwork (1961-1983), I felt that the East Germans had awakened from the dead and could now get on with their lives. I often discussed the new freedom with many East Germans and 99% of them expressed a feeling of being released from captivity. A few remarked that they got along alright under the communist regime, but most expressed joy and delight about their newly found freedom.

My next venture into the newly freed area of the Eastern Block was into Budapest and that came in August of1994. I flew to Frankfurt, attended my daughter's wedding, and decided to take a 3-day trek to the beautiful city of Budapest, Hungary.

Believe it or not, my curiosity about Budapest was first awakened when a young lady I dated in 1958, gave me a book to read about Budapest. She was a delightful person and had to leave her husband because he remained in the beautiful city under the rule of the communists. She escaped after the 1956 Budapest revolution and received passage to the United States. She often longed for homeland and missed many of the socialist provisions provided by the communist government, especially the medical benefits.

Buda being on one side of the Danube and Pest on the other. Budapest is a most unusual and beautiful city with about the best food I have found outside of Paris. Both areas are filled with interesting sites and stimulate a visitor's appetite for exploration, dining, and sightseeing.

Hungary has a population of about 10,375,000 (January1, 1990) but the population has dropped by about 130,000 as a result of natural decline. Budapest has a population of 1,885,000 and one recognizes the city as quite large and densely populated when moving about on foot, bus, or by taxis.

I was once told, by a Hungarian-American friend of mine, Otto Thomas, who taught with me in Brunssum, the

Netherlands, that the Hungarian language is linguistically connected to Finnish. Actually the Hungarians are of Finno-Ugric origin and as a people have lived in their present homeland, the Danube Basin, for more than 1,000 years. So there is definitely a Finnish connection, and the language, when I heard it, had completely unfamiliar sounds to me, since my languages were English and German, with a little knowledge of Italian.

So, which language came in handy for me, and was well respected in the lovely city? German, of course, and it worked about 80% of the time. The reason it worked is because there is a large population of German speakers.

Again I learned from a web site on the Internet and I learned this: "Large numbers of ethnic Germans settled along the western borders, the Transdanubian central hills, around the capital, and in the Mecsek hills, Southern Slavs (Serbs, Croats, Slovenes, Slkac, and Bunevac) are concentrated in the southwest, Romanians along the southeastern border, and the Slovaks in the southeastern county of Bekes and near the capital."

I also learned in my research that the religion breakdown of the country is as follows: 70% of the population are Roman Catholics, 20% Calvinists, 5% Lutherans, 5% Jews, and 4.5% other religions.

During my visit, the streets were bustling with activity, and one would hardly have believed that at the time of my visit, the unemployment rate was about the same as the European average is presently and that is 10%. I saw no indication of closed buildings, because of slow business activity. Business in Budapest was stimulated and seemingly dynamic.

The only thing I did notice was that when I visited the world famous restaurant, the Gundel, not too far from where Russian tanks overthrew the attempted overthrow of the

Communist regime in 1956, the restaurant was not completely filled as such a first class restaurant would have been in Western Europe.

An excerpt from "The Hungarian Revolution of 1956 & How it Affected the World", by Zoltan Csipke, Copyright 1998, reveals some of the events that occurred when the Hungarians tried to break the bonds of the Soviet Union in 1956.

"Hungarians have long sought freedom, only to have it dissolve time and again. The events that unfolded from October to December of 1956 symbolized man's endless yearning for freedom. In it, an oppressed people rose up against their oppressors in a feat of such courage that will not be challenged for some time. In the eyes of the Western nations, the revolution at first seemed an act of foolishness. Soon, they realized it was not. The freedom fighters of Hungary had risen because they could no longer stand the iron fist of communism. Their only goal was to free Hungary from foreign occupation."

The attempt failed, and two years after this dastardly military assault on the Hungarians, I met a young lovely Hungarian, dark haired lady in New Orleans. In quoting from the results of the refugees in the description by Zoltan Csipke, 1998, I reflect back on this young lady I met in 1958, and who came to the United States as a Hungarian refugee. Her name is Liz Kulin, and after leaving her husband, who elected to remain under the reign of communism and cooperate with the "Dogs of Russia," she came to the United States. She was not alone in her escape from Communism because many more escaped with her in their success at breaking the chains of satellite bondage imposed by the Soviets.

"All in all, it is estimated that about three hundred thousand people left Hungary seeking freedom after the Soviets reentered. Tens of thousands were deported to Sibeia to Soviet slave-labor camps. The infamous Gulag was one of the places "welcoming" Hungarians.

It has been said that the Western country who helped the most was Austria. By November, the Hungarians had realized the promises of Radio Free Europe were empty. No support came for Hungary. Hungary was left alone in her confrontation of the Soviet Union.

In America, some of the refugees were taken to Camp Kilmer in New Jersey. Here, in a cold deserted section of the base, the refugees were placed in barracks. They were given a speech on freedom and told that this is America. After an unfavorable report by the New York Times, Camp Kilmer was transformed into the warm place it should have been from the start.

All the while, the world was in shock that a country the size of Ohio with greater Los Angeles' population dared rise against the Soviet Empire. As a result of the utter courage of men and women, these people were not looked upon as refugees, but as heroes. Due to this remarkable courage, Time Magazine gave "Man of the Year" honors on its cover to the unknown Freedom Fighter. In reference to the Hungarians Freedom Fighter, Time magazine said:" This man was seen to have shaken history's greatest despotism to its foundations." (Time)."

As I walked down the streets of Buda and Pest, I visualized the charming smile of Liz Kulin, and thought of what she left behind. Because of the attempt of thousands to break away from the terrible grasp of communism, Liz found her freedom, but almost lost her identity as a Hungarian. Her culture shock upon coming to the United States, and vociferously expressed to me, was surprising because I thought there was no place in the world like the United States. But when I was around Liz, I knew there was a tragic loss when she left the warmth and love of her Budapest!

Budapest is a city with spirit, and I thought of the friendliness of its citizens as I enjoyed the fantastic meals, great wine, the excellent restaurant, the Gundel, and admired the magnificent architecture of Buda and Pest. My beautiful ride along the Danube was enchanting and captivating.

This is superb city in the eastern part of Europe that will regain its status and excel because it never truly accepted communism in the first place. It is truly a city of deep cultural splendor and I would encourage all people of the world to visit, enjoy, and admire in its beautiful setting along the Danube!

After the pleasant experience of visiting enchanting Budapest, I decided my next venture into another previous Eastern Block city would be a visit to Prague, The Czech Republic. While riding back to Germany from Budapest I chatted with two New York correspondents who advised me to visit Prague because of its beauty and ease of movement contrasted to Budapest. Walking, I was told, was much easier, and I found out with the concentrated layout in its structure, it was most inviting to pedestrian movement.

On the train returning to Vienna, the correspondents, a young lady and young man told me everything happened in Prague and it would be very romantic and as beautiful as Budapest. So on my return to Germany in 1997 I planned a 3-day trip to the beautiful city of Prague by train. The city was everything they told me it was. I was even approached by two lovely street ladies in the heart of the city who wanted an evening escort. A couple of glasses of wine for each were the extent of my venture. The common language, of course, was German. My Czech knowledge is about nil.

My visit to Prague was in the summer of 1977. I left Bad Kreuznach and within about 5 or 6 hours train ride, I was in the beautiful, bustling, and exciting city. The country, The Czech Republic, has a population of 1,304,302 people and was another city reveling in its freedom from the past chains of the Soviet Union. Tourists were everywhere, people walking, enjoying restaurants, scenery, architecture, and just enjoying the excitement of being in Prague.

In researching information about the beauty of Prague I found that the city "(Praha) is one of the least "eastern" European cities one could imagine. Architecturally it is a revelation: few other cities anywhere in Europe look so good and no other European capital can present six hundred years of architecture so completely untouched by natural disaster or war. Hardly surprising, then, that a staggering ninety percent of Western visitors spend all their time in and around the capital and that Praguers exude and air of confidence about their city.

"After World War II, which it survived substantially unscathed, Prague disappeared completely behind the Iron Curtain. The city briefly re-emerged onto the world stage during the cultural blossoming "Prague Spring" in 1968, but the decisive break came in November 1989, when a peaceful student demonstration, brutally broken up by police, triggered off the Velvet Revolution which eventually toppled the Communist government. The exhilarating popular unity of that period is now history, but there is still a great sense of newfound potential in the capital.

The River Vltava (Moldau in German) divides the capital into two unequal halves: the steeply inclined left bank, which accommodates the quarters of Hradcany and Mala Strana and the more gentle, sprawling right bank, which includes Stare Mesto, Josefov and Nove Mesto. Hradcany, on the hill, contains the most obvious sights-the castle itself, the cathedral and the former palaces of the Aristocracy. Below Hradcany, Mala Strana (Little Quarter), with its narrow eighteenth-century streets, is the city's ministerial and diplomatic quarter, though

Baroque gardens are there for all to enjoy. Over the river, on the right bank, Stare Mesto (Old Town) is a web of alleys and passageways centered on the city's most beautiful square, Staromestske namesti. Enclosed within the boundaries of Stare Mesto is Josefov, the old Jewish quarter, now down to a handful of synagogues and a cemetery. Nove Mesto (New Town), the focus of the modern city, covers the largest area, laid out in a long wide boulevards-most famously Winceslas Square-stretching south and east of the old town."

I found the city to be intriguing, and saw tourists from all over Europe, because of the multiplicity of languages heard just walking the streets. There are also about 40,000 young American people in Prague. I saw youth on every street corner, on the bridges across the Moldau, and also many Italians, Germans, French, and Scandinavians all about the city in the month of August 1997, the year I made my visit.

Though the unemployment is just a little below the European average of 10%, it is about 9% in the Czech Republic but only about 3.5% in Prague. The average wage is about 1300 Kc ($340) a month. But with the complete integrating and with the tremendous tourist trade of this charming, exciting city, I feel certain Prague and the Czech Republic will continue to grow economically.

The largest Church is Roman Catholic but Czechs are mostly atheists, because of the systematic oppression of religion during Communism. I found the people there to be helpful and to be very friendly. I utilized my German as a mode of communication quite extensively as I also did while in Budapest and the locals were very receptive to the language.

My visit to fantastic Prague was just another piece of the jigsaw puzzle I am putting together in my visits to unseen places of Eastern Europe. I will be watching for a full integration into freedom and exciting things for the future. In the future I would expect to see strong capitalistic entrepreneur ventures, and a progressively expanding society, especially after the tremendous burdens placed on these people and the other East Europeans by the chains of Communism.

In 1999 I returned to Germany and decided to make my next venture into a city I had always dreamed of seeing. Since restrictions by the Communist government restricted me from visiting it during my stay in Germany from 1961 to 1984, I was eager to go there. This city was one I read was bombed almost flat from the Second World War, and the city is Dresden. I only spent about 25 days total in Europe, just short of one month, on this summer I flew back to Germany to see Liane and my ex wife, Brigitte. I only spent two days in Dresden, but it was an impressive experience.

Dresden is a city with 484,646 inhabitants. It is the 14th largest city in Germany and located in the State of Sachsen. I was completely taken back by the beautiful Frauenkirche that is being completely rebuilt because it is one of the most significant masterpieces of European architecture.

This beautiful and friendly city, with more Lutherans (17.5 percent) than Roman Catholic (4.7 percent) lies on the beautiful Elbe River and is the ultimate in cities. I found it to be charming, and a city I hope to revisit in the very near future because of its convenience and charm.

This city was unscathed during the Second World War until the night of February 13, 1945. In a matter of hours it was reduced to ruins in the most extreme saturation bombing ever conducted until the Vietnam War. The official figures cite 35,000 civilians, since people fleeing from the advancing Red Army packed the city.

The post-communist authorities are restoring all the beautiful historic buildings left as rubble. I arrived at the Hauptbahnhof and saw the Prager Strasse, a vast Stalinist pedestrian precinct with the standard cocktail of high-rise luxury hotels, public offices, box like flats and cafes and restaurants, with a few fountains and statues. At the far end, beyond the inner ring road, is the Altmarkt, which was much extended after its wartime destruction, but interesting. After that is the Kreuzkirche, a church that mixes a Baroque body with a neoclassical tower. Behind it stands the Rathaus, built early in the 1900s in a lumbering historical style.

I saw, at the end of nearby Auguststrasse, the Baroque Hofkirche (or Dom) which is a Catholic Church in a staunchly Protestant province and is explained by the fact that the Saxon rulers converted in order to gain the Polish throne. The church's gleaming white interior features a very ornate pulpit by the great sculptor of Dresden Baroque, Balthasar Permoser.

The elaborate Opernhaus opposite the Hofkirche was built by the leading architect of nineteenth-century Dresden, Gottfried Semper, and saw the first performance of Wagner's "The Flying Dutchman and Tanhauser, and Richard Strauss' Der Rosenkavaler.

I lived on the outskirts of town in a quaint and inexpensive hotel but found the bus system for getting about the town absolutely one of the most convenient I have seen for a city with almost a half million residents. I checked the hotels in town and they were quite expensive compared to what I paid for the nice bed and breakfast hotel only about 1.5 kilometers from the heart of town. My price was no more than $45 a night with breakfast.

On one bus ride I encountered a lovely elderly lady and talked with her about pensions, cost of living, what conditions were like under the communists, and she told me her pension, especially with the cold winters barely got her by. If I remember correctly she only received about $450 a month.

People were friendly, seemingly grateful that they no longer lived under the terrible reign of communism. This seemed to be the status quo of most people I talked with all over Eastern Europe.

My next venture should take me to Poland, and eventually up to the corridor of Russia. I plan to do this within the next two years, if not sooner. I enjoy making my trips during the summer since the days are nice and long and the temperatures are delightful throughout Europe at this time of year.

My visions for Eastern Europe in the future are ones that will illuminate the beauty of free enterprise, freedom, and a modern and advance technological world because of the new technology permeating Europe and the world. With the chance to build new infrastructure, roads, phones, modern buildings, and modern transportation, the vicinity of Eastern Europe should someday even exceed, especially in East Germany, that of most of Western Europe.

One would expect to see progress that never had a chance to develop under the chains of communism and the people of Eastern Europe can be thankful that the bonds of Red Imperialism did not last longer than the useless fifty plus years since the end of World War II.

My expectations of Poland are not great as far as the technological development and what I have heard from my Polish friends here in San Diego, and several acquaintances I know from Germany it is natural with friendly and down to earth people. I expect more of a laid back country with freedom loving people who have a past of dynamic multicultural exposure. It should be a nice place to visit because of its diverse history and interesting sights.

I hope to eventually travel to the area my ex wife lived in and was known as East Prussia, but much of the area is now under the control of Russia and Poland. The memories my ex wife expressed in the years of our marriage relate an interesting setting that might be even similar to Kiel, Germany. Since the descriptions often include Danzig, or what is known as Gdansk, which sits right on the Baltic, I can imagine areas of great beauty. I often heard her speak of Elbing, East Prussia, which is now Elblag, Poland.

After my visits to Hungary, The Czech Republic, and various cities in East Germany that were previously occupied by and under control of the Soviets, I was extremely pleased. The enlightenment I had into the potential for growth and development under more democratic settings was very pleasing to me. I can only imagine what tours of Poland will be like visiting these freedom loving people who pulled so drastically at the chains of bondage under the Soviet Union.

The potential for travel into Eastern Europe now stand unrestricted compared to what they were for me in the 1960s, 1970s, and even the 1980s. Today the road is open and the possibility to travel, meet people, take photographs of lands and its occupants will be readily available to me. There will be an avenue of exploration to be devoured by my unending appetite for new adventure.

Limitations will be language, but fortunately most of the Eastern European countries have a facility for German, and I found it to be one of my most important tools for communication while traveling to the east.

Most of all, the excitement of unrestricted visits excite me and ignite my wanderlust. The restrictions I had while living abroad during the Cold War will no longer be a deterrent. The domination of the eastern part of Europe by the Communists and the many barriers impeded my desire to go beyond the borders of West Germany previously. Now all this has changed with the potential for exciting and awaiting revelations of Eastern Europe only a plane and train ticket away.

Eastern Europe, which had formed a monolithic bloc during the triumphant rule of the Soviet Union, appeared in 1995 to be split between such countries attached to the Western world (the Czech Republic, Hungary, and Poland), countries finding it difficult to emerge from their Communist past (Slovakia, Romania, Bulgaria and perhaps Russia) and, finally, areas with much turmoil (former Yugoslavia and the Caucasus).

Now Eastern Europe is clearly free. What are its desires and aspirations? Are they seeking prosperity and a democratic mold? Or will ethnic identity cause future problems? Western Europe and its support for these countries should help make the difference for ultimate success. Will Western Europe be imaginative enough to build an integrated region with Eastern Europe founded on progress toward common economic desires?

The people Hitler left behind are beginning to experience the profits of democracy that will fully integrate them into, hopefully, an exciting exchange of ideas, technology, tourism, and positive interchange of friendship, along with cultural understanding.

Chapter 14

~✝~

German Autocracy

As a person having spent many years on German soil, I feel my experience places me in a position to analyze the mood and ideas emanating from German society because I had the various levels of contact provided through associations with various strata from the everyday people to aristocrats.

One of the clues I first got, as far as insight, into the thinking and mental processes of the German people was in a conversation I had with Frau Lang, my German instructor who taught for the University of Maryland, Kaiserslautern High School, in 1962. She was quite a self-critic of the past adventures of Germany brought about by the rise of the Third Reich and its domination of Europe during the Nazi era.

It was about 1961 when I started taking my first course in German. The course was German 101 or some code name indicating the very first German class I could take at my level at the University Extension of the University of Maryland. The courses were held either in Ramstein Junior High where I taught or at nearby Kaiserslautern High School, during the evenings.

One morning I was conversing with her, because she also taught as regular staff at Ramstein Junior High School,

Ramstein Air Base, Germany, where I was a teacher of general science. I made a comment related to the societal behavior of the German people, how they fell under Nazi Germany, and what a progressive group of people the Germans were.

She reflected for a moment, then she said, "Herr Stell, I really attribute the autocratic behavior of our German people to the school system. Yes, it is the way they are taught in the schools which breeds the concept of discipline, and the way we conduct ourselves. We probably never would have fallen under the dictatorship of Adolf Hitler had we have been freer thinkers like the Americans. Our strict codes of order and discipline, along with the autocratic superiority of the school master are coherent parts of German society Herr Stell."

I too reflected on this for a moment and agreed that she might be completely correct in her analysis. The processes of blind obedience and extremely high respect for the pedagogical processes in structuring education in Germany must impart a lasting influence on behavioral modes in the minds of the German people.

I have no criticism about the tiered structure of German education because I think it has tremendous techniques and strong characteristics as far as the types of schooling which siphons students, ability wise, then channels them into the proper setting for life's work.

Who is to say whether or not it is the structure in German society that imparts the autocratic processes or the integral autocratic mode that sets the tone for them and their modal behavior? I would guess it is not the structure but autocracy that leads to strict structure. They have a broad basic respect for education, and follow rules of society and education with almost blind obedience. The German people follow their rules, in their day by day living, which makes them obedient to the headmaster, der Rektor (headmaster or principal).

This places them into this overwhelming arena of respect for school, education, the teachers, and the administrators all the way up to the State level in administrative authority.

It is absolutely gratifying to endure, as I did for over twenty years, the love, respect, almost blind respect, for someone who is in the profession of teaching. Even though I was, and still am, an American teacher, families, children, adults, professionals, and workers, in German society, showed utmost respect for me, once they learned of my profession. This is a breath of fresh air when I compare myself to the lack of respect and attitudes I endure in our great country, the United States, of public school teachers.

From the moment I set foot on German soil, I began to feel the kindness and acknowledgment cast upon me as a secondary teacher. I had never felt this extreme, almost pedestal like status that was imparted to me until I lived in Germany for the twenty years. This is difficult to impart to other Americans unless one has had the experience and exposure.

The German people in their social activity, businesses, schools, military and institutions manifest the intrinsic concept of discipline in society. The positive attitudes toward me, as a teacher, were the perennial ghosts of conversation between my social contacts and me. The almost pedestal like respect upon which I was placed, because I was a teacher was a never-ending reminder that I was something special to the German people. Any teacher is held in high esteem in Germany.

The autocratic mode of German society, from the time of the Franco-Prussian War (1870-1871) under the leadership of Otto Eduard Leopold von Bismarck, to the First World War, and also the Second World War, illuminates autocracy as an integral part of the German nation. The strict discipline of the military forces of the Kaiser, in World War I, to the fanatical leadership of Adolf Hitler in World War II are merely manifestations that the German people can quickly adhere and render to from the call of a strong leader.

In questions to myself regarding German society, I question if the Germany of the twentieth-century is a result of seventeenth and eighteenth century philosophers such as Hegel and Kant, or are the roots much deeper?

One would think that the educational theories gleaned from some of the European philosophers would have cast a strong influence into promoting more autocracy in German schools from the way they are administered.

Actually, some of the educational philosophers, who influenced some of the concepts of some of the United States science programs, such as Pestalozzi, the Swiss educational reformer, and others tended to liberalize some of the theories of learning, and break away from too much autocracy. Many of these views lean toward because they respect the varied levels of children's learning and gear the programs in a structured manner that adapts to the different age levels. The age levels of development are acknowledged and the work begins with the concrete, then builds to developing concepts in the abstract.

American schools are quick to innovate these concepts into their educational modes, but from what I saw, even at the elementary levels of German schools, strict discipline and a great deal of regimentation ensued in the learning processes. Obviously, the various philosophies of various educational philosophers might be adapted in German society, but the basic foundation of intense structure and discipline can still be adhered to.

The philosophy of Maria Montesorri (1870-1952) is also a popular concept often adapted in the United States and the children learn self discipline, move at their own pace, and learn in a natural way. This is, seemingly diametrically opposed to concepts to regimented processes often used in Japan and also in Germany. But I must say I have seen very good elementary German teachers utilize some of the Montesorri concepts, and especially on my own child. And Montesorri schools still prevail throughout Europe because many parents, even in Germany pursue private education for their children.

I also noted that the advancement of the classes of children in the Grundschule (primary or elementary school) in Germany does not tend to wait for the child. Once Liane, my daughter hit the abstracts in about the third grade and the mathematical abstracts began to be administered, she began to fall back in performance, and that is when I let her repeat the third grade so her maturity could catch up with the demands of the system.

In information from "britannica.com," on the web, I found an interesting quote of the philosopher, born during the eighteenth century but died in the nineteenth century, Georg Wilhelm Friedrich Hegel. I often hear his name associated with Adolf Hitler.

This is a quote from the briticannica.com: "Georg Wilhelm Friedrich Hegel (1770-1831) is widely regarded as the most influential philosopher of the 19th century. Indeed many consider him one of the greatest of all modern thinkers. Yet he was not without his detractors: Arthur Schopenhauer, his contemporary called him a "vulgar, dull, repulsive, witless charlatan." Karl Popper accused him of being an "enemy" of the "open society." Hegel's ideas have been blamed for everything from Nazism to Communism.

Maybe Hitler used some of his ideas, but this dictator had a concept, and it seems that the autocratic society, in which Adolf Hitler lived, fit right into his plans. Because he and the German people were an integral part of a regimented and autocratic society, with strict form and high standards of man prevailing, the mold seem to fit perfect.

From another source on the Internet, Hitler's Holocaust," I found an interesting quote and it ties into his concept of German society. Then, in 1932, when Hitler became chancellor of Germany, the quote below matches the man.

"For Hitler and the Nazi official ideology, the individual was a "non-entity." Those individuals who thought of themselves as individuals before they considered themselves of a greater German culture were in essence going directly against German official ideology. Theoretically they posed no direct threat to Hitler's own stability in the Nazi State. Hitler's total belief in this ideology is evident in his statement that "one being drink the blood of another. By dying the one furnished food for the other. We should not blather about humanity." 1) It appears that Hitler's total disregard for the rights of the individual were directly related to the perceived security of the collective state.

Hitler also appears to have believed that the preservation of the German race/nation (the Aryan nation as he and other Nazi's thought of it) was key to the survival of and stability of the German nation-state itself."

The autocratic society of Germany, perpetuated by an educational system, highly regimented, as well as the corporate and state and military structure, during the time of Hitler's rule, were successful in the propagation of the totalitarian state of Germany. As far as the attitudes of the German people today go, one must examine their present attitudes. During my twenty plus years of being among them, I would say that there is definitely an atmosphere, among the elderly people who suffered from the failures of the Third Reich, that a great mistake was made because their allegiance to the dictator. The youth are somewhat detached, except from historical accounts.

But I did meet some very adamant Germans, once I became familiar enough with them, and some of them being my wife's family, with Prussian background (East Prussia), who expressed animosity toward Winston Churchill, the British Empire, and their successful attempt to hold back the Germans. Some even chastised the great American president, Franklin D. Roosevelt, and lay blame upon him and Churchill for strong leadership and eventual success in stifling the Third Reich expansion of Europe.

Of course, I as an American, and being in the presence of many Germans, when they were voicing their feelings about losing the war, never attacked the United States or me as they did the British and the Russians. For obvious reasons, though, I often heard some respectful comments about the might of the vast land of the USSR and their strength. I often heard many American military make comments that the Germans hated the Russians, and they, no doubt did, especially after their surrender at Stalingrad in 1943.

Sometimes I think the Germans voiced the respect of the giant bear, Russia, because so many actually found out about the will of the Russians in their successful attempt to hold back the German military on the Russian front. The discovered that the size of Russia, along with its bitter cold winters was a barrier only Napoleon's defeat should have driven home. But the German military, along with Adolf Hitler's leadership had to learn the lesson the hard way.

One of elements of the German people exemplified in the past, and still seems to be, again reiterated, is their extreme respect for authority. Americans seem to revel in their oftentimes disdain toward authority. In the American family, problems are often solved through conferences or discussion and working together on a solution. The democratic approach for us is often a method we value in the family.

In a German family, if the father is there, he, is the dominant leader who traditionally most often guides the family through crises. If the mother exerts influence, it is often done through clever nuances and manipulation. These were my observations, unless the family was without the father, as was the case of my ex wife's family. The psychological processes of matriarch in this case seemed to transfer rather well. I have first hand knowledge in that I had to deal with my mother-in-law the many years I was married to Brigitte.

But the overwhelming idea of obeying the schoolteacher, the father of the family, the corporate leader or CEO, in business, seems to prevail in the German setting. I found that authority tended to be strongly top-down in German society. It readily explains the prevalent traditional processes of strong monopolies and cartels exhibited in corporate Germany since the end of the Third Reich and the re-establishment of new post World War II Corporate Germany.

I would imagine that my acquaintance, Alfons Heck, author of <u>A Child of Hitler,</u> might not like to hear my opinion regarding the German people, especially in this light, and as an opinion of modern German society. I often feel that Mr. Heck, now an American citizen is quick to praise me, when I pass on compliments toward modern day Germany and its people. I know this because of a response I had from him when my opinion toward German jurisprudence was expressed in the super conservative Union Tribune, for which Mr. Heck often writes editorials. Alfons Heck called me, unsolicited, after he read the very complimentary article about German courts. And what I wrote was truly my opinion.

What I said in the article was that our judges here in San Diego, sometimes appear to be dictators, and in Germany, my treatment in court was much more humane than what I had experienced here in San Diego. I really believe this is true. There may be a creeping totalitarianism in our society, and it could possibly happen through some of the extreme processes that take place by autocratic and dictatorial judges. When confronting judges here in this country, as by my example in the San Diego Union Tribune, one sometimes feels he or she is facing a dictator. This is especially true with some judges. Whereas while I was in Germany and went through a court proceeding, I felt I was treated in a more humane manner than my treatment has been here.

However, after viewing newsreels in the 1940s, some of the trials that took place under Nazi Germany, and the way the sentencing judges yelled at the defendants, I cannot help but believe that the way the wind was blowing at that time with Nazi control, was the way the judges acted. But after the war was over and the courts yielded to the sweeping changes that the allies deemed necessary for complete de-Nazification, then the tide turned. The Germans fell under the line of authority and if that is what the allies wanted, then that is what they got.

The civil and congenial processes, legal, business, or what the circumstances may be, that prevail under the German people today will be in effect until a political change occurs. If a sweeping change in German society evolves, and it very well could, then the German people could also change their direction. But today Germans will respect minorities, follow the civilized rules in court, and continue to vociferously support Democracy. They are under international pressure to do so. Their regimes would take too much international pressure if they were to act otherwise.

Until a dynamic shift in economic structure reappears in Germany, the status quo of a portrayed non-authoritarian society will continue to exist. But, innately, I feel the German people are more prone toward the basic conditioning and concept of authority, and that is, what the boss says do, you do. He is my supervisor, teacher, CEO, father, or political leader, so we do what we are told. Right now the German people are very much aware and sensitive to political criticism. The multi-party involvement, and the outward appearance of the German people today, are those of one of the most democratic people in Europe.

But I assume the British and French will be cautious in their dealings with Germany in geopolitical goals for Western Europe. They know the natural instincts of the Germans and that is that they could someday fall back under an autocratic leadership that could again could possibly cast a political and foreseeable military dominance of Europe, provided the proper elements emerge.

As an exemplary individual who is a product of German society, I suspect Alfons Heck, now an American citizen, and an excellent writer, is innately German, will never lose his genetic propensity and attitude toward the great people of his heritage. And I probably would not lose my innate democratic attitude if the situation was reversed and I became a German citizen. Inculcation in a society tends to cast strong bonds on the individual, especially if the adaptation is generally strong and positive.

What Mr. Heck, most likely, wants to perceive, is a completely democratized Germany, with a complete reversal of any characteristics it had during the Third Reich. I, personally, do not believe this will ever totally happen. The innate "autocratic" mold in Germany is too prevalent and ubiquitous to shake the perpetuating nuances cast by traditional processes.

The reason I say this is because of the innate structure and autocratic leanings of the German people. They have hundreds of years conditioning in their predilection toward an autocratic existence. In contrast to the American, sometimes extreme leanings toward freedom for all, and our rugged individualism, the Germans will never lose their preference toward authoritative rule.

When my daughter, Liane, was raised by her mother and me, we both shared extreme love for the child, but the concept of child rearing differed. Brigitte, even sometimes more diplomatic than I, is still more authoritative than I. She still has ingrained into her being, the concepts of autocracy and I have ingrained in me, the inherent processes of democracy.

This, in essence, is the difference between a German and an American. I am a living testimony of the differences in basic philosophical concepts of rule. I, would, if confronted by a dictator in society, probably be a freedom fighter. My ex wife, Brigitte, on the other hand, would probably fall into line very quickly.

Even reformed citizens like Alfons Heck, whom I consider to be innately a very conservative person, must often feel that the bickering and extreme measures American society tolerates for criminals, is extraneous and foolish. He is, basically, German in nature, bright, methodical, and has a great command of English, as well as German. I am sure that his impatience with democratic bickering in this country oftentimes emerges because of his desire to get to the crux of problems.

I also feel that democracy in the United States often goes to the extremes in its freedom, especially in accessibility of guns, drug acquisition, and excessive freedom in schools. But to reduce crime, or completely eliminate it, a society would have to be on the order of the old Marxist State controlled society, or that of Nazi Germany. Crime was almost eliminated under the Führer, and also Stalinist Russia. The democratic processes seem to work and continue to produce splendid results for us Americans as a great society.

In the arena of American public schools, ironically, the courts, in the past thirty or so years, have upheld most of the cases which work to deter student action toward rules regulating parental coddling of their children. Where we have failed is in the overall discipline and teacher control in the classrooms of our schools. Here is where more concepts of authority should be utilized. More authority by the teacher and less assertion of parents who coddle their children might improve the decaying authority once wielded by teachers in the classroom. The over protective parent can sometimes hinder the progress of direction by the teacher. The counselor movement as a sounding board for the student has also deteriorated teacher control of students in our schools in the Untied States.

The lack of respect for the teacher's authority and control of students, because of the protection of them through extreme tolerance via counselors and overprotective parents might be just the element that will completely tear down the structure of the American education system. And it looks like it is on its way.

The lack of respect for the teacher in the United States is an element we in America need not be proud of. The respect for the American public school teacher as compared to the German public school teacher tends to leave the public school teacher at a loss when it comes to positive control in the learning environment.

A lot of this might come from the fact that the school administrators, once they get out of the bondage of the classroom, rarely associate with students in the classroom setting. The school administrator loses focus on the s vital part of the education process and that is the student-teacher interaction that occurs on a day by day basis between the teacher and student.

The teacher control has almost been eliminated in American public schools, where it is most needed, and that is in the classroom. Though this concept of strong teacher control is still propagated in German society, and the teacher still retains his or her respect, teachers are regarded on a level with doctors, dentists, or lawyers in Germany. This element of prestige for the American public school teacher seems to be quickly deteriorating and with the proliferation of individualism and ultimate student/parent choice. With the support of counselors pampering the student, a strong education system will most certainly fail or be replaced by either private schools or some type of voucher system in this country.

The element of authority in both the United States and Germany should be sociologically examined more thoroughly. The idea of dominant control by the authoritative leader is not always for the good of all, but the element of the teacher being authoritative in the German school setting seems to levy much more prestige for the German teacher. The idea of American teachers losing the control in the classroom is a phenomenon that should be reexamined in American society, especially in public school education.

Private schools maintain discipline because they have the freedom to be selective and if the student is nor performing or is a discipline case, then the student and the parent are removed from that particular institution. The extreme forces created by freedom allowed in public schools may someday lead to the complete demise of public education in this country.

The analogy here is complex, but the underlying idea of authority, especially in schools, seems to be the element, along with the tiered or selective structure, especially in Germany and most European schools that has seemingly helped maintain scholarly results for student performance in Europe and the orient. Or this might just be a manifestation of the school structure in Germany and Europe. If the school is structured properly, student achievement can be elevated. But along with a proper structure there needs also to be strong teacher control, and that has deteriorated in our society. School structure in the United States is, no doubt, the critical element, especially in public schools.

The continuing exchange programs, which prevail between the United States and other countries, in order to promote understanding, should be explored and continued extensively. Even a strong central "federal" funding process to exchange students and teachers should be expanded beyond Fulbright scholarships or exchange programs.

This coming July I have invited two eighteen-year old students from Germany to visit me for about 6 weeks. During that time I expect to travel about Southern California. Last year, 2000, I had the pleasure of having one of these young men, Matthias Jagow, the nephew of my ex wife, Brigitte, spend 6 weeks during the months of July and August.

The value of such visits is rich because it continues the extension of my interaction with German people, and also opens avenues for youth in German-American relations. Such private arrangements and state or federally promoted exchanges can only increase basic understanding between two nations.

Matthias' visit last year must have been profitable for him because before March of this year his parents bought him a ticket to return to California, and that was even before I consented to host Matthias. I, of course, consented, because I feel the opportunity is profitable for both of us. The lad was most eager to again explore more parts of California and the surrounding area. This year we shall probably extend our visit into Reno, Nevada, Lake Tahoe, and perhaps Northern California where we hope to do some fishing on the Sacramento River with my nephew.

The young lad, Matthias, is a typical product of Germany. He is athletic, a Gymnasium student (the college preparatory secondary school) and highly regimented in his practicing ice hockey. He was, last year, the youngest player in the German Bundisliga or German National Hockey League. He is highly disciplined, follows his father's rules, and practices hockey at least once or twice a week. I expect that he will bring his hockey gear this year because of his love of the game. The burden of weekly practice seemed to be rather burdensome for both of us, but he in his highly disciplined fashion, followed his own will and that of his father. We attended hockey practice once or twice a week.

It might be time, at this point in this book to make a comparison between the somewhat autocratically reared German teenagers and the American teenagers. It was observed by me, and articulated by some of my German colleagues who are teachers, many years ago, while I was teaching in the American Dependent Schools in Germany, that German children are kept children as long as possible. They are not given the freedom of decision making as soon as American teens are. This is obviously observable if one has the opportunity to in any way deal with German and American teens in a social setting. Oftentimes, American offspring, teens especially, seem to be more socially precocious than are German offspring. Obviously the democratic process is at work in the development of the American, whereas the German has the more autocratic setting and independent thinking is not as prevalent in the German as in the American.

This might have endless avenues for research in the realm of sociology or psychology.

I notice that Matthias readily went with me on drives or destinations and was not prone to be dictated to by his local American peers regarding his social life. That may be because he has not yet built a social base here and obviously that he has not made the number of acquaintances he has in Germany. But while under my jurisdiction, he is quite obedient, washes the dishes when he is told, and abides by my apartment rules. I also know he does these things at home, when told by his mother or father. His father, very autocratic, makes demands and Matthias obeys them. This even happened to him here because commands were coming from his father via telephone calls from Germany about every day. If there was something Matthias was to do while visiting, the father told Matthias to take care of it and it was done with no argument.

He is not the independent thinker that most teens his age in the United States are. And maybe this may not be so bad. It is not so bad when viewing the statistics of criminality of many school children in our country and observing the classroom conduct that permeates American society.

At any rate, keeping children in their role as children as long as possible may not be a bad idea. German children tend to follow the rules and do what they are supposed to do as a general rule. Also, while my daughter was going through her childhood and teens I observed that the German teenagers and children were not free to make decisions as quickly as our children and teens in the United States.

The concept of autocracy and obeying the parent might not be such a bad idea, especially for child or teen control, by the parent while rearing children. I have a Filipina friend whom I have known for about three years and I respect her to the utmost. She was a woman I actually dated for a couple of years and I grew quite fond of her. Now the relationship seems to be fading, but I still work with her son, serving as a mentor for him, Joseph, the youngest who is now 13 years of age.

She has two children and when I want to associate with the younger or the older one who is almost 17, she insists that I ask them if they want to go to a movie with me or join me for a social expedition. I consider this too liberal. She, however, expects them to meet her standards at home and in school and they are good students. Both are quite well behaved in school from the reports I get through her.

I believe that the overall process of bringing up children in Germany is profitable because of the mold by which their schools are founded on. The school system in Germany and its demands for performance and preparation for the right vocation or profession seem to work well in that country. The needs are being met for the German and European students, and the molds the students are placed in seem to fit the child who eventually completes his or her education with viable skills for viable function in society.

However, during the time of the Third Reich, it must have been quite convenient to organize such functions as the Hitler Jugend (Hitler Youth), and make them conform to the nation's rule about what they were to do toward the promotion of the Third Reich.

Alfons Heck, the author previously mentioned, fell under this mold during the Second World War and has a lot to say about the autocratic setting under which he was raised. He later broke away from these chains and he came to this country and wrote about his experiences of the past as a child of Hitler.

In perspectives other than education and looking at the further mechanisms of such things as military setting, political stance, and societal evolution of Germany in its presence arena, one can analyze them in their contemporary setting. Germany's progress as a nation certainly depends upon its solid and well-structured institutions. One trend worth examining is the role that Germany plays in NATO.

With the guidance of NATO and the evolving European Community, German society should be dynamic in its contribution to the expansion and progress of Europe. But if the concept of, especially the European Community does not work, and Germany gets shortchanged, which they could with their strong currency, there could be a day of retribution. Germany must fit willingly into the link for complete European unification. In order for the European nations to fully extend their economic and cultural blend, Germany must be one of the strongest players.

The inherent concept of progress through exertion of strong political and economic leadership will have to have ample input and participation from Germany because they are a nation much too strong to sit back and watch other nations take advantage of them from an economically, politically, or militarily.

It is sometimes mind boggling to think that in the year 2001, that most of Europe suffers from about a 10% unemployment rate. With unemployment numbers being higher that those in the United States, one wonders why, and how long the United States can maintain its lead? The dynamics of the economic factor of macro and microeconomics no doubt influence the outcome of the eventual success of nations so the comparative factors have endless avenues for exploration. The economic development of East and West Germany will, no doubt, reflect political stability in Germany and full integration into the European setting as a whole will, no doubt influence German political stability.

How, on the other hand, with our present and faltering school system, can the United States hold the lead over the

European Community? Are there some unexplainable results of our so-called democratic processes in our schools, which continue to give the United States highly successful economic results?

Do the faltering processes, with the extreme lack of uniformity, in the American education system really have an advantage over such a highly structured and productive school system exemplified by Europe? Maybe it is because the American School in its diverse and numerous local and state processes really breed highly successful products.

I have often, as a teacher, conjectured, as to why we do have leading astronauts, computer soft and hardware geniuses, and some great producers in the world. Maybe it is because our secondary students have the opportunity to reflect and observe the high number of high school dropouts, drug users, and many citizens in prisons. Do those who are successful, have the opportunity to reflect, see all the flaws, laugh about it, and take the opportunity to become truly successful because they see so much failure and it impels them to achieve at the highest level?

Does the autocratic setting, in its essence, really prohibit eventual success, whether it is in business, winning wars, putting men on the moon, and leading in high tech adventures? Not to discard some of the high technological advances Europeans made in certain fields of technology and science. Just take a look at Albert Einstein, Enrico Fermi, and Wehrner von Braun! Their contributions to atomic energy and later von Braun's spearheading much of our satellite achievements would support the concept of strong structured and disciplined scholastic processes. Maybe the siphoning off of German scientists gave Americans the impetus we needed to succeed during World War II and thereafter.

Maybe, in some instances, the autocracy of the German people, in the end processes, and their desire to follow the mold set up in society, whether it be in nationalism, military leadership, or societal progress, causes them to sometimes trip over their own feet. This definitely happened with the culmination of the Third Reich. The chains of a dictator actually led to an almost complete annihilation of Nazi Germany.

How can a country such as Germany, that was shooting rockets at England toward the end of World War II, and that almost developed the atomic bomb before we did, not succeed with their autocratic processes in industry, business, schools, and the family, not have conquered the world? Maybe it could have, if the United States had not been propelled into the war by the attack on Pearl Harbor on December 7, 1941. When the United States did shake its veil of pacifism worn prior to the infamous Japanese Pearl Harbor venture, its dynamic potential allowed it, once unveiled, to become one of the greatest military nations the world had seen.

Does autocracy, especially the brand that Germany still renders as the proper edict for running a highly structured school system, really spell success in the long run? Actually there are elements that should be, in my opinion, investigated in Germany's strong selective school system. The structural part of their school system, because of Germany's success in placing students, according to their needs, in productive places in society, warrants close analysis.

But the overall concept of blind obedience through following, without questioning, might be the basic difference in German society and that of the United States. Germany has much to offer, and I do not believe they should alter their school system too much, possibly select what good elements the United States does have, which might be seen by many countries, as too few, and integrate them into their processes of education.

And I definitely think the United States should view the structure of the German school system with adaptation of the structural scheme, because there is much to be learned from it.

German autocracy will most likely continue to permeate their society because of its historically hard cast dye. It must merely be tempered with the continued process of questioning when and if government leadership tends to veer in the wrong direction. Extreme and strong unquestioned leadership should always be questioned in Germany as well as in this country. Strong leadership, with proper balances is fine, but the voice of the people must be heard.

Germany fell into their dastardly exigency because of an economic setting that allowed a tyrannical leader to take Germany on the wrong course during the Nazi era. Questioning should have been more prevalent, and the "blind obedience" to authority lead a great nation down the wrong trail. It is obvious that today, especially with the direction Europe is now heading, blind authority will not sucker the German people into another Third Reich.

The make-up and structure, because of the propensity toward autocracy could be an element still underlying the make-up of German society. However, with the present world setting, speedy communications, and fast transportation, the elements that prevailed, in Germany, from 1932 through 1945 would be difficult, but not impossible to replicate today.

The people left behind by Hitler, especially in a modern European society, have a chance to excel in all arenas of the world. Their technology is superb, their people progressive, and above all, the end products of their school system, at least what I have seen, seem to be extremely well educated.

Chapter 15

Sieg Heil!, Niemals Wieder!

ail to Victory! Never again! That is the translation of the above title to this chapter. Could this ever happen to Germany again? Millions of Germans utilized the "Sieg Heil" greeting as well as the "Heil Hitler" (Hail to Hitler) greeting. It was a standard greeting for military personnel and all citizens showing allegiance to the dictator and German State from the early 1930s, after Hitler became chancellor of Germany in 1932 until the end of World War II.

It is very interesting that while I was teaching German at, especially Lincoln High School, with 68% African American students, the fascination with Hitler and the idea of the Nazi era was foremost in the students' minds while taking German.

I sensed the fascination and, of course disdain, of Nazi Germany by my African American students, even in U. S. History classes. The subject of Hitler and Nazis were often brought up simply because I had lived in Germany, working there for over twenty years and because of my past experience in the German nation. My African American students had an innate suspicion of anyone associated with the German people or who lived in the country as long as I did.

Because of their, sometimes lack of historical knowledge, and unfamiliarity with a changed modern contemporary society in Germany, many students do not know the status of modern Germany contrasted to Nazi Germany. My African American students were quite vociferous in their attempt to articulate their concepts or attitudes related to German society, past or present. Suburban students with whom I have also dealt tend to be better informed because of intensive reading about the Nazi era. Many suburban students have parents, relatives and friends who have traveled in Germany, but display more tolerable attitudes towards, at least, the high technological successes of the German people today and in the past.

Even the movies and television which over the past fifty years have illuminated the highlights of the Nazi era and have familiarized students with the colorful uniforms, flags, and goose stepping soldiers of those times. It left a distinct impression on African American students who interpreted a strong hand aimed at eliminating minorities such as the Jews. Also it left many of the students not yet exposed enough to accurate information and the historical progress and development of modern Germany with varied impressions.

With the African American students, it is understandable that they look, with disdain, on a society that Germany produced through the leadership of Adolph Hitler, who was dedicated to eradication of another minority in that society, the Jews. When teaching the suburban students in San Diego, I found in them, a definite fascination toward Nazi Germany, but not in the same vain as I found with African American students. Many of the African American students, with preponderance, often alluded to the demonic and disdainful aspects of Nazi society as depicted by many films and television. That is obviously where they got their major

Impressions of German society. These impressions were extrapolated to mould in the African American students' minds, a conception of the Nazis as if they still prevailed in modern day society.

It was also very difficult to try to impart the German language to most of African students, because of their attitude toward the sound inflections of the German language and also because of the stigma the Nazis left stamped on Germany and its people.

The suburban students had more of a fascination toward the uniforms, the polarization and conservative leadership of the country during the Third Reich. I found my suburban students more willing to delve into the Nazi era via reports and library research than my African American students.

It is certainly no wonder the African American students had such an attitude toward a nation steeped in a goal of wiping out a minority of people, the Jews, during the Third Reich. Also, because of past experience and unjust minority treatment stemming from the time of slavery in our country, the African American student has, definitely, a strong suspicion of anything related to the Hitler era or a society that focuses on eliminating a minority group. They relate the Nazi era to what they feel has unjustly been cast upon them since inception of slavery in the United States.

The racist element, of course, still prevails toward African Americans in the United States, but the intensity since the 1950s and the Civil Rights Movement has certainly improved since I was a teen-ager living in Little Rock, Arkansas in those turbulent years of the early 1950s.

The focus of German society on democracy and the positive socioeconomic development in Germany during the years I was there (1961-1984), has propelled Germany into a dynamic and highly developed and modern nation. Certainly since the fall of the Berlin Wall, events seem to have brought Germany even further away from any semblance of leaning toward strong leadership akin to such episodes evolving from the Third Reich.

If anything, the German people and the numerous political parties outside the two main parties, CDU (Christian Democratic Union) and SPD (Social Democratic Party) tend to be very multi-party in attitude and think democratically today. The two main parties have most of the political clout, but with a total of about nine parties in Germany, there is certainly a strong semblance of balance in the nation. The two controlling parties, having about 70.6% of the political control in the Bundestag (Federal Assembly held September 27, 1998) wield most of the political control.

There are nine parties ranging from PDS (Party of Democratic Socialism) which had 4.4% of the population in 1998 to the controlling SPD with 36.4%. This is indicative of diverse thinking that exists in Germany today.

The focus on the German people as contrasted to the time Hitler became chancellor in 1932 and the formation of the NSDAP (Nationalsozialistische Deutsche Arbeiterpartei) which numbered just over 3,000 members then, is definitely more democratic and multi-party today.

From a historical perspective, it might be noted that by December 7, 1921, the Völkische Beobachter, a German newspaper, called Adolf Hitler the leader of this party. (Reference: The Face of the Third Reich by Joachim C. Fest). This was about eleven years before Hitler became chancellor, so things were starting to become formatted for his keen perception as to the needs of the German people in trying times.

In another reference, I found some interesting ideas about some of the motivations of Hitler and his desire to do what he did with the German nation and the people. (Reference: http//

www.lemworld.com/genocide/hitler.asp) quoted in the next several paragraphs.

"There is an evidence pertaining to Hitler's regime and of Hitler's own actions and intents that support the belief that he did indeed honestly (at least to some extent) feel that the protection and expansion of Nazi ideology was the key to the overall stability of the state itself. It appears that Hitler not only thought to homogenize the German nation, but he also intended to "purify" the German race itself. It seems that he believed that through an ideology of racial non-tolerance and "blood purity", not only the German people would profit, but the nation-state would in turn find stability and growth.

For Hitler and the Nazi ideology, the individual was a "non-entity." Those individuals who thought of themselves as individuals before they considered themselves members of a greater German culture were in essence going directly against German official ideology. Theoretically they posed no direct threat to Hitler's own political power, but under Nazi official ideology they would theoretically endanger the stability of the Nazi State."

It also appears that Hitler thought the individual's rights were directly related to the perception of the state as a whole. It is here that the extreme fanaticism which seemed to be conveyed to us as Americans during the Second World War portrayed the Nazis as completely dedicated to nationalism, winning the war, with little regard for human life, especially if it meant sacrificing oneself for the Führer and the country."

Such fanaticism appeared to be also prevalent in Japanese, especially as manifested in the air battles with their Kamikaze raids on American ships in the Pacific. We also were led, in the United States, to believe that such things as honorable Hari-Kari or suicide was part of all the Japanese people. Americans were propagandized, and with just cause, against all aspects of the two Axis nations. Nazis and the Japanese were portrayed as evil, almost mechanized, almost non-human, and fanatical in their endeavors against Americans. I was a great reader of comic books that certainly emphasized the complete fanaticism of both Germans and Japanese during the Second World War.

After the war, and talking with many German people, I did not feel the fanaticism that was portrayed in the press, comic books, and news, about German people and their military during the time of the Third Reich. In fact, the German people with whom I spoke and associated with during my almost twenty years there, did not seem so different from my many American friends and me, especially when it came to their attitudes and dedication toward authority of the state or the leader of the state. I found some of my friends who must have certainly been dynamic converts if they were fanatical worshippers of Adolf Hitler! It is difficult to believe that the Germans I knew would have worshipped a leader in the manner depicted by so many writers if the Nazi era.

It seems as though, after the end of Hitler and the Third Reich, the German people were freed from such magnetic and fanatical admiration that seems to have been generated by the bonds of Nazism. I am sure, however, that many of the people with whom I conversed, had different attitudes when they were living under the preponderance of strong and dictatorial Nazi Germany.

The convenient position Adolf Hitler held as dictator and leader of a nation would lead one to believe that the tremendous dislike of the Jews was prevalent among the German people. I personally found that many Germans, with whom I spoke, during the 1960s, expressed compassion when it came to the ubiquitous and disdainful treatment of the Jews in Germany during the Second World War. Some even said certain attitudes of good will or non-disdain for Jews and political enemies of the state could have meant their own imprisonment. Many merely did not speak out, and that is why the whole effect of the Nazi era snowballed and propagated the forces of Nazism.

It seemed that the propaganda and concept of the "Final Solution" or Hitler's push to eradicate all the Jews from Europe was a personal Vendetta. Again, a quote from http://www.lemworld.com/genocide/hitler.asp leads one to believe the extensive pursuit of Jewish eradication was a personal vendetta of Hitler.

"There is a converse argument to support the camp that Hitler was in no way compelled by any inherent instability of the nation-state to murder millions who did not agree with his ideology. There is evidence or at least long-standing historical belief to support the statement that Hitler simply used the Nazi State to fulfill a personal vendetta against the Jewish people and to murder anyone who attempted to stand in his way." "And so I believe today that my conduct is in accordance with the will of the Almighty Creator. And standing guard against the Jew, I am defending the handy work of the Lord." This passage demonstrates Hitler's slanted spin on his actions that he used to win the support of the German people by feigning a threat to the nation-state, and to the foundation of German society from the Jewish nation. Evidence to this fact is the effective abolishment of religion as a counter ideology against state official ideology. Yet in his own words, Hitler used religion to win the support and create fear among the German people. Perhaps the instability of the German state was in part created by Hitler's own contrived "threats" to the state. If Hitler acted upon his own personal needs instead of as a response to the instability of the nation-state, then Hitler's inherent inadequacies of the nation-state, are to blame for German democide."

Mental illness was also a possibility of Hitler's extreme disregard for the Jewish population. I again quote from http://www.lemworld.comgenocide/hitler.asp

"The alternate theory in addition to the above quotes, is that Hitler was mentally ill. Some historians take this stance as an explanation of Hitler's radical views of culture and the state as well as his inhuman actions. It is also believed that Hitler, for at least part of his reign as ruler of the German State was addicted to barbiturates and eventually committed suicide. This opens the possibility that it was Hitler's own possible madness and childhood hatred of the Jews that prompted the ideological genocide under his regime and not solely the problems of the nation-state."

For the German people to ever fall under the spell of such a fanatical leader is actually beyond one's imagination. And the danger of the German people ever being misled again is seemingly improbable.

But the fact that the military tendency of the German nation as exemplified in World War I and World War II, there seems to be a greater danger of the country becoming involved in a military conflict than falling in the hands of a completely strong, overwhelming leader. Maybe, because of the extreme measures taken by the enemies of Germany during the First World War, to punish the German Nation would have propelled Germany into a Second World War, even without Hitler. There is, no doubt, however, that Hitler's dynamic leadership certainly spurred the event of World War II on!

The mistakes of World War I and World War II cost the German people drastically in human lives, as it did the United States. The United States was certainly brought into the war by the Japanese retaliation toward the United States in their attack on Pearl Harbor in 1941. There was no way out because of the Pearl Harbor action so the United States had a great reason to cast away the bonds of pacifism and join their allies on the European front. One would think the German nation, after the terror and nearness to annihilation brought on by home front action probably never wants to see a repeat of the fiasco.

But the lily-white hands of the Americans were no longer innocent with the tragic years of the Vietnam War in the 1960s and 1970s. It is indicative of how a nation can fall into a well-veiled trap of political-military-industrial turmoil.

Who would ever have thought that the Americans, who were so instrumental, with their allies, in winning the Second World War and becoming the industrial leaders in helping win the war, would have fallen into the Vietnam trap?

The two world wars we fought in were propelled by the gigantic movement of nations in the natural alignments brought on by balance of power. If Japan had not attacked Pearl Harbor when they did, we would, most likely, have eventually lost our chains of isolationism and realized that the world was slowly becoming endangered by the military expansion of the Axis movement to take over Europe and eventually the rest of the world. The Pearl Harbor, no doubt, propelled us much sooner into the conflict.

With the modern advances in technology and communications, it is highly unlikely that Germany would ever be let alone long enough to expand, militarily and propagate another war. The world, today (1950-2000) is not the same, as it was in the 1930s and 1940s because of rapid communications, and military awareness of other nations. Germany is too much at the forefront on political and economic leadership in Europe to fall into the same military adventure, seemingly, unless NATO eventually disbands and leaves Europe alone to forge a new military cloak.

On the other hand, with the development of the European nations with their multi-national complexities, the only danger of Germany ever causing problems again might come from economic inequities. These might be brought on by the Euro as a dominant currency of most of Europe, along with injustices toward Germany from other European nations. Conflicts might arise because of the leveling of the currencies in Europe, with Germany receiving the short end of the stick. Germany is one of the most productive countries and has the technological clout and curiosity to develop in a vanguard capacity and economically reign over all of Europe. If its currency is dragged down by less productive countries there could be some repercussions from Germany because of inequities.

It is, highly inconceivable that Germany would ever again be pushed to the brink of war, but it could, with the right mixture of **iniquities economically**, cause some turmoil if it feels it is being taken advantage of by less advanced nations. **Lebensraum** or a need for other territories in order to expand the borders of a highly a highly progressive nation could also be a contributing factor that might motivate Germany to become more aggressive.

The German people, if faced with the multi-ethnic infusion such as the United States already endures, and with their almost ethnic purity (95.1% German citizens; 2.3% Turkish citizens; 0.7% Italians; 0.4% Greek; 0.4% Poles, and 1.1% others who are mostly those fleeing from Yugoslavia), could possibly become reactionary in its desire for equity. (2002 statistics) Actually the German immigration is minor compared to the allowed immigration status of the United States. Much of the past infusion, of Germany, with multi-nationals has come from political refugees and the Gasarbeiter movement in Germany. (Guest Worker Program)

Contrasted to the German post World War II years of peaceful existence, the nearest the United States has come to international disdain as a country emanated from the Vietnam War. We are lucky that we got out of that war when we did because the mighty military power of the United States was obviously misused. The extension of that war was basically because of political control and a Washington policy that tied the hands of the military. Had the military have had the upper hand in this particular war and time frame of history, the Americans might have honorably won the war. Already, some of the ex leaders have already proclaimed that war was one we should never have gotten into.

The Germans, with their current attitudes, on the other hand, would never have wanted to become involved in such a quagmire and has, since the end of the Second World War, minded their own business. Some think they should have aligned with France and other European countries during the ethnic flare-ups in Yugoslavia, and gotten more involved. But the tendency, unfortunately, of many Europeans, as in World War I and World War II, is to mind their own business and not get involved. France and such countries as Belgium and the Netherlands certainly displayed an attitude of pacifism at the beginning of the Second World War. Americans today, on the other hand, with our poweful military force, have tended to play a gigantic role as world peacekeepers, though Vietnam, Iraq, and now Afghanistan, without our military idustrial complex may cause us to seemingly NOT be peacekeepers of the world!

Maybe the Americans, as previous peacekeepers of the world learned a costly lesson in Vietnam, and will be cautious enough to refrain from involvement unless the causes are right and we know we can win. And with the economic and productive potential, the Americans are strong enough to win most anything they support militarily because of our present military strength. Along with our economic potential so well displayed during the Second World War the United States has quite a world advantage of might.

There is another element that will probably prevent the German people from ever getting into the "Sieg Heil!" syndrome again, and it is probably the awareness of the other European countries of Germany's potential. Along with France and Great Britain's constant awareness of Germany, especially after World War II, the dominating factor some people think will keep Europe at peace is NATO.

Could it be that NATO is not only a protector of the North Atlantic Treaty Organization, but also a watchdog over Germany just so she will never again fall into the "Sieg Heil" syndrome? I have had many military officers tell me that that is one of the reasons NATO continues its existence is to keep a pulse on the military heartbeat of Deutschland.

There are some disturbing factors that seem to emerge in relation to German purity today. Each time I return to Germany, I hear complaints about minorities in Germany, and most of the complaints are about the Turkish people who came into Germany as Gastarbeiter (guest workers). But with only 2.3%, it does not seem that the Turkish population would really make a dent into the ethnic purity of Germany. Each time I go to Germany, there is always talk about the Turkish population and their reluctance to fit into German society. Their ethnic difference seems to be, sometimes, looked upon by many Germans as somewhat inconsistent with German order and cultural attitudes.

I think the infractions perceived by the German people is that the Turkish people really do not assimilate into the culture but are highly visible, with different cultural practices and tend to be highly visible among the German population.

These problems will, most likely, be foremost in German political maneuvers for future goals of societal improvement. The Germans brought on the problems of the cheap labor through the Gastarbeiter program and they must work solve it.

The strong, conservative element of the German people that I have observed often is through their (the German peoples') comments about the social infractions of the Turkish people. Expressions of disdain toward many Turkish people is often expressed because of the housing support and social services rendered by the German people in helping many of them who chose to remain in the country.

But again, with 95.1% purity, I do not perceive a great social problem in the German nation. Maybe the Germans do. The liberalization of the German people in their present sociological mode should propel the nation into one that can cope with the ethnic breakdown of only about 4.1% of other nationalities than German.

The Turkish people do hold on to their own language, but seem quite adept at communicating in the German language, sometimes imperfectly, but many also speak German quite well. Sometimes criminal escapades tend to be, in my estimation, quite exaggerated but usually by Germans who are basically conservative and tend to want to hold on to traditional German purity.

The German people today seem to be quite content with the status quo of their sociological conditions. On any given night one can see in the city of Bad Kreuznach, where I have spent many years, people getting together in bars drinking wine or beer in the many restaurants and guesthouses. They are doing what Americans do not tend to do nearly as frequently and that is conversing from Tuesday evening through Sunday evening.

The intensity of conversation, and I mean extended conversation and socializing, is much more pervasive in Germany than in this country. Even in a city with only about 45,000 population (Bad Kreuznach) there is excitement, frequenting restaurants and coffee bars, to a lesser degree than in the United States.

People in Germany and many more areas of Europe tend to continually expand the art of conversing and living intensely via the art of verbal intercourse and communication. I find that restaurants and bars are frequented on weekends in San Diego, but not throughout the week as is done in Europe. Maybe that is a good sign that things are going quite well for the Germans and other Europeans.

Maybe the Americans are more attuned to baseball and picnics or outdoor adventures, but we do not have the pervasiveness of wine and beer festivals, and in my opinion, we do not have the intense art of communicating during the leisure time after work. These seem to be cultural elements that tend to bond the German people into the pleasant mode of enjoying life day by day.

Who can predict, however, just what direction the German people will take. Maybe they will never fall into the same military and fanatical adventure they did under Adolph Hitler. Or, maybe there will never be a "Sieg Heil!" episode by the German people. I do know that when talking with some citizens, many of them are almost apologetic in regards to the Nazi era of history. This might be an indication that the two world war experiences have taught them a fundamental lesson and they want no more!

Some, on the other hand, are outspoken, and even profess that some elements of the Third Reich were not completely wrong. They are referring to the military and socialist programs of the NPSAD, along with the strong control of the Nazis had over criminal activity. These ideas are often expressed as a protest of existing crime rates and sometimes unpopular government programs not favorable to all parties and citizens.

The underlying causes that propelled Adolph Hitler are certainly not germane to modern German society because the unemployment rate is only about 6 % (1950-2014=5.98%) and even with East Germany now integrated with West Germany, the society is economically ALIVE!. Also with the need for complete East German uplifting and new infrastructure, Germany should be rather dynamic in its economic ventures for years to come.

The German people are content and Europe, along with Germany is absolutely fantastic to visit. The economic and political success of Germany will, most likely, remain intact for years to come. There are far too many lessons that have been learned from such a great country as Germany, through the turmoil of the Third Reich. We can also hope that we in the United States have learned them from Vietnam.

Germans can be proud of modern day Germany. The highly cultivated society one feels while visiting this great country tends to make you pause and wonder, "How could it ever happened to such a great people and nation?"

The people Hitler left behind surely have learned a significant lesson from the losses of two World Wars. The Germans should now have a future of positive contributions to Europe and the world. Let them revel in the tremendous accomplishments and stability that prevail. May there be no more "Sieg Heils".

The world still has a fascination for the Nazi era, mostly because of its significant impact upon the world. How the Germans ever fell into the Third Reich trap, is still an enigma. Visitors today (1960s through 2015), however, can easily see a country that is modern, friendly, and one that is outstanding in the European composition. The order and beauty of a highly developed society with its colorful landscapes, mountains, forests, lakes, varied sights, and friendly people, will be one of the most exhilarating of all European countries to visit!

Most of my concepts in this book have been presented as a person, speaking German since the 1960s are observation of the Germans, via conversing, having many German friends, working with German educators, teaching in their schools, travels, and having a German family!

Could Germany fall back into the **STRONG LEADER, "SIEG HEIL"** syndrome? With the right elements of economic pressure, military circumstancs, and infusion of outside cultures, **I believe, because of their desire for a strong leader, it is possible for Germany to SOMEDAY, fall into a possible military/political debacle!** Though so many Germans I have discussed this with, tend to believe, because of the **DISASTER OF THE WW II and their defeat** and tremendous efforts to recovery, **it will never happen again!**